KU-531-504

GREAT MENUS

FROM

MAGAZINE

BBC BOOKS

by a recipe denotes that this dish is suitable for vegetarians who eat cheese and eggs, and will buy rennet-free cheeses if required.

Because of concern over the risk of salmonella, MAFF advises against serving uncooked eggs. While you may wish to make your own decision on this issue, we strongly recommend that vulnerable groups such as babies, pregnant women, the sick and the elderly should avoid eating any dishes containing raw eggs.

57**8**2**3**7

MORAY COUNCIL
Department of Technical
& Leisure Services
641.5

Published by BBC Books,
an imprint of BBC Worldwide Publishing,
BBC Worldwide Limited, Woodlands,
80 Wood Lane, London W12 0TT

First published 1996
© BBC Worldwide Publishing 1996
ISBN 0 563 37175 7

Designed by Louise Morley
Charts by Lydia France

Photographers: Lunches - Gus Filgate, Martin Brigdale, Vernon Morgan, Ken Field
Dinners - Vernon Morgan, Martin Brigdale, Gus Filgate, Howard Allman, Ken Field, Diana Miller, Janet Smith
Al Fresco - Nick Carman, Martin Brigdale, Graham Kirk, Vernon Morgan
Buffets - Vernon Morgan, Ken Field, Martin Brigdale, Jess Koppel
Children's Parties - Ken Field, Vernon Morgan
Weddings - Gus Filgate, James Duncan, Vernon Morgan
Special Occasions - Gus Filgate, Vernon Morgan, Martin Brigdale, Simon Wheeler, Nick Carmen

Home Economists: Lunches - Maxine Clarke, Louise Pickford, Mandy Wagstaff, Kathy Mann,
Linda Tubby, Bridget Sargeson
Dinners - Mary Cadogan, Carola Weise, Berit Vinegrad, Bridget Sargeson, Ricky Turner, Sara Lewis, Kathy Man
Al Fresco - Pete Smith, Jane Charlton, Linda Fraser, Sarah Barrass, Jacqueline Clarke
Buffets - Joanna Farrow, Jacqueline Clarke, Annie Nichols, Mandy Wagstaff
Weddings - Joanna Farrow, Mitzie Wilson, Bridget Sargeson
Special Occasions - Ailsa Cruickshank, Bridget Sargeson, Joanna Farrow, Angela Nilsen,
Jane Suthering, Janet Smith, Maxine Clarke, Louise Pickford

Set in Perpetua and Palatino
Printed in Great Britain by Cambus Litho Ltd, East Kilbride
Bound in Great Britain by Hunter & Foulis Ltd, Edinburgh
Colour separations by Radstock Reproductions Ltd, Midsomer Norton
Jacket printed by Lawrence Allen Ltd, Weston-super-Mare

CONTENTS

FOREWORD

PAGE 5

INTRODUCTION

1. LUNCHES

2. DINNERS AND SUPPERS

3. AL FRESCO

4. Buffets and Drinks Parties

5. Children's Parties

6. Special Occasions

7. Weddings

Index

FOREWORD

I know from the stack of post that I get each week at *BBC Good Food* magazine that our readers really do enjoy the challenge of planning something special like a grand buffet for a daughter's wedding, a barbecue for the kids on a hot summer's day or a stylish dinner party for friends. But whatever the occasion, the questions I get asked most frequently are how much do I serve and what can I prepare ahead so that I am not frantically cooking instead of enjoying myself?

Whether you are catering for 6 or 60 I hope that *Great Menus from Good Food* will provide all the answers and give you enough information and practical tips to make your party go with a swing. There are menus for a variety of occasions from a cocktail party to a Christening tea, an Easter Sunday lunch to a ruby wedding anniversary celebration, a quick pasta supper to a smart vegetarian dinner. The recipes have been devised in smaller quantities which can easily be multiplied to serve as many guests as you like. There is valuable preparation and storing advice and many of the larger menus have countdowns to help you plan ahead and spread the workload.

We have created an especially useful quantities chart, listing almost every ingredient you might need to consider when entertaining on a larger scale. If you need to know how much bread, butter, tea, coffee, cold meat, strawberries or whatever to buy in order to cater for more than the average-sized dinner party, the chart will help. And because forgetting the really obvious can be a dilemma when planning a big event, we have provided handy checklists of anything and everything you might ever need to remember; invitations, marquees, entertainment, hiring equipment like tables, chairs, linen and cutlery, providing enough rubbish bins, ashtrays and even loo rolls!

Catering for friends and family on any scale can be hard work, but it is always very rewarding and I hope you'll enjoy using *Great Menus from Good Food* to help you. Remember that the most important rules of all are to write plenty of checklists and plan ahead – then you can be sure that you, too, will get the opportunity to relax and enjoy the party with your guests.

Have fun!

Mitzie

Mitzie Wilson
Editor-in-Chief
BBC Good Food magazine

INTRODUCTION

PLANNING YOUR PARTY

Planning a party can be a daunting prospect, especially if you haven't had much experience of organising an event like it before. It doesn't matter whether it's your first proper dinner party or celebration for a ruby wedding anniversary, the task will always require thought and careful organisation.

These days, most large parties, especially wedding receptions, take place in hotels, restaurants and hired rooms. The main advantages of this form of entertaining is that it requires little work and almost no involvement in the planning. The disadvantages are that it can be impersonal and expensive.

But you can easily do a great deal of the organising yourself, especially if you plan carefully and enlist the help of friends and family. In this introduction, you will discover that the secret to successful entertaining is in the planning, whether you are hosting a dinner party for 4 or a wedding reception for 50.

Once the party is approached in bite-sized pieces, it becomes manageable. The information here will help you to take your party one step at a time, from working out the budget to decorating the table.

ASSESSING YOUR BUDGET

The main factor that will determine what sort of party you will eventually give, apart from the occasion itself, is money. The first decision you will need to make is how much you want to spend. Your budget will affect all of your other decisions so, first of all, be realistic about what you can afford, and second, work out the minimum you will need to spend on each guest. If there is a huge discrepancy you will either have to revise what you originally planned to do or cut the number of guests you invite.

Whether you are planning a small or large affair as far as numbers are concerned, you will need to consider the cost of food, drink, hire of the venue (if you are not planning on using your home) and accessories such as decorations, serviettes, cutlery, crockery. Here is a list of other items you will need to consider in your budgeting in order to get a realistic idea of what you can afford to plan and spend.

BUDGETING CHECKLIST

Invitations; printing, and postage
Hire of hotel, room, hall or marquee
Cost of food
Cost of drink
Hire of equipment (see Hiring Equipment
Checklist on page 8 for an idea of
the sort of equipment you may
need to consider)
Hire of staff (see Hiring Staff to Help
on page 7 for guidance on how
to assess your needs)
Flowers/decorations
Music/entertainment

CHOOSING A VENUE

There are lots of unusual venues available for hire including museums, local gardens, boats either afloat or berthed, college halls, church vaults, even private homes, film studios, swimming pools, ice rinks and steam trains. It is fun to entertain in a place which has some novelty value, and so it is worth making a few enquiries about the cost and availability of hiring an unusual place. The phone book is always a good starting point, local restaurant/pub guides, local newspapers and friends, too, can provide useful inspiration.

Your budget will probably decide for you where the party is going to be held. If the budget is low and if you have a lot of space at home, you may choose to hold your party there. Whatever you decide, make sure that you have enough space to accommodate all the guests you plan to invite.

If you have the money and decide that you definitely need more room than just your house can provide, consider renting a marquee which you can erect on the lawn, or hire tenting to attach over a small back garden, or yard, to make an extra room.

But if your home and garden combined are just not large enough, you could consider hiring a room elsewhere, although some have caterers attached so if you want to make your own food, you should check this before going ahead. In some cases, cooking facilities may be limited which means that you will have to plan your menu accordingly. Choose dishes which can be prepared in advance, like patés, terrines which can be served cold and casseroles and soups which can be re-heated and kept warm in hot cupboards. Most puddings can be made in advance with just a little assembly work being required on the premises and any vegetables can be cooked at the venue too. With careful thought, you could easily choose food which only requires you to hire some electric rings and hot cupboards.

If you are considering a venue that has no kitchen facilities at all, find out if there is a room where you can set up a temporary one. If not, you may have to consider screening off part of the main room so that you have some space to prepare the food, keep used cutlery and glass and to generally be able to organise yourself unseen by the guests.

HIRING STAFF TO HELP

If you are entertaining a large number of people, then it might be worth considering hiring some professional staff. It makes all the difference if you can rely on the expertise of two or three professionals.

Trained waiting staff can be found through agencies, but this can be costly, and you never know who you will be sent so it's better to find people by word of mouth, if possible. If you know somebody in the catering trade they may be able to advise you. If not, try the local pub – their part-time help might be interested in some waiting work. Usually, waiters and waitresses work in 'packs', which can be useful if you're looking for more than one pair of hands. The bonus is that they will be used to working together, and will make a good team.

How Many to Hire?

Discuss with the staff themselves or their agency, when booking, how many waiters/waitresses you will need. They have the experience and should be able to advise you.

As a guide, for a sit down meal, you will need 1 member of staff for 10 guests, plus 1 butler or bar person to serve the drinks. For a buffet you will need 1 member of staff for about 20 guests and for a cocktail party, 2 staff for up to 30 guests; one to hand round food and the other to serve drinks.

Uniforms

When you book staff, make it clear what you would like them to wear. Most professionals prefer to work in uniform – white jacket and black trousers for men, and white blouse, black skirt and white pinny for the women. This gives a clear indication of who's who, and gives your party a professional air.

Timing

Make sure you arrange for the staff to arrive in plenty of time to help get the party organised. They will give you a good indication of how much time they need. A small party may take 45 minutes to set up, but a big function could take between 2 and 3 hours. Remember, too, to calculate how long it may take to clear up after the last guests have gone.

Pay

Generally, waiting and bar staff prefer to be paid in cash. There is usually a standard fee for a lunch, cocktail or evening party up to a certain time, then you start paying overtime. Weekend and public or bank holidays are also paid at overtime rates. Again, discuss with the staff how they would like to be paid and if you have any doubts concerning tax etc. consult the Inland Revenue for advice.

Bear in mind that staff will expect to be offered tea and coffee on arrival and if they are working a very long day, remember they will need a break at some point. It's a good idea to provide some sort of food too – sandwiches, biscuits etc. – as they will be working hard and so will need fuelling as much as your guests. They will also appreciate somewhere to relax and a safe place to put their personal belongings.

HIRING EQUIPMENT

Wherever you have decided to hold your party, you will almost certainly need to hire china, glass, cutlery and linen. Some companies will request that their china and glass is washed before being returned, so make sure you have facilities to be able to do this – even if it's only buckets of water. If this is too daunting or impractical a task, you may be able to persuade the hire company to take the crockery back, unwashed, for a supplementary fee. Linen (tablecloths, napkins, etc.) is always returned dirty.

When compiling a list of items to be hired, there are certain things which may not be immediately obvious, but can make all the difference towards an efficiently run event. For example, planning where 50 guests will leave their coats and how to chill 25 bottles of champagne.

HIRING EQUIPMENT CHECKLIST

China
Soup bowls and saucers
25 cm (10 in) plates
23 cm (9 in) plates
16 cm (6$\frac{1}{2}$ in) plates
Dessert bowls
Cruet sets

Cutlery
Soup spoons
Table knives and forks
Small knives
Small forks
Dessert spoons
Tablespoons
Serving spoons and forks
Salad spoons and forks
Salad servers
Pie slices
Soup and sauce ladles
Cheese knives
Butter knives
Wedding cake knife

Coffee and tea crockery
Large cups and saucers
Small cups and saucers
Dessert spoons
Teaspoons
Milk jugs
Cream jugs
Sugar bowls
Teapots
Coffee pots
Kettles
Coffee machine
Tea urn

Glasses and bar equipment
Large tumblers or water glasses
Small tumblers or spirits glasses
$\frac{1}{2}$ pint or pint glasses
Red wine glasses (250 ml/8 fl oz)
White wine glasses (175ml/6 fl oz)
Champagne flutes
Sherry or port glasses
Brandy balloons
Jugs for water and soft drinks
Measuring jug

Trays
Ashtrays
Ice buckets and spoons
Cocktail shaker
Lemon plate and knife
Can opener
Bottle openers
Corkscrews
Large plastic bins
(for chilling wine/champagne in ice)
Tea towels (allow plenty for polishing glasses)
Tablecloths (and drawing pins to fasten them)
Trays
Ashtrays

Miscellaneous items
Tables and chairs
Trestle tables
Table for wedding cake
Coat rail and hangers
Hot rings/plates
Oven
Hot cupboards
Saucepans
Serving dishes
Colander
Butter dishes
Bread/biscuit baskets
Cheese boards
Oil and vinegar sets

Linen
Cloths
70 x 144 cm (28 x 58 in)
90 x 90 cm (36 x 36 in)
70 x 70 cm (28 x 28 in)
Napkins
Serving cloths
Tea towels

Apart from the hire items, there are a few things which you can easily supply from home: rubbish bags, dish cloths, cling film, oven gloves, mop and bucket, extension flex, adapters, matches, candles (in case of emergencies!) cocktail sticks, trays, ashtrays, napkins, cloths and tablecloths, tea towels, aprons and coffee filters, if needed.
It's also a good idea to check the supplies of loo rolls and to take along a few large plastic containers with lids, to store and take home any left-over food.

CONSIDERING THEMES AND DECORATIONS

Give a little thought to how you want to decorate the room and tables – it makes all the difference to the atmosphere. As before, check your budget before launching into the realms of fantasy – you can do a lot without breaking the bank.

Consider the sort of event you are planning and decide whether to give yourself a theme to work around. Here are some ideas: Colours, masks, 'P' party – come as anything beginning with the letter P ... or any other letter of the alphabet, hats, medieval or any other historical period, flags – incorporate your favourite flag or its colours into a costume, days of the Raj, science fiction, circus, Dickens – come as any one of his countless characters, etc.

There are the more obvious events, such as Burn's Night, which would take a tartan theme. Try tying tartan ribbon around the napkins, making swags of tartan fabric round the tables and filling little baskets with dried thistles, heather, etc. Hallowe'en could take on a black and orange theme using coloured tablecloths and napkins and a pumpkin to light the tables. Lengths of muslin, or any other cheap fabric, can be used to cover walls and can be draped from the centre of the ceiling to the edges of a room to create an exotic, tented, effect.

The seasons of the year can suggest attractive themes if your party has no particular occasion attached to it. An autumn dinner table could be decorated with golden and red leaves and pretty berries, winter with evergreen branches and pine cones, spring with little pots of spring flowers, and summer with an abundance of colourful flowers and fruits. Make pyramids of fruit and vegetables on cake stands or in bowls as centrepieces for your table, or hollow out apples, globe artichokes and different coloured peppers and use them as candle holders. Paper flowers can also be fun and are easy to make using crêpe paper. Cover a wall with a blanket of them or surround a doorway to make a stunning entrance. Enlist the help of creative friends to make the flowers, the more the better as the effect is achieved by the quantity.

If you decide you do want a theme, one really good source of inspiration is home-style magazines. They are full of exciting and inspirational ideas on decorating rooms and creating special effects. If all this sounds too fiddly, there is a huge selection of party decorations available in specialist shops – look in the phone book for names and addresses. Balloons are also popular and are a fairly inexpensive way of decorating a large space. Some balloon companies make huge sculptures and arches for parties which can be matched to your colour scheme. Let your imagination go and have some fun.

FLOWERS

Flowers are the most obvious and probably the most popular decoration of all, but they can be expensive. If you have a natural talent for flower arranging, you can save on cost by buying the flowers in bulk from a local market early in the morning. Bear in mind the season and buy accordingly. Masses of one type of flower can look stunning and can often be a cheaper way of buying than smaller quantities of a selection of flowers. Think about your venue and plan where you want the arrangements – small ones look good on tables while large ones can be very effective at the entrance, on the buffet table or mantelpiece or in a window that may not have a particularly attractive view.

If you are using a florist, discuss the colours, types and numbers of arrangements you think you will need, and he or she will advise you. Ask for a quotation and, again, work the cost into your overall budget. If flower arranging is not one of your skills and you don't know a friend who could do it for you, a professional florist will be able to decorate the room on the day.

MUSIC AND ENTERTAINMENT

If you are planning a special party, you will probably plan to have some kind of music or entertainment and maybe some dancing. You need to think what form it should take. As with the theme and decorations, the entertainment will create an atmosphere. For example, a pianist playing Cole Porter melodies sets the right atmosphere at a cocktail or drinks party while a harpist or string quartet lends a civilised and relaxed air to a small, romantic reception.

On the other hand, if you are holding a large party and have a dance floor, you can consider anything from a steel band to a rock band. Most professional musicians should be able to supply you with a demonstration tape to enable you to hear them before making a firm booking. Remember, if they are hired for a full day or evening, they will need a break as well as food and drink to keep them going.

Discos are also popular and some specialise in period music – 1950s, rock and roll etc. – or more general present-day popular music. Many of them supply a light show of some kind, maybe even lasers and a smoke machine. Unlike a live band, a DJ can provide non-stop music if this is more suitable to your requirements.

Entertainers can be a saving grace at a children's party, and can provide a period of quiet and calm for a while at least! Choose from magicians, clowns, Punch and Judy, or even face painters. Recommendations are best by word of mouth, but the phone book can be a useful source of information. As well as making enquiries about price, always remember to ask about arrival and set-up times, duration of performance, content of act and enquire if there are any special requirements or points to note like will they make a mess or noise and are they covered for insurance for dangerous stunts.

WEDDING EXTRAS
Invitations and Printing
Make sure you get your invitations sent out in good time so that your guests reply early enough for you to have a good idea of numbers before getting too far ahead with your plans. Decide whether you want seating plans and place cards on the tables and make arrangements to get these printed, too.

Basic wording for a wedding invitation:

Mr and Mrs Peter Green request the
pleasure of your company
at the wedding of their daughter
Anne Jane Sarah to James John Grant
at St Mary's Church, Perth, on
Saturday, 14th September, 1995 at 2 o'clock
and afterwards at Camphill House.

RSVP
Camphill House
Scone Road
Perth
Angus   Morning Dress

Seating Plans
Have photocopies of the seating plan for your tables available next to the bigger, wall-sized plan. Guests can then take one with them to the table and avoid the confusion that often occurs when people are wandering about, trying to find their table.

Wedding Favours
It is customary to present the guests with a small gift or token when leaving a wedding. Sometimes a token is put at each lady's place at the table. Perhaps a few sugared almonds wrapped in a piece of net and tied with a ribbon. You could invent your own ideas, using a miniature posy of dried flowers, a heart-shaped ginger biscuit piped with white icing and tied with a ribbon, or some scented rose petals tied up with ribbons and lace.

Wedding Cakes
These will often be the centrepiece of the dining area for a wedding reception. Give some thought to using the right table and cake stand for maximum show and ease of photography with the bride and groom. A decorative, but sharp knife will be a necessity as will some form of sensible packaging if you are planning on sending people home with a souvenir piece of cake.

PLANNING YOUR MENU AND FOOD

Because it is often easy to choose a dish but not so easy to plan a menu for a whole meal or occasion, we have provided menus in this book with balanced and complimenting dishes to save you the planning and thinking time. However, you can always mix and match the dishes in these menus to bring together your favourite recipes in each to create new menus.

When planning your food, always remember to consider vegetarian alternatives. Give thought to the actual ingredients of each recipe and how they come together as a whole meal. Consider the colours, flavours, textures and richness of the dishes and bear in mind the time of day and season of the year you are holding your event to avoid an inappropriate choice of recipes.

PLANNING YOUR TIME AND STORAGE FACILITIES
Once you have decided what you are going to cook, make a time plan and organise the shopping well in advance. Get hold of as many plastic storage containers of varying sizes as you can as you will certainly need them! Establish which dishes can be made in advance. Biscuits or meringues can be made a week in advance, and kept in airtight containers. Soups, patés, terrines, casseroles, pies and many puddings freeze very successfully for 3–4 weeks. It would be wise, in the weeks before the event, to run down your freezer

stock in readiness for the quantity of food to be stored. If you're short of freezer space, it is possible to hire domestic freezers. Alternatively, you may be able to persuade a kind friend to lend you the use of theirs.

If you are entertaining during the cold winter months, some foods, such as vegetables, fruit and salad ingredients can be stored outside, either in cool boxes or in plastic crates, which means that you don't need to worry about extra fridge space. Meat and poultry can also be kept outside, but the temperature must be sufficiently low, to avoid any risk of bacteria forming. (Make sure everything is securely sealed, to avoid tempting any local predators like cats or foxes.) It is advisable though to give these foods priority when storing in the fridge. You can chill large quantities of wine and beer overnight, outside in the garden shed, as long as you have a lock on the door.

PLANNING THE SHOPPING
Compiling a shopping list can be complicated, when there are several recipes to consider. To make it easier, list the ingredients under various headings, such as fruit and vegetables, dairy, meat and poultry, fish, dry goods, frozen goods, drink, and miscellaneous. Set your list out either on one sheet of paper, or give a separate sheet for each heading and work your way through each recipe listing the ingredients needed as you go. This will also make life a lot easier in the supermarket, as everything is displayed collectively, so hopefully, you shouldn't forget anything.

Make sure you order large quantities of meat or fish well in advance. The butcher will need to know if he has to prepare any special cuts of meat, and the fishmonger will need ample warning if you want 3 or 4 salmon, as he may not carry this quantity on a day-to-day basis. If you plan to shop in a supermarket, it may also be worth checking that they'll have what you want.

Dry goods and frozen foods can be bought 2–3 weeks in advance. Certain fruit and vegetables – potatoes, carrots, onion, apples – can be bought up to 2 weeks in advance and stored somewhere cool and dark (the garage is perfect). More perishable items – tomatoes, courgettes, mushrooms – can be purchased 2 days beforehand. Soft fruits, like strawberries, should be bought the day before and stored in the fridge or another suitably cold place. Salad leaves can be prepared the day before, and kept in plastic bags in the fridge, and bunches of herbs can be plunged into jugs of cold water.

The morning before the party, go through your original shopping list, and check off all the items, making a final trip to the supermarket for anything you might have forgotten.

PLANNING FOR CHILDREN
A little forward planning is well worth the effort to keep the younger guests happy! Children may not be interested in the food provided for adults and may prefer something with a little novelty value. 'Mini' foods are fun, and one or two of the leading food stores sell mini hamburgers and hot dogs, and little muffins and chocolate eclairs. Of course you can make your own, if time allows. Cocktail sausages on sticks, mini meatballs, sausage rolls and cheese straws are guaranteed to please and thin chips with tomato ketchup are always a success.

It is often easy to please the younger ones, not by creating another menu for them but just by presenting the adult one in a more fun way. Serve the food on brightly coloured plates, make faces or designs out of the food, or give each child a 'lunch box' – a small cardboard or plastic decorated box – and let them have fun discovering what's inside. Chips could be served in pages from a favourite comic and snack-type foods are often sold in mini bags which can be popped into the lunch boxes along with tiny bags of sweets and goodies. Ice-cream is always a favourite – especially in cones. The children should enjoy the party as much as everyone else, and by giving a little thought to their tastes, everyone should be happy!

PLANNING THE DRINKS

If you are going to be entertaining on a large scale it is best to serve a selection of wines and soft drinks. Serving spirits to a large crowd is complicated, time-consuming, and may get the party atmosphere off to too quick a start. It's also expensive and so best kept for smaller dinner parties, where one drink is served before dinner.

Consider those who won't be drinking and have an imaginative selection of low- and non-alcoholic beverages on offer. There is a huge selection of such drinks available nowadays, and non-drinkers should be catered for with as much care as drinkers. You can never have too much sparkling or still mineral water, fruit juice and fizzy drink available and remember it often gets consumed by the alcohol drinkers, too, especially later on during longer parties so be prepared. If there are going to be children at the party, make sure you also give some thought to their needs.

WORKING OUT DRINK QUANTITIES

Once you have established the number of guests you expect, consider the type of party you are giving. For a dinner party, allow $^{1}/_{2}$–$^{3}/_{4}$ bottle of wine per person, although, if it is to be drunk at a leisurely pace over more than 2 hours, you may have to allow about 1 bottle per person. This quantity includes the variety of wines that you may choose to serve with the different courses – red, rosé, white or sweet and any wine you may have chosen to serve as an aperitif. A standard 75 cl bottle of wine will yield about 6 glasses. People tend to drink less at lunchtime so $^{1}/_{2}$ bottle per person is ample.

Quantities for drinks parties will vary according to the length of the party. If it is to be held in the early evening from about 6–8 pm with a few nibbles on offer, $^{1}/_{2}$ bottle of wine per person should be fine, particularly if you plan to dilute it with orange juice to make Buck's fizz or with crème de cassis to make kir. However, if it is to be a longer party with more substantial food being be served, (whether a buffet or 'finger' food) allow 1 bottle per person. For punches and mulled wines, allow 2 glasses per head.

If you plan to serve cocktails, then expect guests to drink $1^{1}/_{2}$ cocktails per hour for the first 2 hours, then 2 per hour after that, and hope the party doesn't last too long! An average 75 cl bottle of spirits will yield 30 measures.

These quantities are just guidelines, and, after all, it's your party, so if you are of a generous nature, or you have very thirsty friends, then adjust them accordingly.

BUYING YOUR DRINK

If supplying your own wine and drinks, check if the venue you are hiring charges corkage - a fee to cover the lost profit they would have made if selling their own drinks.

Supermarkets, off-licences, wine merchants, wine warehouses, even shippers are all good sources for drink. Make sure you buy on a sale or return basis to avoid either running out or being left with huge quantities you will never use or cannot store. Sale or return means that your money will be refunded on every unopened bottle, giving you the flexibility of buying on the generous side, but remember not to uncork all your bottles to save time before your party, as you won't be able to

return them if you do. Supermarkets, unfortunately, don't provide a sale or return service but often their stock is more competitively priced.

Wherever you decide to buy, do a little homework first. Visit all your potential suppliers and compare prices, discounts and special offers. Establish whether your supplier will deliver the drink and supply you with ice, and possibly even your glasses, before making your choice. Finally, make sure you invest in a bottle of each wine and have a tasting at home before committing yourself to buying in quantity. You can then decide whether you have made the right choice.

SERVING WINE

It is important to serve your wine at the correct temperature. There is nothing worse than a glass of warm white wine (or worse still, warm champagne) or a glass of chilled red.

To chill wine, plenty of ice is essential. If you are not getting ice from your wine supplier, try other ice suppliers and check that they will deliver. Ice is cheap to buy and saves the work and freezer space needed to make it. If you're holding a large party and have a lot of wine to chill, stand the ice in a bath, large sink, or in large plastic bins (these can also be hired and if you're setting up a bar, the bins can be stored underneath, which will save you running to and from the bathroom or kitchen). Fill the bins with ice and cold water, making sure it comes up to the necks of the bottles. You'll need to start chilling the wine at least 2 hours in advance of the start of the party. Make sure you have plenty of glass cloths to hand to wrap round the wet bottles when serving.

Red wine should stand in a warm room for 1–2 hours and be opened 1 hour before serving so that it can breathe; this will improve the flavour of even the most humble reds. But remember your sale or return arrangement and don't uncork all the bottles at once – start with an average of 1 bottle for every 5–6 people who may drink red not white.

RUNNING A BAR

If you plan to have a paying bar, you will need to consider getting a licence to sell alcohol. Anyone is entitled to buy wines and spirits by the case and sell them on to a third party for consumption at a private function. However, if the drinks are to be sold in a public place, you will have to apply to the local town hall for a licence. Alternatively, you could ask your local publican to give you an extension to their licence for an agreed fee.

If you are only serving wine, then obviously, you will need several corkscrews to avoid the constant 'hunt the corkscrew' dilemma! Other things you need to consider, which are not included on the bar section of the Hiring Equipment Checklist (page 8) are plenty of ice, lemons, cocktail fruits or glass decorations and olives, peanuts or nibbles to serve with drinks before food arrives. It's also a good idea to consider putting down an old piece of carpet or a mat behind the bar to protect the floor from spillage.

DEALING WITH STAINS

Don't make a huge fuss if someone spills red wine over your damask tablecloth – just deal with the situation calmly and efficiently, and as quickly as possible. Never use hot water – it will just 'set' the stain– and treat the stain from the wrong side of the fabric if possible.

Check the effect of stain remover on coloured fabric, by testing on an inconspicuous area. If using chemical remover, rinse with lukewarm water afterwards.

• Beer: sponge off immediately with plenty of cold water.

• Candle wax: scrape off as much as possible, then place a sheet of non-waxed brown paper over it, and press gently with a warm iron.

• Coffee: pour on soda water, then sponge with a solution of washing-up liquid in water.

• Red wine: pour on soda or ordinary water, or salt and leave to soak (this can be messy, but if applied to the stain quickly it can be very effective.) If the stain has been allowed to dry, apply a solution of equal parts glycerine and warm water, leave for 15 minutes, then sponge out.

• Tea: as with red wine, treat with salt.

• White wine and champagne: these shouldn't stain if rinsed with cold water

QUANTITY CHARTS

These quantity charts are a comprehensive guide to planning food for varying numbers of guests and a range of occasions. When you are catering for large numbers of people, it is not always necessary to increase the quantities you serve by the same amount. If, for example, you wanted to increase the your guestlist from 50 to 100, you may only have to increase the quantity of some foods by one third (or thereabouts) rather than double up. These charts are here to help you.

KEY TO CHARTS

Chart A
is for barbeques, picnics and cold buffet-type entertaining

Chart B
is for Sunday lunches, dinner parties and meal-based special occasions

Chart C
is for cocktail parties and events requiring finger food to nibble on

Chart D
is for miscellaneous extras

A LAST WORD

Remember to be well-organised and to leave as little as possible to do on the day of the party or wedding. Make lots of checklists and try to delegate tasks to others if they are volunteering to help. Above all, relax – you should enjoy yourself too! Good luck!

CHART A

Chart A covers buffets, barbecues, picnics and cold buffet-type entertaining. The amounts indicated allow each person 'some of everything' presuming they are choosing from a selection of 3 or more dishes.

	10	25	50	100
Quiche	2 x 20 cm (8 in)	2 x 25 cm (10 in) or 4 x 20 cm (8 in)	4 x 25 cm (10 in) or 8 x 20 cm (8 in)	9 x 25 cm (10 in) or 17 x 20 cm (8 in)
Sausages	Allow 2-4 per person			
Burgers	Allow 1 burger and 1 bun per person			
Chicken legs	Allow 1 chicken leg per person			
Salmon/chicken for mousses and pâtés	450 g (1 lb)	1.25 kg (2½ lb)	1.8 kg (4 lb)	5.75 kg (12½ lb)
Cold meats and antipasto	Allow 4 slices	Allow 3-4 slices	Allow 3 slices	Allow 3 slices
Pies	1.75 kg (4 lb)	4.5 kg (10 lb)	9 kg (20 lb)	18 kg (40 lb)
Chicken salad	1.75 kg (4 lb)	4.5 kg (10 lb)	8.5 kg (19 lb)	19 kg (43 lb)
Salmon off the bone	1.75 kg (3½ lb)	3.75 kg (8 lb)	7.5 kg (17 lb)	15.75 kg (35 lb)
Roast meats on the bone	1.5 kg (3¾ lb)	2.9 kg (6½ lb)	6 kg (14 lb)	14.5 kg (32 lb)
Finished casseroles	2.25 kg (5 lb)	4.5 kg (10 lb)	9 kg (20 lb)	20 kg (45 lb)
Baked fries	1.7 kg (3½ lb)	3.5 kg (8 lb)	7.25 kg (16 lb)	14.5 kg (32 lb)
Potato salad	1.7 kg (3½ lb)	3 kg (7 lb)	7 kg (15 lb)	14.5 kg (32 lb)
Rice salad	500 g (1¼ lb)	1.25 kg (2¼ lb)	1.8 kg (4 lb)	5 kg (11 lb)
Salads	1.25 kg (2¾ lb)	2.25 kg (5 lb)	4.5 kg (10 lb)	8.5 kg (19 lb)
Fruit cake	1 x 15 cm (6 in)	1 x 23 cm (9 in)	1 x 30 cm (12 in)	2 x 30 cm (12 in)
Mince pies	Allow 1-2 per person			
Gateau (round)	1 x 25 cm (10 in)	2 x 30 cm (12 in)	5 x 25 cm (10 in)	10 x 25 cm (10 in)
Strawberries	1.5 kg (3 lb)	3 kg (7 lb)	6 kg (13 lb)	11.75 kg (26 lb)
Ice-cream	1 litre (1¾ pints)	1.5-2.5 litres (2½ -4½ pints)	2.25-4.5 litres (4-8 pints)	6-12 litres (10-20 pints)

CHART B

Chart B covers Sunday lunches, dinner parties and meal-based special occasions. The amounts indicated allow each person 'just enough room' for a starter, a main course and a pudding and/or cheese.

	10	25	50	100
Soup	2 litres (3½ pints)	5.5 litres (10 pints)	12 litres (20 pints)	24 litres (40 pints)
Smoked salmon	1 kg (2½ lb)	2.75 kg (6 lb)	5.75 kg (12½ lb)	11.5 kg (25 lb)
Finished mousses and pâtés	1.5 kg (3 lb)	2.75 kg (6 lb)	5.75 kg (12½ lb)	11.5 kg (25 lb)
Salmon as a main course off the bone	1.75 kg (3¾ lb)	4.5 kg (10 lb)	9 kg (20 lb)	22.5 kg (50 lb)
Pheasant/guinea fowl (roasted or casseroled)	4 birds	8-9 birds	15-18 birds	30-32 birds
Duckling quarters	3 birds	6 birds	12½ birds	25 birds
Venison steaks	1.75 kg (3¾ lb)	3.75 kg (8½ lb)	7.5 kg (17 lb)	15.5 kg (34 lb)
Sirloin roast	1.75 kg (3¾ lb)	4 kg (9 lb)	7.5 kg (17 lb)	15.5 kg (34 lb)
Pork fillet	1.6 kg (3½ lb)	3.5 kg (8 lb)	7.25 kg (16 lb)	15 kg (33 lb)
Turkey on the bone	2.75 kg (6 lb)	6 kg (13 lb)	11.5 kg (25 lb)	23 kg (50 lb)
Meat for casseroles off the bone	1.5 kg (3 lb)	3 kg (7½ lb)	7 kg (15 lb)	13.5 kg (30 lb)
Stuffing	675 g (1½ lb)	1.6 kg (3¼ lb)	3 kg (6½ lb)	5.75 kg (12½ lb)
Gravy/sauce	600 ml (1 pint)	1 litre (2¼ pints)	2 litres (4½ pints)	4 litres (9 pints)
Creamed potato	1.5 kg (3 lb)	2.75 kg (6 lb)	5.5 kg (12 lb)	10 kg (22 lb)
Vegetables	1 kg (2¼ lb)	2.25 kg (5 lb)	3.5-4.5 kg (8-10 lb)	8 kg (18 lb)
Mushrooms	450 g (1 lb)	1.25 kg (2½ lb)	1.5 kg (3 lb)	2.75 kg (6 lb)
Pasta to accompany a main dish	1.25 kg (2½ lb)	2 kg (4½ lb)	3.75-4 kg (8¾ lb)	8 kg (17¾ lb)
Parmesan	150 g (5 oz)	275 g (10 oz)	500 g (1¼ lb)	1.5 kg (3 lb)
Cold mousses and soufflés	1.7 litres (3 pints)	4 litres (7 pints)	8.5 litres (15 pints)	17 litres (30 pints)
Tarts and flans	2 x 20 cm (8 in)	2 x 25 cm (10 in) or 4 x 20 cm (8 in)	4 x 25 cm (10 in) or 8 x 20 cm (8 in)	9 x 25 cm (10 in) or 17 x 20 cm (8 in)

CHART C

Chart C covers cocktail and drinks parties, and events requiring finger food. Allow each person 2-3 bites from each of about 6 different canapé recipes.

	10	**25**	**50**	**100**
Mini sausage rolls	Allow 2 per person			
Cocktail sausages	Allow 3 per person			
Pizza toasts	Allow 2 per person			
Mini sandwiches	Allow approximately 1 round per person			
Crostini (baguettes)	1 x 60 cm (24 in) baguette	1½-2 x 60 cm (24 in) baguettes	2-3 x 60 cm (24 in) baguettes	4-6 x 60 cm (24 in) baguettes
Bacon rolls (devils, angels)	Allow 2 per person (made using 1 rasher)			
Dips	450 g (1 lb)	675 g (1½ lb)	1.5 kg (3 lb)	2.25 kg (5 lb)
Palmiers and twists	175 g (6 oz)	450 g (1 Ib)	750 g (1¾ lb)	1.75 kg (3¼ lb)
Mini roulades	450 g (1 Ib)	1.5 kg (3 lb)	2 kg (4½ lb)	4 kg (8¾ lb)
Tiger prawns	900 g (2 lb)	2 kg (4½ lb)	4 kg (9 lb)	8 kg (18 lb)
Chicken for satay	500 g (1¼ lb)	1.5 kg (3 lb)	2.25 kg (5 lb)	4.5 kg (10 lb)
Meatballs	675 g (1½ lb)	1.5 kg (3 lb)	2.25 kg (5 lb)	4.5 kg (10 lb)
Cheese sablé dough	175 g (6 oz)	350 g (12 oz)	500 g (1¼ lb)	1.25 kg (2½ lb)
Pancake/blini batter	600 ml (1 pint)	1 litre (2 pints)	2 litres (3½ pints)	4 litres (7 pints)
Mini choux bun pastry	100 g (4 oz)	225 g (8 oz)	450 g (1 lb)	1 kg (2 lb)
Scone dough	450 g (1 Ib)	1 kg (2¼ lb)	2 kg (4½ lb)	3.75 kg (8½ lb)
Tuiles	225 g (½ Ib)	500 g (1¼ lb)	1.25 kg (2½ lb)	2.25 kg (5 lb)
Shortbread	500 g (1¼lb)	1.25 kg (2½ lb)	2.25 kg (5 lb)	4.5 kg (9¾ lb)
Fruit for chocolate fruits	450 g (1 lb)	900 g (2 lb)	1.75 kg (4 lb)	3 kg (7 lb)
Chocolate for chocolate fruits	75 g (3 oz)	175 g (6 oz)	350 g (12 oz)	500 g (1¼ Ib)

CHART D

Chart D covers all sorts of miscellaneous extras which don't appear in any particular categories covered by the previous three charts. Some of the amounts are estimated per head rather than in weights. Quantities given in this way make this chart easier to interpret.

	10	25	50	100
Dressings	450 ml (¾ pint)	750 ml (1¼ pints)	1.25 litres (2¼ pints)	2.5 litres (4½ pints)
Mayonnaise	600 ml (1 pint)	1.25 litres (2¼ pints)	2.5 litres (4½ pints)	5 litres (9 pints)
Pickles/chutneys	175 g (6 oz)	450 g (1 lb)	900 g (2 lb)	1.75 kg (3½ lb)
Softened butter for spreading	350 g (12 oz)	450 g (1 lb)	900 g (2 lb)	1.75 kg (4 lb)
Cheese (chart A)	675 g (1½ lb)	1.6 kg (3½ lb)	2.75 kg (6½ lb)	6 kg (13 lb)
Cheese (chart B)	1 kg (2 lb)	2.1 kg (4¾ lb)	4.25 kg (9½lb)	8.5 kg (19 lb)
Cheese biscuits	Chart A allow 3 per person		Chart B allow 4 per person	
Fruit bowl	Chart A allow 1 piece per person		Chart B allow 1½ per person	
Sandwiches	Chart A allow 1½ -2 rounds per person (each sliced loaf contains about 20 slices)			
	2 loaves	5 loaves	10 loaves	20 loaves
French sticks	60 cm (24 in) stick - allow 2 sticks per 10 people and 3 per 10 people if serving with soup			
Mineral water	2 x 1.5 litre bottles	5 x 1.5 litre bottles	10 x 1.5 litre bottles	20 x 1.5 litre bottles
Sugar	75 g (3 oz)	175 g (6 oz)	350 g (12 oz)	675 g (1½ lb)
Milk	450 ml (¾ pint)	750 ml (1¼ pints)	1.25 litres (2¼ pints)	2.5 litres (4½ pints)
Cream for coffee	450 ml (¾ pint)	600 ml (1 pint)	1.2 litres (2 pints)	2.25 litres (4 pints)
Cream for desserts	600 ml (1 pint)	1 litre (1¾ pints)	2.25 litres (4 pints)	3.50 litres (6 pints)
Tea	Allow 1-1½ teabags per person			
	1.75 litres (3 pints)	4 litres (6½ pints)	8 litres (13 pints)	19.5 litres (32½ pints)
Coffee	Allow 1 cup per person			
instant	25 g (1 oz)	50 g (2 oz)	100 g (4 oz)	225 g (8 oz)
ground	50 g (2 oz)	100 g (4 oz)	225 g (8 oz)	450 g (1 lb)
After dinner coffee	1.6 litres (2¾ pints)	2.5 litres (4½ pints)	5 litres (9 pints)	12 litres (20 pints)
Non-alcoholic punch	1.5 litres (2½ pints)	3.5 litres (5½ pints)	6 litres (11 pints)	12.2 litres (22 pints)
Sherry (minimum 1 glass per person)	1 bottle	2 bottles	4 bottles	8 bottles
Wine (2 glasses per person)	4 bottles	9 bottles	17 bottles	35 bottles

LUNCHES

A long lunch with good conversation is a delight.
Here are seven different menus – formal and
informal – so whatever the occasion, there is a
menu to match.

From the far right clockwise: *Chervil Potatoes (page 21), Cherry Tomato
Compôte (page 22), Mixed Seafood Cocktail (page 20), Steamed Carrots
and Turnips (page 21), Chocolate Mousse Cake (page 23)* and
Chicken and Ham Terrine in a Pastry Crust (page 20)

CELEBRATION SPRING LUNCH

MIXED SEAFOOD COCKTAIL

CHICKEN AND HAM TERRINE
IN A PASTRY CRUST

CHERVIL POTATOES

STEAMED CARROTS AND TURNIPS

CHERRY TOMATO COMPOTE

CHOCOLATE MOUSSE CAKE

The terrine and cake can be prepared (and even frozen) in advance leaving almost no work to be done on the day.

MIXED SEAFOOD COCKTAIL

Ready-prepared cooked seafood and bags of mixed salad are easily available from most supermarkets but you could also buy a selection of cooked prawns, mussels or squid.

Serves 6

1 x 120 g (4¹/₂ oz) bag mixed salad leaves and herbs
2 celery sticks, sliced
675 g (1¹/₂ lb) prepared cooked seafood
4 tablespoons mayonnaise

For the dressing
6 tablespoons olive oil
4 tablespoons white wine vinegar
¹/₂ teaspoon Dijon mustard
Salt and freshly ground black pepper

For the garnish
A little ground paprika, for sprinkling
Fresh dill sprigs
Fresh chives
Lemon slices
Lime slices

1. Place the salad and celery in a large bowl then make the dressing by shaking together the oil, vinegar, mustard and seasoning in a screw-top jar. Pour over the salad serving and toss well.
2. Arrange the leaves and celery on six plates. Tip the seafood into the bowl used to toss the salad

leaves and coat the seafood in the remaining dressing. Spoon the seafood over the leaves. Add a little mayonnaise to each plate and sprinkle with the paprika. Garnish with the dill sprigs, chives, and lemon and lime slices.

Mixed Seafood Cocktail

CHICKEN AND HAM TERRINE IN A PASTRY CRUST

Serves 6–8

225 g (8 oz) unsmoked, rindless streaky bacon
50 g (2 oz) crustless white bread, diced
50 ml (2 fl oz) milk
1 tablespoon sunflower oil
1 onion, finely chopped
1 celery stick, finely chopped
450 g (1 lb) ham, diced
2 teaspoons Dijon mustard
2 tablespoons dry sherry
1 egg, lightly beaten
25 g (1 oz) unsalted, shelled pistachio nuts
2 large chicken breasts, cut into long strips
2 tablespoons chopped fresh parsley
450 g (1 lb) ready-made puff pastry
1 egg white, lightly beaten
1 egg, beaten, to glaze
Salt and freshly ground black pepper

1. Drag the back of a knife along the bacon rashers to stretch them. Line the base and long sides of a 900 g (2 lb) loaf tin or terrine mould with the bacon overlapping the rashers. Reserve a few for later use. Place the bread in a bowl and pour over the milk; leave to soak.

2. Heat the oil in a pan, add the onion and celery and cook over a medium heat until softened. Remove from the heat and cool. Place in a food processor with the ham, soaked bread and mustard and whiz for 2–3 minutes until smooth.

3. Pre-heat the oven to 160C/325F/Gas 3. Add the sherry, the lightly beaten egg and seasoning to the mixture in the food processor, whiz to combine, then turn into a large bowl and stir in the pistachio nuts. Spread one third of the mixture in the bacon-lined tin, lay half of the chicken strips on top, then scatter with half the parsley.

4. Continue layering the ingredients in the same way, finishing with a layer of ham mixture. Flip the ends of the bacon rashers over the top and finish with a layer of the reserved rashers. Cover the terrine with foil or a lid and place in a roasting tin half filled with boiling water. Bake in the oven for 1 1/2 hours, then remove. Cover the tin with a piece of card, place weights or cans of food on top, leave to cool, then chill for about 2 hours.

5. When chilled, pour off the excess juices from the tin. Roll out the pastry to a 33 x 46 cm (13 x 18 in)

Chicken and Ham Terrine in a Pastry Crust, Chervil Potatoes, Cherry Tomato Compote (page 22) and Steamed Carrots and Turnips

rectangle and cut away the corners. Brush the surface of the pastry with the egg white. Run a blunt knife around the edges of the terrine and carefully invert it on to a board then back on to the pastry. Wrap the pastry around it, trimming and reserving any excess. Dampen the edges to seal.

6. Turn over the terrine and place on a baking sheet. Use the trimmings to make leaf shapes, dampen with water and place on top. Chill for at least 30 minutes.

7. Pre-heat the oven to 220C/425F/Gas 7. Brush the top of the terrine with the beaten egg and bake for 25 minutes then reduce the oven temperature to 200C/400F/Gas 6 and bake for a further 10 minutes or until the pastry is browned and cooked through. Serve hot or cold.

CHERVIL POTATOES

Fresh herbs make all the difference to the flavour.

 Serves 6–8

900 g (2 lb) new potatoes
50 g (2 oz) butter
2 tablespoons chopped fresh chervil or mint
Salt and freshly ground black pepper

1. Scrub the potatoes and cut into equal pieces. Place in a pan and cover with cold salted water, bring to the boil and simmer for 15 minutes or until tender. Drain.

2. Melt the butter in a pan and add the chervil or mint, the potatoes and seasoning. Toss lightly to coat and serve hot.

STEAMED CARROTS AND TURNIPS

 Serves 6–8

350 g (12 oz) baby turnips, with their stalks
350 g (12 oz) baby carrots, with their stalks
6 tablespoons olive oil
1 tablespoon red wine vinegar
Salt and freshly ground black pepper

1. Scrub the vegetables, place in a steamer and steam for 15 minutes or until just tender.

2. Remove and place in a warmed serving bowl. Add the oil, vinegar and seasoning and toss to coat. Serve hot.

CHERRY TOMATO COMPOTE

Serves 6–8

2 tablespoons olive oil
1 yellow pepper, seeded and sliced
350 g (12 oz) cherry tomatoes
4 tablespoons white wine vinegar
3 tablespoons golden caster sugar
2 teaspoons mustard seeds
Salt and freshly ground black pepper

1. Heat the oil in a pan and fry the pepper for 10 minutes or until softened. Add the tomatoes and fry for 1 minute. Add the vinegar, sugar, mustard seeds, seasoning and 2 tablespoons of water.
2. Bring to the boil and boil rapidly for 5 minutes, stirring occasionally. Remove from the heat and serve cool.

Chocolate Mousse Cake

CHOCOLATE MOUSSE CAKE

Serves 10–12

175 g (6 oz) plain chocolate
350 g (12 oz) plain flour
50 g (2 oz) cocoa
2 teaspoons baking powder
2 teaspoons bicarbonate of soda
175 g (6 oz) butter, softened
350 g (12 oz) light muscovado sugar
3 eggs, beaten
150 ml (5 fl oz) milk
3 tablespoons apricot jam, sieved

For the filling
2 teaspoons powdered gelatine
175 g (6 oz) plain chocolate
100 g (4 oz) butter
3 egg whites
25 g (1 oz) golden caster sugar

For the topping
175 g (6 oz) white chocolate
175 ml (6 fl oz) double cream
25 g (1 oz) butter, softened
50 g (2 oz) each plain, white and milk chocolate,
to decorate

1. Pre-heat the oven to 180C/350F/Gas 4. Grease and line 2 x 20 cm (8 in) round spring-release tins.
2. Place the chocolate in a bowl with 150 ml (5 fl oz) of boiling water. Stir to melt. Sift flour, cocoa powder, baking powder and bicarbonate of soda.
3. Beat together the butter and sugar in a bowl until pale and fluffy, then add the eggs a little at a time, beating well after each addition. Fold in the sifted ingredients alternately with the melted chocolate and milk. Divide equally between the two tins and bake for about 45–55 minutes or until well risen and just firm to the touch.
4. Remove from the oven and leave the cakes to cool in the tins for 30 minutes. Turn out on to a wire rack and allow to cool completely. Wash one tin and line with cling film.
5. To make the mousse, sprinkle the gelatine over 2 tablespoons of cold water. Place bowl in saucepan containing a little hot water and heat until gelatine dissolves and liquid runs clear. Melt the chocolate in a heatproof bowl over a pan of gently simmering water. Stir in the butter, leave to cool a little, then beat in the gelatine. Whisk the whites and sugar together in a bowl over a saucepan of gently simmering water until stiff. Gently fold into the chocolate mixture then chill for 10–15 minutes until the mousse is starting to set.
6. Cut each of the cakes in 2 horizontally, giving you 4 circles of cake. Cut a 13 cm (5 in) round from the centre of one split cake and repeat with another; leave the other two circles of cake whole. Set aside the cut-out centres to use in a trifle. Place a whole circle in the tin, spread the edge of the cake with apricot jam and top with a cake ring. Spread as before with jam and top with the second ring. Spread as before with jam. Spoon the mousse into the centre of the cake. Place the second whole round on top then chill for 1 hour until the mousse is set. Remove from the tin.
7. To make the topping, heat the white chocolate, cream and butter in a pan, stirring occasionally until melted. Remove from the heat, leave to cool then whip until smooth. Chill in the fridge for 30–40 minutes until thickened, then spread over the top of the cake.
8. Melt the plain, white and milk chocolate in separate bowls over hot water and place in separate paper piping bags. Wrap a rolling pin with non-stick baking paper and drizzle the chocolate back and forth over the rolling pin. Leave to cool and set before peeling off the semi-circles of chocolate and arranging them on top of the cake.

COUNTDOWN

• Make the dressing for the seafood cocktail in advance and wait until the last minute before tossing the salad. You can even arrange the leaves and seafood on the plates and chill in the fridge for up to 2 hours; drizzle over the dressing just before serving.

• The chicken and ham terrine can be made a day in advance, or frozen. To freeze, follow the recipe up to step 6, freeze without covering until firm, then seal well and freeze for up to 3 months. Thaw at room temperature for 4–6 hours.

• The chocolate mousse cake can also be prepared in advance, or frozen for up to 1 month. To freeze, follow the recipe completing step 6 but only chilling for 30 minutes, then remove from the tin, wrap in cling film and place in a rigid container. Thaw at room temperature for 4 hours, then complete.

AMERICAN DEEP-SOUTH LUNCH

LOUISIANA CRAB CAKES WITH TOMATO

AND CORIANDER SALSA

JAMBALAYA

BAKED BANANAS WITH CINNAMON ICE-CREAM

PECAN PRALINES

MINT JULEP

LOUISIANA CRAB CAKES WITH TOMATO AND CORIANDER SALSA

The crab cakes and salsa can be prepared the day before you need them. Just fry the crab cakes and bring the salsa to room temperature on the day.

Serves 6

25 g (1 oz) butter
1 shallot, finely chopped
15 g (¹/₂ oz) plain flour
150 ml (5 fl oz) hot milk
1 teaspoon Dijon mustard
Juice and finely grated rind of 1 lime
1 tablespoon chopped fresh parsley
2 pinches of chilli powder
450 g (1 lb) crab meat, defrosted if frozen
75 g (3 oz) toasted white breadcrumbs
Salt and freshly ground black pepper
Oil, for frying
Crisp lettuce leaves, to garnish
Lime wedges, to garnish

For the salsa
450 g (1 lb) ripe tomatoes, preferably plum
1–2 red chillies
1 red onion, finely chopped
100 ml (3¹/₂ fl oz) tomato juice
2 garlic cloves, finely chopped
2 tablespoons chopped fresh coriander
2 tablespoons red wine vinegar

1. Melt the butter in a small pan, add the shallot and cook for about 5 minutes until softened but not

From the top clockwise: Jambalaya (page 26), Mint Julep (page 27), Tomato and Coriander Salsa and Louisiana Crab Cakes

browned. Stir in the flour and cook, stirring, for 1 minute. Gradually add the milk, stirring continuously until thickened and smooth. Cook for 2 minutes, stirring.

2. Remove from the heat and stir in the mustard, juice and rind of the lime, parsley, chilli powder and seasoning. Mix well, cover and leave to cool.

3. Drain the crab meat in a sieve over a bowl, then press gently with the back of a wooden spoon to extract any excess moisture. Turn into a bowl with the sauce and breadcrumbs and mix lightly to avoid breaking up the flakes of crab meat too much. Taste and add more seasoning if necessary. Cover and chill for 1 hour to firm up the mixture.

4. To make the salsa, quarter and seed the tomatoes, then finely chop the flesh. Halve and seed the chillies and chop very finely. Place the tomatoes and chillies in a bowl with all the remaining ingredients and mix well. Cover and store in the fridge until needed.

5. Shape the crab meat mixture into 12 patties. Heat about 2.5 cm (1 in) oil in a large frying pan. Add the crab cakes, in batches if necessary, and fry on both sides until crisp and golden. Remove with a slotted spoon and drain on kitchen paper. Serve hot with the salsa and garnish with the lettuce leaves and lime wedges.

Louisiana Crab Cakes with Tomato and Coriander Salsa

JAMBALAYA

Prepare this dish ahead but once you've added the rice it needs to be cooked and served quite quickly.

Serves 6

900g (2 lb) boneless chicken thighs and breast, skinned
$1/_2$ teaspoon chilli powder
4 tablespoons sunflower oil
175 g (6 oz) thickly sliced cooked smoked ham,
cut into cubes
2 onions, chopped
1 red pepper, seeded and chopped
1 green pepper, seeded and chopped
3 celery sticks, chopped
4 garlic cloves, crushed
450 g (1 lb) long-grain rice
900 ml ($1^1/_2$ pints) chicken or vegetable stock
400 g (14 oz) can chopped tomatoes
225 g (8 oz) peeled prawns, preferably large,
tail segments retained
1 teaspoon Tabasco sauce
4 tablespoons chopped fresh parsley
1 bunch spring onions, chopped
Salt and freshly ground black pepper

1. Cut the chicken pieces into 2.5 cm (1 in) cubes and place in a shallow dish. Sprinkle with salt, pepper and the chilli powder and turn the pieces in the seasonings until evenly coated.
2. Heat half the oil in a large pan, add the chicken and cook quickly on all sides until lightly browned. Remove from the pan and keep warm. Add the ham to the pan and cook, stirring, for 5 minutes. Remove from the pan and add to the chicken. Set aside and keep warm.
3. Heat the remaining oil in the pan, add the onions, peppers, celery and garlic. Fry for about 5 minutes, scraping the base of the pan to incorporate all the flavours. Return the chicken and ham to the pan, sprinkle in the rice and mix until all the rice grains are glistening with oil.
4. Add the stock and tomatoes to the pan, check the seasoning, and bring to the boil, stirring. Cover and simmer for about 25 minutes or until the rice is just tender, adding more stock if it seems dry.
5. Stir in the prawns, Tabasco sauce, parsley and spring onions and cook for a further 5 minutes. Serve piping hot.

BAKED BANANAS WITH CINNAMON ICE-CREAM

Serves 6

100 g (4 oz) unsalted butter
100 g (4 oz) light muscovado sugar
6 ripe bananas, peeled and thickly sliced diagonally
$1/_2$ teaspoon ground cinnamon
100 ml ($3^1/_2$ fl oz) dark rum
2 tablespoons banana liqueur (optional)

1. Melt the butter in a large frying pan, then add the sugar and stir until it has melted. Add the bananas and cook gently for about 3–4 minutes or until tender.
2. Sprinkle over the cinnamon and mix well. Pour over the rum and banana liqueur (if using), shake the pan, then ignite. Shake the pan until the flames die down. Serve hot with the *Cinnamon Ice-cream*.

CINNAMON ICE-CREAM

Serves 6

3 egg yolks
90 g ($3^1/_2$ oz) light muscovado sugar
2 cinnamon sticks, broken in half
300 ml (10 fl oz) milk
300 ml (10 fl oz) double cream

1. Whisk together the egg yolks and sugar until thick and pale and the mixture leaves a trail when the whisk blades are lifted. Slowly heat the cinnamon sticks in the milk until just boiling, then remove from the heat, discard the cinnamon and stir milk into the egg yolk mixture.
2. Return the mixture to the pan and cook, stirring, over a low heat for about 15 minutes or until thickened. The custard should just coat the back of the wooden spoon.
3. Remove from the heat, strain into a clean bowl and leave until cold. Stir occasionally to prevent a skin from forming.
4. Stir the cream into the custard. Place the bowl in the freezer and leave until the mixture has set 2.5 cm (1 in) in from the edges. This will take about 2–3 hours. Whisk the mixture to break down the large ice crystals, return to the freezer for a further hour, then whisk again. The ice-cream should be softly set.

5. Transfer to a rigid container and freeze until firm. Transfer to the fridge 30 minutes before serving to soften and make it easy to serve.

PECAN PRALINES

These sweets are really good with coffee. They keep well in an airtight tin layered between waxed paper for up to two weeks.

 Makes about 20

25 g (1 oz) unsalted butter
350 g (12 oz) granulated sugar
175 g (6 oz) tin evaporated milk
1 teaspoon vanilla extract
100 g (4 oz) shelled pecan halves

1. Melt the butter in a large heavy-based pan. Add the sugar and milk and cook over a low heat, stirring, until the sugar has dissolved.
2. Bring the mixture to the boil, then boil for about 10 minutes or until it reaches the soft ball stage or 114C on a sugar thermometer. Test to check if the mixture is ready by dropping a tiny amount into a bowl of cold water. If it forms into a soft ball then it is ready. Sit the pan in cold water to stop the mixture cooking further, stir continuously as it cools until it develops a fudge-like consistency.
3. Quickly stir in the vanilla and pecans, then spoon blobs on to baking sheets covered with foil. The pralines should be about 5 cm (2 in) across. Leave to cool, peel off foil and store until required.

MINT JULEP

This is a refreshing drink to serve as your guests arrive. The syrup base can be stored in the fridge for several days.

 Serves 6

100 g (4 oz) granulated sugar
A handful of mint leaves, stripped from their stalks
225 ml (8 fl oz) bourbon
Crushed ice, to serve
Mint sprigs, to decorate

1. Place the sugar in a small pan with 120 ml (4 fl oz) water and heat gently, stirring, until the sugar has dissolved. Bring to the boil, then simmer for 5 minutes or until slightly syrupy but not coloured. Leave to cool.
2. Put the mint leaves into a large glass jug. Add the syrup and crush the leaves against the side of the jug with a wooden spoon. Fill the jug three-quarters full with crushed ice, then pour in the bourbon. Mix well and decorate with a sprig of mint. Serve in tall glasses.

Crushed Ice
Sandwich ice cubes between two non-fluffy tea towels and crush with a rolling pin.

Baked Bananas with Cinnamon Ice-cream

FABULOUS FISH LUNCH

Lemon Sole and Prawn Mousse
with Tomato Sauce

Salmon Rosti

Grilled Fresh Figs with Raspberries

LEMON SOLE AND PRAWN MOUSSE WITH TOMATO SAUCE

This sauce can be made in advance and then heated before serving or can be served at room temperature.

Serves 4

450 g (1 lb) lemon sole, filleted and skinned
2 egg whites
150 ml (5 fl oz) double cream
175 g (6 oz) cooked peeled prawns
A little finely grated lemon rind
2 shallots, finely chopped
1 tablespoon sunflower oil
450 g (1 lb) ripe tomatoes, skinned and finely diced
100 g (4oz) cooked prawns in their shells, to garnish
Butter, for greasing
Salt and freshly ground black pepper

1. Butter four individual ramekin dishes. Cut the fish into 2.5 cm (1 in) cubes. Put in a food processor with the egg whites and mince finely. Blend the cream into the fish mixture and season with black pepper.

2. Spoon half of the fish mixture into the ramekins and level the surface of each one. Divide the peeled prawns and grated lemon rind between the ramekins. Top with the remaining fish mixture and smooth the tops with a round-bladed knife. Cover each ramekin with buttered foil. Keep chilled in the fridge until ready to use.

3. Place the ramekins in a wide-based saucepan. Pour in enough water to come half way up the sides of the ramekins and cover the pan. Bring to the boil, then simmer gently for about 8 minutes or until set.

4. Meanwhile, make the tomato sauce. Gently fry the shallots in the oil until transparent and softened. Add the tomatoes and 2 tablespoons of water. Cook for 6–7 minutes or until the tomatoes break down a little but keep some shape. Season to taste.

5. Turn out each mousseline on to a serving plate and spoon round some of the sauce. Garnish with prawns in their shells and serve with Melba or wholemeal toast.

Lemon Sole and Prawn Mousse with Tomato Sauce
and *Salmon Rosti*

SALMON ROSTI

Make sure that the grated potato is well rinsed to wash off the excess starch. Dry well in a clean tea towel to remove all moisture; this will prevent the rosti from becoming soggy. To make the rosti crisp, get the butter really hot before adding the mixture.

Serves 4

675 g (1¹/₂ lb) floury potatoes, coarsely grated, rinsed and dried
225 g (8 oz) celeriac, coarsely grated
175 g (6 oz) fennel, chopped
A small bunch of chives, finely snipped
675 g (1¹/₂ lb) fresh salmon, filleted and skinned
50 g (2 oz) butter
Juice of ¹/₂ lemon
Salt and freshly ground black pepper

1. Mix the potato, celeriac, fennel, chives and seasoning together. Cut the salmon into 1 cm (¹/₂ in) strips.
2. Melt half the butter in a 23 cm (9 in) non-stick frying pan. When it is hot and foaming spoon in half of the potato mixture and press down lightly and evenly. Lay the salmon evenly over the potato and sprinkle over the lemon juice and season with black pepper.
3. Cover the salmon with the rest of the potato mixture then cook over a medium heat for 7–10 minutes. Shake the frying pan from time to time to make sure the potato does not stick.
4. To turn the rosti, remove the pan from the heat and place a plate that is larger than the frying pan over the top of it. Carefully invert so that the rosti transfers to the plate.
5. Return the frying pan to the heat and melt the remaining butter. Carefully slide the rosti back into the frying pan and cook for a further 7–10 minutes. The fish should be just set and the outside of the potato crisp.
6. Slide the rosti on to a serving dish or cut into wedges and serve straight from the pan with a *Mixed Green Salad with Walnut Vinaigrette* (see page 68).

GRILLED FRESH FIGS WITH RASPBERRIES

Serves 4

8 fresh figs
225 g (8 oz) crème fraîche
8 teaspoons light muscovado sugar
225 g (8 oz) raspberries
Butter, for greasing

1. Pre-heat the grill to high. Lightly butter a shallow flameproof dish, large enough to accommodate the figs in a single layer.
2. Cut the figs into quarters without cutting through the base and gently open each one out a little. Spoon a dollop of crème fraîche into the centre of each fig.
3. Pile a teaspoon of sugar on top of the crème fraîche. Put the figs in the dish and put under the hot grill for 2 minutes or until the sugar has melted and the crème fraîche starts to run. Scatter the raspberries around the figs and serve immediately.

Grilled Fresh Figs with Raspberries

GREEK MEZE

FETA CHEESE SALAD

COUNTRY SAUSAGE AND
SWEET PEPPER CASSEROLE

GRILLED SQUID WITH FETA CHEESE

GRILLED CHEESE

CHARRED COURGETTES AND AUBERGINES

YOGHURT AND CUCUMBER SALAD

TARAMASALATA

LAMB KEBABS

FRIED MUSSELS

AUBERGINE SALAD DIP

BAKLAVA

This Greek meal makes a perfect buffet. It combines meat, vegetables, fish, salads and dips in a colourful array of dishes. Serve lots of bread with this meal.

FETA CHEESE SALAD

Serves 4–6

450 g (1 lb) ripe tomatoes
2 small onions, thinly sliced
1 green pepper, seeded and thinly sliced
10 cm (4 in) piece cucumber, peeled and sliced
8–12 black olives
100 g (4 oz) feta cheese, cubed
A pinch of dried oregano
5–6 tablespoons olive oil
Salt
Fresh oregano sprigs, to garnish
Crusty bread, to serve

1. Quarter the tomatoes. Mix all of the ingredients together in a salad bowl and toss gently. Serve with fresh crusty bread.

COUNTRY SAUSAGE AND SWEET PEPPER CASSEROLE

Serves 4–6

2 tablespoons olive oil
450 g (1 lb) good-quality spicy sausages, cut into 5 cm (2 in) slices
675 g (1½ lb) green or red peppers, seeded and sliced
225 g (8 oz) tomatoes, skinned, seeded and quartered
1 teaspoon chopped fresh oregano
2 tablespoons chopped fresh flatleaf parsley
Salt and freshly ground black pepper
½ pitta, to serve

1. Heat the oil in a pan and gently fry the sausages until lightly browned. Add the peppers and fry for a further 3 minutes, stirring continuously.
2. Add the tomatoes, oregano, parsley and seasoning to the pan, then cover and cook gently for about 10 minutes until the sausages are cooked through. Serve hot with pitta bread.

GRILLED SQUID WITH FETA CHEESE

Serves 4–6

6–8 small squid, about 450 g (1 lb) in total
5 tablespoons olive oil
2 tablespoons lemon juice
1 garlic clove, crushed
1 teaspoon chopped fresh oregano
100 g (4 oz) feta cheese, sliced
Salt and freshly ground black pepper

1. To prepare the squid, pull the head and tentacles away from the body and discard. Remove and discard the body contents, ink sac and plastic-like quill; rinse well. Rub off the dark purplish skin from the outer body and rinse again. Place in a shallow, non-metallic bowl.
2. Shake together the oil, lemon juice, garlic, oregano and seasoning in screw-top jar. Add to the squid and toss to coat well. Cover and leave to marinate in the fridge for 2 hours.
3. Remove the squid from the marinade and insert 1–2 pieces of cheese into each body cavity. Grill or barbecue for 5–6 minutes on each side until the flesh just begins to brown but not burn.

GRILLED CHEESE

Serves 4–6

175 g (6 oz) Kefalotyri or Haloumi cheese
3 tablespoons olive oil

To garnish
Fresh mint sprigs
Lemon wedges

1. Cut the cheese into 1 cm (¹/₂ in) slices. Brush with oil and grill lightly until golden brown. Alternatively, heat the oil in a cast-iron or non-stick frying pan and fry the cheese slices for 1–2 minutes. Turn the slices over and cook until the edges start to brown; drain on kitchen paper.
2. Serve hot, garnished with the mint sprigs and lemon wedges.

CHARRED COURGETTES AND AUBERGINES

Serves 4–6

5–6 tablespoons olive oil
Dried thyme or oregano, to taste
450 g (1 lb) aubergines, sliced lengthways
450 g (1 lb) courgettes, sliced lengthways
Salt, to taste
Yoghurt and Cucumber Salad, *to serve (see right)*

1. Mix together the olive oil and herbs in a small bowl. Brush the aubergines and courgettes liberally with the oil and herb mixture and grill until golden on both sides, turning and brushing frequently with more of the herb-flavoured oil.
2. Arrange the grilled vegetables on a platter and sprinkle with salt. Serve hot with the *Yoghurt and Cucumber Salad.*

YOGHURT AND CUCUMBER SALAD

Serves 4–6

2 tablespoons olive oil
1 teaspoon red wine vinegar
1 garlic clove, crushed
225 g (8 oz) Greek yoghurt (preferably sheep's yoghurt)
13 cm (5 in) piece cucumber, coarsely grated
1–2 tablespoons chopped fresh mint
Salt and freshly ground black pepper

1. Lightly beat the oil, vinegar and garlic in a bowl, then stir in the yoghurt and beat well until smooth.
2. Add the cucumber and mint and mix well, then adjust the seasoning to taste. Cover and chill before serving with the *Charred Courgettes and Aubergines.*

From the left: *Feta Cheese Salad, Country Sausage and Sweet Pepper Casserole, Grilled Squid with Feta Cheese* and *Grilled Cheese*

TARAMASALATA

Serves 4–6

100 g (4 oz) crustless stale bread
175 g (6 oz) smoked fresh cods' roe, skinned
Juice of 1½ lemons
150 ml (5 fl oz) olive oil
Salt and freshly ground black pepper
4–5 black olives, to garnish
Pitta bread, to serve

1. Place the bread in 150 ml (5 fl oz) water. Leave to soak for 20 minutes then squeeze out the excess liquid but leave the bread fairly moist.
2. Place the moist bread, cods' roe and lemon juice in a food processor or liquidiser and blend to form a purée. With the machine still running, gradually add the olive oil until the mixture becomes smooth. If the mixture is too stiff, add a little cold water and blend briefly, then taste and adjust the seasoning.
3. Spoon the taramasalata into a serving dish and scatter over the black olives. Serve with pitta bread.

LAMB KEBABS

Serves 4

500 g (1¼ lb) boneless leg of lamb
4–5 tablespoons olive oil
2 garlic cloves, crushed

Charred Courgettes and Aubergines (page 31), Yoghurt and Cucumber Salad (page 31) and *Lamb Kebabs*

2 bay leaves, crumbled
3 teaspoons chopped fresh oregano
1 red pepper, seeded and cut into 4 cm (1½ in) squares
1 green pepper, seeded and cut into 4 cm (1½ in) squares
2 small onions, quartered
Salt and freshly ground black pepper
Fresh oregano sprigs, to garnish

1. Trim the lamb and cut into 5 cm (2 in) cubes. Mix together the oil, garlic, bay leaves and 2 teaspoons of the oregano in a shallow, non-metallic dish. Add the lamb and toss well, ensuring that all of the cubes are evenly coated, then cover and marinate in the fridge for 4–6 hours, turning occasionally.
2. Thread the lamb on to greased skewers, alternating the meat with the peppers and onions. Sprinkle over the remaining oregano, then season.
3. Grill or barbecue for 8–10 minutes, turning the skewers frequently until the meat begins to brown at the edges. Serve garnished with oregano sprigs.

FRIED MUSSELS

Serves 4–6

675 g (1½ lb) fresh mussels
1 egg
25 g (1 oz) plain flour
A large pinch of baking powder
1 garlic clove, crushed
1 tablespoon chopped fresh parsley
1 tablespoon chopped fresh dill
Vegetable oil, for frying
Salt and freshly ground black pepper
Lemon wedges, to serve

1. Wash the mussels thoroughly under cold running water and scrape off any barnacles and 'beards' with a sharp knife. Discard any mussels that do not close when tapped sharply with a knife.
2. Place the mussels in a large pan, cover and cook over a medium heat for 3–4 minutes, shaking the pan frequently, until the mussels open. Lift the mussels out of the pan and discard any that have not opened. When they are cool enough to handle, pull the meat away from the shells and discard the empty shells.
3. Place the egg, flour, baking powder, garlic, parsley and dill in a bowl with 4 tablespoons of water and beat to a smooth batter. Season to taste.
4. Heat about 4 cm (1½ in) oil in a heavy-based

frying pan. Dip the mussels in the batter then drop them into the hot oil. Fry in batches over a medium heat until they are lightly browned. Remove the mussels and drain on kitchen paper. Serve hot with the lemon wedges.

AUBERGINE SALAD DIP

 Serves 4–6

2 large aubergines, about 675 g (1¹/₂ lb) in total
2 garlic cloves, crushed
Juice of 1 lemon
5–6 tablespoons olive oil
2 tablespoons chopped fresh flatleaf parsley
Salt and freshly ground black pepper
Country bread or pitta bread, to serve

To garnish
Fresh flatleaf parsley sprigs
Black olives

1. Pre-heat the oven to 190C/375F/Gas 5. Prick the aubergines all over with a fork and place on a baking sheet. Cook in the oven for 50 minutes to 1 hour, turning occasionally. Once the aubergines are cool enough to handle, cut in half and scoop out the flesh into a colander. Press the flesh lightly to drain off any bitter juices.
2. Transfer the flesh to a liquidiser and add the garlic and lemon juice. With the machine running, gradually add the oil to form a smooth purée. Add the parsley and blend briefly, then taste and adjust the seasoning.
3. Transfer to a serving bowl and garnish with flatleaf parsley sprigs and black olives. Serve with slices of toasted country bread or pitta bread.

BAKLAVA

 Serves 8–10

450 g (1 lb) walnuts finely chopped
3 tablespoons caster sugar
A pinch of ground cinnamon
275 g (10 oz) packet filo pastry, thawed if frozen
100 g (4 oz) butter, melted

For the syrup
Juice of 1 lemon

Baklava

150 g (6 oz) sugar
¹/₂ teaspoon ground cinnamon

1. Pre-heat the oven to 180C/350F/Gas 4, then lightly grease a 25 cm (10 in) loose-bottomed cake tin. Mix the walnuts, sugar and cinnamon in a bowl.
2. Unfold the filo pastry and cover with a damp tea towel to stop it drying out. Brush a piece of the filo with melted butter, fit it into the bottom of the tin with the buttered side down. Let the edges spill over and brush with butter. Repeat with 3 more buttered pastry sheets making sure that the whole tin is lined.
3. Sprinkle with half of the nut mixture. Repeat with 4 more layers of buttered filo and scatter over the remaining nut mixture. Place 2 more layers of buttered filo on top, then fold the edges in and under.
4. Cut the last 2 pieces of filo so that it fits the tin, place on top and brush generously with butter. Bake for 40 minutes, then increase the temperature to 200C/400F/Gas 6. Mark the surface of the pastry with the tip of a sharp knife to make fan-shaped slices and bake for 20 minutes or until golden brown.
5. Meanwhile make the syrup. Gently heat the lemon juice, sugar and cinnamon until the sugar dissolves and the syrup has reduced slightly. Pour over the cooked baklava and leave to cool in the tin for 1-2 hours. Cut into wedges and serve.

SUNDAY ROAST PORK

Roast Pork with Sage and Onion Crust and

Crackling Chips

Sherry Gravy

Spicy Roast Parsnips

Stir-fried Brussels Sprouts

Cheese-topped Carrot and Potato Purée

Cranberry Red Cabbage

ROAST PORK WITH SAGE AND ONION CRUST AND CRACKLING CHIPS

Serves 6–8

1.5 kg (3 lb) boneless joint roasting pork (i.e. loin, leg or shoulder)
3 tablespoons sunflower oil
1 onion, chopped
2.5 cm (1 in) piece fresh root ginger, finely chopped
2 tablespoons chopped fresh sage
4 tablespoons chopped fresh parsley
100 g (4 oz) fresh white breadcrumbs
1 egg, beaten
Salt and freshly ground black pepper

1. Pre-heat the oven to 180C/350F/Gas 4. Remove the skin and a thin layer of fat from the pork. Cut the skin into thin strips 1 cm ($^1/_2$ in) wide. Lay in a metal, ovenproof dish, add 1 tablespoon of oil, mix to coat, then sprinkle with salt.
2. To make the crust, fry the onion and ginger in the remaining oil for 5 minutes or until softened. Add the sage, parsley and breadcrumbs, remove from the heat and mix in the egg, then season.
3. Place the pork in a roasting tin. Press the crust evenly over the fat, loosely cover with foil, then roast in the centre of the oven with the crackling strips on the shelf above for 30 minutes per 450 g (1 lb), plus 30 minutes. Thirty minutes before the end of cooking, remove the foil to brown the crust.
4. Transfer the pork to a warm serving platter reserving the pan juices for the gravy. Cover with foil and leave to rest for 15 minutes while you make the *Sherry Gravy*.

SHERRY GRAVY

Serves 6–8

Pan juices from roast
2 teaspoons plain flour
1 teaspoon mustard powder
4 tablespoons medium dry sherry
300 ml (10 fl oz) stock or vegetable cooking water
Salt and freshly ground black pepper

1. Pour off all but 2 tablespoons of the pan juices. Heat the roasting tin on the hob until the juices are bubbling; stir in the flour and mustard powder.
2. Stir in the sherry and stock, scraping the base of

the tin to incorporate all the flavours. Bring to the boil, season and simmer for 5 minutes before serving.

To carve
If you choose a boned joint always remove the bone before you carve. Your butcher could chine the backbone to make it easier to remove the bone from the cooked joint. Alternatively, loosen the meat from the bone with a sharp knife, then cut down into slices using a sawing movement.

SPICY ROAST PARSNIPS

Serves 6–8

675 g–1 kg (1¹/₂–2 lb) parsnips, trimmed and quartered lengthways
2 tablespoons sunflower oil
2 teaspoons mustard seeds
2 teaspoons cumin seeds
1 teaspoon paprika
¹/₂ teaspoon turmeric
Salt and freshly ground black pepper

1. Cut out the tough cores from the parsnips. Toss with the oil, mustard, cumin seeds, paprika, turmeric and seasoning until evenly coated. Roast around the joint for the last 30 minutes of its cooking time.

STIR-FRIED BRUSSELS SPROUTS

Serves 6–8

2 tablespoons sunflower oil
675 g (1¹/₂ lb) Brussels sprouts, trimmed and halved
2 tablespoons freshly squeezed lemon juice
Salt and freshly ground black pepper

1. Heat the oil in a pan, add the sprouts and stir-fry quickly until glistening.
2. Reduce the heat and add the lemon juice and seasoning. Cover and cook for 3–4 minutes or until just tender.

From the left: *Roast Pork with Sage and Onion Crust and Crackling Chips, Spicy Roast Parsnips, Sherry Gravy, Cheese-topped Carrot and Potato Purée, Stir-fried Brussels Sprouts* and *Cranberry Red Cabbage*

CHEESE-TOPPED CARROT AND POTATO PURÉE

Serves 6–8

8 medium-sized baking potatoes
450 g (1 lb) carrots, chopped
25 g (1 oz) butter
1 teaspoon demerara sugar
1 tablespoon chopped fresh parsley (optional)
2 tablespoons grated Parmesan or mature Cheddar
Salt and freshly ground black pepper

1. Pre-heat the oven to 180C/350F/Gas 4. Bake the potatoes on the shelf above the joint for 1–1¹/₄ hours or until tender. Place the carrots in a pan with the butter, sugar and seasoning and 4 tablespoons of water. Bring to the boil, then cover and cook for 10 minutes or until the carrots are tender and the liquid has almost evaporated.
2. Purée the carrots in a food processor. When the potatoes are cooked, split them in half and scoop the flesh into a bowl. Mash with a fork, then mix in the carrot purée until evenly mixed. Season to taste and add the parsley (if using).
3. Set the potato shells on a baking sheet and fill with the purée. Sprinkle over the cheese and return the potatoes to the oven for 15–20 minutes or until the filling is golden.

CRANBERRY RED CABBAGE

Serves 6–8

2 tablespoons sunflower oil
1 onion, chopped
675 g (1¹/₂ lb) red cabbage, shredded
4 tablespoons red wine vinegar
50 g (2 oz) light muscovado sugar
100 g (4 oz) cranberries, thawed if frozen
Salt and freshly ground pepper

1. Heat the oil in a large pan, add the onion and fry for 5 minutes until softened. Add the cabbage and stir well to coat in the oil.
2. Stir in the vinegar and sugar and bring to the boil. Cover and cook gently for 25 minutes. Stir in the cranberries and seasoning, cover and cook for a further 10 minutes or until the cranberries have popped. Serve hot.

VEGETARIAN SPLENDOUR

MELON AND ORANGE CUPS

STUFFED AUBERGINES

ROASTED RED PEPPER SAUCE

TAHINI SAUCE

TWO-COLOUR CABBAGE AND TANGERINE SALAD

SPICED POACHED PEARS

This menu is perfect for entertaining vegetarians, vegans and anyone following a healthy diet.

MELON AND ORANGE CUPS

 Serves 4

2 small honeydew melons
1 grapefruit, peeled and segmented
2 oranges, peeled and segmented
50 g (2 oz) roasted, unsalted peanuts
25 g (1 oz) light muscovado sugar
$\frac{1}{4}$ teaspoon ground cinnamon
Fresh mint sprigs, to garnish

Melon and Orange Cups

1. Halve the melons, scoop out the seeds and discard, then remove and chop the flesh. Reserve the melon shells.
2. In a bowl, mix together the melon and citrus fruits. Pile the fruit back into the melon shells.
3. Chop the peanuts and mix with the sugar and cinnamon. Sprinkle over the fruit and serve with mint sprigs.

STUFFED AUBERGINES

Choose between *Roasted Red Pepper Sauce* and *Tahini Sauce* (see right) as an accompaniment to the aubergines. If you want a more substantial main course, serve with a mixture of basmati and wild rice, and a green vegetable.

 Serves 4

4 small aubergines
1 tablespoon vegetable oil
1 large onion, chopped
2 garlic cloves, crushed
1 teaspoon cumin seeds
1 teaspoon ground coriander
175 g (6 oz) mushrooms, chopped
2 large tomatoes, skinned, seeded and chopped
1 tablespoon tahini
1 tablespoon dark soy sauce
50 g (2 oz) wholemeal breadcrumbs
2 tablespoons chopped fresh parsley
1 teaspoon lemon juice
Salt and freshly ground black pepper

1. Pre-heat the oven to 180C/350F/Gas 4. Cut a lid from the top of each aubergine and then remove a slice from the base of each so they will stand upright. Place the aubergines on a lightly greased baking tray and bake for 30 minutes. Scoop out most of the flesh, leaving solid walls. Chop the aubergine flesh finely.
2. Heat the oil in a pan and fry the onion, garlic, cumin and coriander over a moderate heat for 3 minutes, stirring occasionally. Add the mushrooms, tomatoes, tahini and dark soy sauce and cook for a further 8 minutes. Add the aubergine flesh, breadcrumbs, parsley and lemon juice. Season mixture to taste.
3. Fill the aubergine shells with the mixture then place them on a baking sheet, replace the lids and bake for 20–25 minutes. Serve hot.

Stuffed Aubergines and *Roasted Red Pepper Sauce*

ROASTED RED PEPPER SAUCE

Makes 300 ml (10 fl oz)

2 large red peppers
300 ml (10 fl oz) vegetable stock
Salt and freshly ground black pepper

1. Pre-heat the oven to 200C/400F/Gas 6. Place the peppers on a baking tray and roast for around 15 minutes or until the skins are blackened and blistered and the peppers are tender. Place in a polythene bag for 5 minutes before peeling off the skin. Remove the seeds and central core.
2. Place the peppers in a liquidiser or food processor with the stock and purée until smooth. Pour into a small pan, season to taste and gently heat through before serving with the *Stuffed Aubergines*.

TAHINI SAUCE

If you wish, and you're not serving the dish to vegans, you could add 100 g (4 oz) natural yoghurt to make a thicker, sharper-flavoured sauce.

Makes 150 ml (5 fl oz)

1 garlic clove, crushed
Salt
4 tablespoons tahini
Juice of 1 lemon

1. In a food processor, combine the garlic, salt and tahini until smooth. Add the lemon juice and 4 tablespoons of water and blend in. You can vary the thickness of the sauce according to taste by using less or more water and lemon juice respectively.

TWO-COLOUR CABBAGE AND TANGERINE SALAD

Serves 4

100 g (4 oz) white cabbage, finely shredded
100 g (4 oz) red cabbage, finely shredded
2–3 tangerines, peeled and sliced
2 tablespoons olive or sesame oil
1 tablespoon lemon juice
¼ teaspoon salt
6 radishes, trimmed and chopped

1. Place the shredded cabbage and tangerine slices in a large bowl and mix well. In a separate bowl, stir together the oil, lemon juice and salt and pour over salad.
2. Toss well and garnish with the chopped radishes. Serve at once, or cover for a few hours and chill until needed.

SPICED POACHED PEARS

Serves 4

175 g (6 oz) sugar
250 ml (8 fl oz) red wine
4 strips orange peel
Juice of ½ orange
2 cinnamon sticks
4 cardamom pods, split
6 whole cloves
4 pears

1. In a pan, heat together all the ingredients, except the pears, until the sugar has dissolved.
2. Peel the pears, keeping the stalks intact, and place them whole in the liquid.
3. Simmer gently, covered, for 35–40 minutes, turning frequently. To serve, arrange in a serving dish or in individual bowls.

Spiced Poached Pears

LIGHT AND EASY VEGETARIAN LUNCH

Baby Beetroot and Leek Salad with
Soured Cream Dressing
Red Chicory and Asparagus Salad
Crusty Sugarsnap and
Mushroom Flan
Peaches in Filo Pastry with
Redcurrant Sauce

This is a lovely menu for that special lunch when you really want to give your guests a treat.

BABY BEETROOT AND LEEK SALAD WITH SOURED CREAM DRESSING

Serves 6

450 g (1 lb) young cooked beetroot, grated
1 tablespoon sultanas
75 g (3 oz) sliced walnuts
1$\frac{1}{2}$ tablespoons walnut oil
2 teaspoons red wine vinegar
1 teaspoon grated orange rind
4 medium leeks, trimmed
150 ml (5 fl oz) soured cream
Juice of $\frac{1}{2}$ orange
Salt and freshly ground black pepper

1. Mix together the beetroot, sultanas, walnuts, oil, vinegar, orange rind and a little seasoning.
2. Cut the leeks into 1 cm ($\frac{1}{2}$ in) slices and cook lightly in boiling water for 2–3 minutes. Drain and refresh in cold water, then drain again.
3. Mix the soured cream and orange juice together. Divide the leeks between 6 serving plates and spoon over the beetroot and sultana mixture. Drizzle over the soured cream and orange dressing just before serving.

Baby Beetroot and Leek Salad with Soured Cream Dressing and *Red Chicory and Asparagus Salad*

RED CHICORY AND ASPARAGUS SALAD

Serves 6

4–6 heads red chicory or radicchio
450–675 g (1–1$\frac{1}{2}$ lb) asparagus

For the dressing
4 tablespoons walnut or hazelnut oil
1$\frac{1}{2}$ tablespoons cider vinegar
1 teaspoon honey or sugar
$\frac{1}{2}$ teaspoon mustard powder
Salt and freshly ground black pepper

1. Wash and separate the chicory leaves and arrange in a wide, shallow serving bowl.
2. Prepare the asparagus by removing the tough base of the shoots and chopping into 10 cm (4 in) pieces. Cook in fast-boiling water for 3–4 minutes or until just tender but still bright green. Drain and plunge into ice cold water to refresh. Drain again and arrange the asparagus over the chicory leaves. Shake together the dressing ingredients in a screw-top jar. Pour over the salad just before serving.

Crusty Sugarsnap and Mushroom Flan

CRUSTY SUGARSNAP AND MUSHROOM FLAN

This flan is best made with a soft bread such as a herb and cheese or sun-dried tomato loaf.

Serves 6

1 herb and cheese loaf
75 g (3 oz) butter, melted
350 g (12 oz) sugarsnap peas
350 g (12 oz) chestnut mushrooms, sliced
1 bunch spring onions, thinly sliced
2 tablespoons olive oil
1 tablespoon chopped fresh thyme
450 g (1 lb) crème fraîche
5 eggs
2 tablespoons freshly grated Parmesan
Salt and freshly ground black pepper
2 tablespoons Parmesan shavings, to garnish

1. Pre-heat the oven to 200C/400F/Gas 6. Cut the bread into 5 mm ($^1/_4$ in) thick slices. Line the base of a 23 cm (9 in) spring-release cake tin with foil, cutting the foil slightly larger than the base to cover the join between the sides and base.
2. Brush the sides and base of the foil and tin with melted butter. Brush one side of each slice of bread with melted butter. Carefully press the slices of bread, overlapping by about one third, around the sides of the tin to give a pretty scalloped edge.
3. Reserve 4 or 5 slices of bread and put the rest on a baking sheet and bake in the middle of the oven for 10 minutes. Make a base for the flan with the toasted bread, then fill all the gaps with the reserved bread, breaking it if necessary.
4. Blanche the sugarsnap peas in boiling water for 1 minute, then refresh in cold water. Fry the mushrooms and spring onions in the oil until the mushroom juices begin to run. Add the thyme. Allow to cool slightly.
5. In a large bowl, whisk together the crème fraîche, eggs and seasoning. Add the mushroom mixture and sugarsnap peas and mix together well.
6. Sprinkle the grated Parmesan over the base of the flan, then carefully pour in the filling, making sure all the bread is still in place.
7. Quickly sprinkle half the Parmesan shavings over the top of the flan. Put the tin on a baking sheet and cook in the top of the oven for about 40 minutes until the filling is set and the bread is golden brown.
8. Once the flan is cooked, the crust can be crisped by removing the flan from the outer ring, leaving

LIGHT AND EASY VEGETARIAN LUNCH

the base of the tin in place. Return it to the oven for 5–10 minutes then remove from the oven and leave to rest for 10 minutes. Serve garnished with the remaining Parmesan shavings.

PEACHES IN FILO PASTRY WITH REDCURRANT SAUCE

 Serves 6

150 g (5 oz) Amaretti biscuits
100 g (4 oz) ricotta cheese
2 teaspoons soft brown sugar
1½ tablespoons Amaretto (almond liqueur)
6 peaches, ripe but firm
450 g (1 lb) filo pastry (large sheets)
100 g (4 oz) melted butter
100 g (4 oz) flaked almonds
350 g (12 oz) fresh or frozen redcurrants
75 g (3 oz) caster sugar

1. Pre-heat the oven to 180C/350F/Gas 4. Place the biscuits in a polythene bag and crush coarsely with a rolling pin. Mix together the ricotta, 75 g (3 oz) of the crushed biscuits, the sugar and liqueur to form a fairly stiff paste.
2. Carefully cut each peach in half and remove the stone. Replace the stone with a spoonful of the ricotta mixture and sandwich the peach halves together again.
3. Open out the roll of filo pastry and, slicing through all the sheets at once, cut into 20–23 cm (8–9 in) squares. You will need 18 squares in total. Keep the filo covered with a clean damp tea towel or cling film while you work.
4. For each peach use 3 of the filo squares. Working with one peach at a time, butter each square of pastry and lay, off set, on top of each other, so you have a 12-pointed star.
5. Spoon one sixth of the remaining Amaretti crumbs in to the middle of the filo. This will absorb some of the peach juices and prevent the pastry from becoming soggy. Put a whole, filled peach on top of the crumbs, stalk side down.
6 Gather up the sides of the pastry and pinch together at the top, securing with a piece of kitchen string. (This is not essential but can prevent the peach halves from separating and the parcels opening up.) Repeat with the remaining 5 peaches.
7. Place the peaches on a greased baking sheet. Brush each parcel with any remaining butter and sprinkle with flaked almonds. Bake for 30–40

minutes until golden brown.
8. Set aside 6 sprigs of redcurrants for decoration. Remove the rest of the redcurrants from the stalks using a fork. Put in a pan with the sugar and 2 tablespoons of water. Gently bring to the boil and cook for 2–3 minutes until the redcurrants have burst and the fruit is tender. Rub through a sieve and allow to cool. Carefully pour the sauce around the peach parcels and decorate with the reserved sprigs of redcurrants.

Peaches in Filo Pastry with Redcurrant Sauce

DINNERS AND SUPPERS

Why not invite friends around for the evening
and treat them to a fun, themed Balti or Mexican
supper, a splendid vegetarian dinner, a relaxed
Italian supper or even just a quick stir-fry
in the kitchen.

From the top clockwise: *Chicken with Parma Ham (page 44)*,
Marinated Squid and Prawn Salad (page 44) and *Tagliatelle with
Spinach and Pine Nuts (page 45)*

ITALIAN SUPPER

MARINATED SQUID AND PRAWN SALAD

CHICKEN WITH PARMA HAM

TAGLIATELLE WITH SPINACH AND PINE NUTS

ICED ZABAGLIONE

MARINATED SQUID AND PRAWN SALAD

Serves 4

For the salad
450 g (1 lb) small or medium prepared squid
300 ml (10 fl oz) dry white wine
1 shallot, chopped
A few parsley stalks
225 g (8 oz) cooked, peeled king prawns
½ red onion, chopped
2 tablespoons finely chopped sun-dried tomatoes
4 tablespoons chopped fresh flatleaf parsley
Ciabatta bread, to serve

For the dressing
6 tablespoons olive oil
1 tablespoon lemon juice
2 teaspoons balsamic vinegar
½ teaspoon Dijon mustard
1 garlic clove, crushed
Salt and freshly ground black pepper

1. Slice the flesh of the squid into rings, leaving the tentacles whole. Put the wine, shallot and parsley stalks into a pan. Bring to the boil, then allow to bubble for 1–2 minutes.
2. Add the squid in batches and cook for 5–7 minutes until firm but still tender. Using a slotted spoon transfer the squid to a shallow dish and leave to cool.
3. Shake together all the dressing ingredients in a screw-top jar. Season to taste.
4. Add the prawns, onion, sun-dried tomatoes and chopped parsley to the squid. Pour over the dressing and toss to mix. Chill for at least 2 hours before serving with plenty of ciabatta bread.

CHICKEN WITH PARMA HAM

Serves 4

4 chicken breast fillets, skinned
8 slices Parma ham
8 large sage leaves
50 g (2 oz) unsalted butter
25 g (1 oz) plain flour
150 ml (5 fl oz) dry white wine
Salt and freshly ground black pepper

1. Place the chicken breast fillets 2 at a time between sheets of cling film or inside a polythene bag. Using a rolling pin beat until very thin, taking care not to tear the flesh. Cut each fillet in half.
2. Lay a slice of Parma ham on top of each piece of chicken fillet, crinkling it to fit. Place a sage leaf on top, securing it with a cocktail stick.
3. Melt half the butter in a large heavy-based frying pan. Dip the chicken in the flour, shaking off any excess. Quickly fry, ham-side down, for 2 minutes. Turn and continue to fry gently until cooked through, adding more butter when necessary. When ready, keep warm in a low oven while cooking the rest of the fillets.

Marinated Squid and Prawn Salad

Chicken with Parma Ham and *Tagliatelle with Spinach and Pine Nuts*

4. Add the wine to the pan and scrape the bottom to incorporate all the flavours. Bring to a simmer, return the chicken to the pan and cook for a further 1–2 minutes until the wine reduces slightly and thickens. Taste and adjust seasoning.
5. Remove the cocktail sticks from the chicken and serve immediately, giving 2 pieces per person, accompanied by *Tagliatelle with Spinach and Pine Nuts.*

TAGLIATELLE WITH SPINACH AND PINE NUTS

 Serves 4

500 g (18 oz) fresh white tagliatelle
2 tablespoons olive oil
2 garlic cloves, crushed
225 g (8 oz) fresh spinach, roughly chopped
50 g (2 oz) pine nuts, toasted

1. Cook the tagliatelle in a large pan of boiling salted water for 3–4 minutes until just tender.
2. Meanwhile, heat the oil in a small pan and gently fry the garlic.
3. When the tagliatelle is ready, drain thoroughly and return to the pan. Pour over the hot garlic oil and toss in the spinach – the heat of the pasta will cause the spinach to wilt. Season if required.
4. Transfer to a warm shallow serving dish, sprinkle over the pine nuts and serve at once.

ICED ZABAGLIONE

For best results it is essential that the marsala is added slowly and the mixture is thick, otherwise it will separate.

　　　　　Serves 4

4 egg yolks
75 g (3 oz) caster sugar
100 ml (3½ fl oz) marsala
300 ml (10 fl oz) double cream
Cantuccini (crisp almond biscuits), to serve

1. Put the egg yolks in a large, heatproof bowl with the sugar then place over a pan of gently simmering water and beat with an electric whisk for about 5 minutes until pale and thick.
2. Gradually add the marsala, a tablespoon at a time, until the mixture is very thick and foamy (this will take about 15–20 minutes). Remove the bowl from the heat and continue to whisk until the mixture is cool.
3. Lightly whip the cream, then gently fold in using a large metal spoon. Pour into four small freezerproof dishes, cover and freeze for 3 hours.
4. Serve straight from the freezer, accompanied by the cantuccini.

COUNTDOWN

The day before
• Prepare, cook and dress the fish for the *Marinated Squid and Prawn Salad*.
• Make the *Iced Zabaglione* and freeze.
• Chill the white wine.

An hour or two before
• Toast the pine nuts.
• Wash and chop the spinach.
• Make the garlic-flavoured oil, ready for re-heating.
• Assemble the *Chicken with Parma Ham* and chill.

Just before serving
• Bring the *Marinated Squid and Prawn Salad* to room temperature.
• Warm the ciabatta bread to accompany the starter.
• Bring a pan of water to the boil, ready for cooking the tagliatelle.
• Re-heat the garlic oil.
• Cook the chicken and tagliatelle between courses.
• Remove the *Iced Zabaglione* from the freezer and serve.

Iced Zabaglione

SZECHUAN CHINESE DINNER

HOT AND SOUR SOUP
CHINESE CHICKEN WITH HOT PEANUT SAUCE
PRAWNS WITH CHILLI AND GINGER SAUCE
PORK WITH GARLIC AND CHILLI SAUCE
PICKLED CUCUMBER
FRIED RICE
FRESH FRUIT SALAD

The Szechuan region of China is justly renowned for its cuisine. This collection of recipes makes a light menu for a large dinner party.

HOT AND SOUR SOUP

You can substitute dried ceps for the shiitake, or fresh black mushrooms which do not need soaking.

Serves 8–10

6–8 dried shiitake mushrooms
225 g (8 oz) pork fillet or chicken breast
550 g (1 lb 4 oz) tofu (bean curd)
225g (8 oz) bamboo shoots
1.2 litres (2 pints) stock or water
2 tablespoons Chinese rice wine or dry sherry
2 tablespoons light soy sauce
2 tablespoons rice or sherry vinegar
2 teaspoons cornflour mixed with 4 teaspoons cold water
2 teaspoons ground white pepper
Salt

1. Soak the dried mushrooms in water for at least 1 hour. Squeeze dry and discard any stalks. Thinly shred the mushroom caps, meat, tofu and bamboo.
2. Pour the stock or water into the pan and bring to a rolling boil. Stir in the meat and tofu then bring back to the boil. Add the mushrooms, bamboo shoots, rice wine or sherry, soy sauce and vinegar. Bring back to the boil, add the cornflour paste and stir until thickened. Season to taste. Serve at once.

Hot and Sour Soup

CHINESE CHICKEN WITH HOT PEANUT SAUCE

Serves 8–10

900 g (2 lb) whole fresh chicken.
1 teaspoon salt
1 tablespoon sesame oil
½ cucumber, cut into matchsticks

For the sauce
2 tablespoons light soy sauce
1 teaspoon caster sugar
1 tablespoon finely chopped spring onion
1 teaspoon red chilli oil
½ teaspoon ground Szechuan pepper
3 tablespoons peanut butter
A drop of sesame oil

To serve
Lettuce leaves
1–2 teaspoons sesame seeds
Tomato roses (optional)

1. Place the chicken in a pan of boiling water, add the salt and bring back to the boil. Cover and simmer for 25–30 minutes. Remove the pan from the heat and allow the chicken to cool in the water, covered, for 3–4 hours.
2. Drain the chicken (reserving the stock for use in other recipes) and pat dry with kitchen paper. Peel off the skin, brush the chicken with sesame oil and leave for 10–15 minutes.

From the left: *Chinese Chicken with Hot Peanut Sauce (page 47), Prawns with Chilli and Ginger Sauce, Pork with Garlic and Chilli Sauce* and *Fried Rice*

3. Remove the meat from the legs, wings and breast bone, pound it gently with a rolling pin to loosen it, then tear into shreds.
4. Toss together the chicken and cucumber, then blend the sauce ingredients in a bowl.
5. Serve the chicken on a bed of lettuce leaves. Pour over the sauce and sprinkle with sesame seeds. Garnish with tomato roses (peel tomato in one long strip and wind into a rose shape).

PRAWNS WITH CHILLI AND GINGER SAUCE

You can substitute ready-cooked king prawns for the uncooked tiger prawns, just omit the poaching step.

Serves 8–10

450 g (1 lb) uncooked tiger prawns, unshelled and heads removed
Cucumber fans, to garnish (optional)

For the sauce
1 tablespoon thinly shredded spring onion
1 tablespoon thinly shredded root ginger
$\frac{1}{2}$ tablespoon thinly shredded and seeded fresh red chilli
1 tablespoon oil
2 tablespoons light soy sauce
1 tablespoon rice or sherry vinegar
$\frac{1}{4}$ teaspoon sesame oil

1. To poach the prawns, place them in a pan of boiling water for 1 minute. Turn off the heat and leave to stand in the hot water for 4–5 minutes. Drain and rinse in cold water then set aside.
2. Place the spring onion, ginger and chilli in a small, heat-proof bowl. Heat the oil and pour over the chilli mixture. Add the soy sauce, vinegar and sesame oil. Pour into a small bowl.
3. Peel the prawns, leaving the tails on. Arrange on a plate with the cucumber. Serve with the *Chilli and Ginger Sauce*.

PORK WITH GARLIC AND CHILLI SAUCE

Serves 8–10

450 g (1 lb) leg of pork, boned and tied with string

For the sauce
2–3 garlic cloves, crushed
2 teaspoons finely chopped spring onion
1 teaspoon caster sugar
2 tablespoons chilli soy sauce or 1 tablespoon soy sauce
mixed with 2 teaspoons red chilli oil
¹/₂ teaspoon sesame oil

To garnish
Carrot fan (see Pom-Pom Sticks *page 134)*
Cucumber matchsticks

1. Place the pork in a pan of boiling water, return to the boil and skim off the scum. Reduce the heat, cover and simmer for 1 hour. Turn off the heat and leave the pork in the liquid to cool, covered, for 2–3 hours. Remove from pan and leave to cool, skin side up, for 4–6 hours.
2. Using a sharp knife, cut the skin off the pork, leaving a thin layer of fat. Thinly slice the pork and arrange on a plate.
3. Mix together the sauce ingredients and pour evenly over the sliced pork. Garnish with the carrot fan and cucumber sticks, then serve at once.

PICKLED CUCUMBER

Serves 8–10

1 slender cucumber
1 teaspoon salt
1 tablespoon caster sugar
2 teaspoons rice or sherry vinegar
1 teaspoon sesame oil

1. Cut the cucumber in half or thirds lengthways, remove and discard the seeds and cut the flesh into strips. Place in a bowl and sprinkle over the salt. Stand for 25–30 minutes until the juices run clear, then rinse under cold, running water and pat dry.
2. Toss the cucumber with the sugar, vinegar and sesame oil just before serving.

A selection of soy sauces

FRIED RICE

Serves 8–10

3–4 eggs
1 teaspoon salt
¹/₂ tablespoon finely chopped spring onion
3 tablespoons oil
450 g (1 lb) cooked long-grain rice
100 g (4 oz) cooked peeled prawns
100 g (4 oz) cooked meat, such as chicken, pork or ham, finely chopped
50 g (2 oz) frozen peas
Spring onion curls, to garnish

1. Beat together the eggs, a pinch of the salt and the finely chopped spring onion.
2. Heat the oil in a wok or frying pan, add the eggs and lightly scramble. Add the rice and stir to separate the grains.
3. Stir in the remaining salt, prawns, meat and peas and stir-fry for 2–3 minutes until heated through. Garnish with the spring onion curls and serve at once.

FRESH FRUIT SALAD

The Chinese do not usually eat dessert after a meal, but fresh fruit makes a refreshing finale. Choose lychees, bananas, kiwi fruit, pineapple, papaya or grapes.

MEXICAN FIESTA

RE-FRIED BEANS

CHILLI BEEF IN TORTILLAS

HOT TOMATO SAUCE

GUACAMOLE SALAD

DEEP AND INDULGENT CHOCOLATE CAKE

TEQUILA SUNRISE

TEQUILA SLAMMER

MARGARITA

NON-ALCOHOLIC MANGO COCKTAIL

MEXICAN HOT CHOCOLATE

Mexican food is the perfect choice for a relaxed, informal evening. This is a real hands-on meal so provide plenty of napkins.

RE-FRIED BEANS

To make the required cooking weight of pinto beans, you will need 225 g (8 oz) of beans dry weight, soaked for several hours or overnight then boiled until tender in unsalted water. If time is short, you can use canned red kidney beans.

 Serves 6–8

500 g (1 1/4 lb) cooked pinto or canned red kidney
Bean liquor from cooking or can
1 medium onion, chopped
2 tablespoons bacon fat or olive oil
100 g (4 oz) mild Cheddar, grated
Salt and freshly ground black pepper

1. Drain the beans, retaining their liquor. Reserve about 50 g (2 oz) then mash the rest with just enough of the liquor to make a chunky paste. Add the reserved whole beans to the paste.
2. Gently fry the onion in the fat or oil until softened, add the beans and stir until heated through, adding more of the bean liquor if necessary. The result should be a thick, chunky paste. Season with salt and pepper and serve very hot, topped with melted cheese and the *Chilli Beef in Tortillas*.

CHILLI BEEF IN TORTILLAS

Wheatflour Tortillas
Tortillas are pancakes and these are the easiest you will ever make.

 Makes 24

750 g (1 3/4 lb) plain flour
4 teaspoons baking powder
1 teaspoon salt
4 tablespoons oil

1. Mix the flour and baking powder with the salt. Mix in the oil with a fork, then add enough lukewarm water to enable you to gather the dough into a ball with your hands. Knead lightly to smooth it, then leave it covered in the bowl for at least 20 minutes.
2. Divide the dough into 24 balls and roll out each one on a floured surface to a thin pancake that will fit into a 20–23 cm (8–9 in) frying pan. Heat the pan without adding any oil and cook each pancake until the top surface bubbles up. Puncture the large blisters, turn, press down and cook until the underside develops brown patches. As they are cooked, wrap in a tea towel or, if they are to be kept for a day or two, in foil in which they can be re-heated in the oven. Serve with the *Chilli Beef*.

Chilli Beef

Serves 6–8

1 large onion, finely chopped
2 teaspoons dried oregano
1 teaspoon ground cumin
1 teaspoon chilli powder
1 teaspoon paprika
50 g (2 oz) dripping or 3 tablespoons vegetable oil
750 g (1 3/4 lb) very lean beef, minced or finely chopped
1 large green pepper, seeded and finely chopped
2 garlic cloves, crushed
50 g (2 oz) tin tomato purée
Tabasco sauce (optional)
Salt and freshly ground black pepper

To serve
24 Wheatflour Tortillas *(see above)*
Shredded iceberg lettuce
Bottled chilli or Tabasco sauce
Soured cream or natural yoghurt

From the top clockwise: *Re-fried Beans, Chilli Beef in Tortillas, Hot Tomato Sauce* and *Guacamole Salad (page 52)*

1. Fry the onion gently with the oregano, cumin, chilli powder and paprika in the dripping or oil until the onion is just soft. Add the beef, green pepper and garlic and stir gently until the meat changes colour and breaks into granules.
2. Empty the tomato purée into a bowl and mix with its own volume (measured in the can) of cold water. Stir into the meat and cook covered for about 10 minutes for minced beef or 15–20 minutes for chopped beef. Season and, if you like hot food, add a dash or two of Tabasco sauce.
3. Serve with the warm *Wheatflour Tortillas, Re-fried Beans*, a bowl of shredded iceberg lettuce, chilli or Tabasco for those who like things hot and soured cream or yoghurt for those who want to cool things down.

HOT TOMATO SAUCE

Large chillies tend to be less fiery than small ones, and since much of the heat is in the seeds, they are gentler when seeded. Adapt the chilli according to your palate: it shouldn't be too blazing, but you can add more if you wish.

 Serves 6–8

400 g (14 oz) can tomatoes
½ Spanish onion, finely chopped
1 large green chilli, seeded and finely chopped
1 tablespoon lemon juice
Sugar and Tabasco sauce, if necessary
Salt and freshly ground black pepper
Coriander leaves, to garnish

1. Drain the tomatoes, mash them and mix with the onion, chilli, lemon juice and seasoning, including a little sugar and a dash or two of Tabasco sauce if you want the sauce to be hotter.
2. Garnish the sauce with the coriander leaves.

GUACAMOLE SALAD

Serves 6–8

3 ripe avocados
Juice of 1 lemon
2–3 sprigs of coriander, roughly chopped
3–4 tomatoes, skinned and coarsely chopped
1 Spanish onion, sliced into rings
2 large green chillies, seeded and finely chopped
A pinch of cayenne pepper
Salt and freshly ground black pepper
Coriander leaves, to garnish

To serve
Lime wedges
Tortilla chips

1. Not more than half an hour before serving (to avoid them discolouring) halve, stone and peel the avocados. Slice half of one avocado thinly and set to one side. Dice the flesh of all the rest. Toss with the lemon juice, the chopped coriander leaves, and seasoning. Pile on to a serving platter, arranging the reserved slices in fans on top to decorate.
2. Season the chopped tomato. Surround the avocado first with the onion rings, then the tomato and a finally a border of sliced chilli. Sprinkle the onion with cayenne pepper and garnish the whole dish with coriander leaves. Serve with lime wedges and tortilla chips.

DEEP AND INDULGENT CHOCOLATE CAKE

Serves 6–8

400 g (14 oz) plain chocolate, broken into squares
1 tablespoon milk
2–3 teaspoons almond oil
150 g (5 oz) unsalted butter, diced and softened
4 large eggs
1 tablespoon caster sugar
$\frac{1}{2}$ teaspoon almond essence
25 g (1 oz) plain flour

To decorate
Whipped cream
Flaked almonds, toasted
Chocolate curls or shavings

1. Heat the oven to 220C/425F/Gas 7. Put the chocolate and milk in a heatproof bowl and place on top of a pan of barely simmering water. Leave to melt gently for 10–15 minutes.
2. Line a roasting tin measuring about 25 x 20 cm (10 x 8 in) with greaseproof paper or baking parchment. Fold so it fits neatly into the edges and corners. Brush the paper liberally with almond oil.
3. When the chocolate has melted, add the diced butter but do not stir. Remove the bowl from the heat and leave to stand. Separate the eggs. Beat the whites until they just form the softest of peaks. Lightly beat the yolks with the sugar and almond essence, then mix in the flour.
4. Mix the butter and chocolate then add to the yolk mixture, beating continuously. Gently fold in the beaten whites. Lightly re-brush the lining paper with more almond oil and pour in the mixture. Bake in the centre of the oven for 20 minutes then turn off the oven, open the door and leave the cake undisturbed to go completely cold.
5. Turn the cake out on to a serving platter or board and carefully peel away the lining paper. An hour or two before serving, decorate the cake with whipped cream, almonds and chocolate curls or shavings. Serve cut into squares.

Deep and Indulgent Chocolate Cake

TEQUILA SUNRISE

Serves 1

120 ml (4 fl oz) fresh orange juice, chilled
30 ml (1 fl oz) tequila
15 ml (¹/₂ fl oz) grenadine
Orange slices, to decorate

1. Pour the orange juice into a tall, chilled glass.
2. Add the tequila and mix well before slowly pouring in the grenadine so that it sinks to the bottom of the glass.
3. Decorate with orange slices.

TEQUILA SLAMMER

Serves 1

40 ml (1¹/₂ fl oz) tequila
Champagne or sparkling white wine, to taste

1. Pour the tequila into a short, sturdy glass and then top up with the champagne or sparkling wine.
2. Put a clean folded napkin on top of the glass and hold it down. Slam the glass on the table so it froths furiously.
3. Remove the napkin, then hand the glass to a guest who must down it in one!

MARGARITA

Serves 1

Lime juice, to taste
Salt
Tequila, to taste

1. Rub the rim of a small glass with the lime juice and then dip the rim in the salt.
2. Mix 2 parts of tequila with 1 part of lime juice in an ice-filled shaker.
3. Strain the liquid into the glass and serve.

From the top clockwise: *Margarita, Non-alcoholic Mango Cocktail* and *Tequila Sunrise*

NON-ALCOHOLIC MANGO COCKTAIL

Mango juice or mango mixed with apple juice, to taste
A squeeze of lime juice
Soda water, sparkling mineral water or lemonade, to taste

To decorate
Strawberries
Mint sprigs

1. Blend the mango juice with the lime juice and top up with the soda water, mineral water or lemonade as preferred.
2. Pour into a jug and add plenty of ice.
3. Decorate with strawberries and mint sprigs.

MEXICAN HOT CHOCOLATE

Serves 1

150 ml (5 fl oz) milk
50 g (2 oz) plain dark chocolate
1 cinnamon stick

1. Heat the milk and add the chocolate, stirring until it is thoroughly dissolved.
2. Pour into a liquidiser and blend until a thick froth has formed.
3. Pour into a mug or cup and add the cinnamon stick as a stirrer. Serve immediately.

MEDITERRANEAN MEDLEY

SUMMER VEGETABLE PLATTER

GRILLED AUBERGINE WITH PARSLEY DRESSING

GARLICKY PLUM TOMATOES

GREEN BEANS WITH TOASTED ALMONDS
AND PARMESAN

COURGETTE RIBBONS WITH SESAME SEEDS

GRILLED PEPPERS AND OLIVES IN MUSTARD
DRESSING

NEW POTATOES WITH FETA CHEESE
AND PESTO DRESSING

MUSHROOMS WITH RED ONIONS AND CHIVES

GARLIC TOAST

SALMON, SCALLOP AND PRAWN KEBABS
WITH BASIL AND GINGER BUTTER

SAFFRON AND CHILLI RICE

HERB SALAD

LEMON CREAM WITH SUMMER FRUIT

ALMOND SHORTBREAD

This supper is perfect for entertaining large groups of people over an extended period, especially long parties that stretch from late afternoon into the evening.

SUMMER VEGETABLE PLATTER

This is a wonderful selection of dishes including aubergines, tomatoes, green beans, courgettes, peppers, new potatoes, mushrooms and garlic toast. If time is short, serve large amounts of two or three dishes given for the platter instead of all of them. You can prepare everything several hours ahead, but serve the platter at room temperature.

All recipes for the
Summer Vegetable Platter serve 6

ⓥ GRILLED AUBERGINE WITH PARSLEY DRESSING

1 medium-sized aubergine, thinly sliced
2 tablespoons olive oil
2 tablespoons balsamic vinegar
2 tablespoons chopped fresh parsley
Salt and freshly ground black pepper

1. Place the aubergine on a grill pan and brush with a little olive oil. Grill on one side until lightly browned.
2. Turn the aubergine and brush with more oil and grill until tender.
3. Arrange the aubergine slices on a plate and sprinkle with the balsamic vinegar, olive oil and the parsley. Season to taste.

ⓥ GARLICKY PLUM TOMATOES

4 ripe plum tomatoes, skinned, quartered and seeded
Salt
2 tablespoons olive oil
1 garlic clove, thinly sliced
Freshly ground black pepper

1. Cut each quarter of tomato in half lengthways and place in a single layer in a shallow dish. Sprinkle with salt and lightly drizzle over the olive oil.
2. Loosely cover the dish with greaseproof paper and leave in a warm place for several hours or even overnight. (The tomatoes will become firm and extra sweet.)
3. Fry the garlic in a little oil until lightly browned and crisp. Sprinkle the tomatoes with the garlic and some black pepper just before serving.

From the top: *Garlic Toast (page 57), Courgette Ribbons with Sesame Seeds (page 56), Grilled Aubergine with Parsley Dressing, Garlicky Plum Tomatoes, Mushrooms with Red Onions and Chives (page 56), Grilled Peppers and Olives in Mustard Dressing (page 56), Green Beans with Toasted Almonds and Parmesan (page 56) and New Potatoes with Feta Cheese and Pesto Dressing (page 56)*

GREEN BEANS WITH TOASTED ALMONDS AND PARMESAN

You can either buy ready-toasted almonds or you can toast them yourself under the grill.

225 g (8 oz) green beans
1 tablespoon lemon juice
3 tablespoons olive oil
Salt and freshly ground black pepper
25 g (1 oz) flaked almonds, toasted
25 g (1 oz) Parmesan, fresh and coarsely grated

1. Steam or boil the beans until just tender and then place them in a dish.
2. Blend the lemon juice with the olive oil and season to taste. Pour this over the beans, and toss in the dressing.
3. Just before serving, sprinkle the beans with the almonds and Parmesan.

COURGETTE RIBBONS WITH SESAME SEEDS

2 courgettes
2 tablespoons lemon juice
2 tablespoons olive oil
Salt and freshly ground black pepper
1 tablespoon sesame seeds, toasted

1. Trim the ends off the courgettes and draw a potato peeler from one end to the other to make thin, flat ribbons.
2. Place the ribbons in a colander and sprinkle with salt. Leave to drain for 30 minutes.
3. Rinse the ribbons under cold running water and pat dry with absorbent kitchen paper and place in a serving dish.
4. Pour over the lemon juice and olive oil and season to taste.
5. Just before serving, sprinkle the courgettes with the sesame seeds.

GRILLED PEPPERS AND OLIVES IN MUSTARD DRESSING

2 yellow peppers, halved and seeded
1 red pepper, halved and seeded
100 g (4 oz) black olives, stoned
1 tablespoon red wine vinegar
1 teaspoon Dijon mustard
3 tablespoons olive oil
Salt and freshly ground black pepper

1. Place the peppers skin side up under a hot grill until the skins have blackened. Remove from the grill and place in a polythene bag until cool enough to handle.
2. Peel the skins from the peppers and slice the flesh into strips. Place in a bowl with the olives.
3. Shake together the vinegar, mustard and olive oil in a screw-top jar and season to taste. Pour over the peppers and toss to coat in the dressing.

NEW POTATOES WITH FETA CHEESE AND PESTO DRESSING

450 g (1 lb) small new potatoes
100 g (4 oz) feta cheese, crumbled
1 tablespoon red wine vinegar
1 tablespoon pesto
3 tablespoons olive oil
Salt and freshly ground black pepper

1. Boil the potatoes in salted water, drain and leave to cool before mixing with the feta cheese.
2. Shake together the vinegar, pesto and olive oil in a screw-top jar and season to taste.
3. Sprinkle the dressing over the potato mixture.

MUSHROOMS WITH RED ONIONS AND CHIVES

If you can't get chestnut mushrooms, use button mushrooms.

175 g (6 oz) chestnut mushrooms, sliced
1 small red onion, thinly sliced
2 tablespoons wholegrain mustard
1 tablespoon freshly squeezed lemon juice
4 tablespoons olive oil
Salt and freshly ground black pepper
Fresh chives, snipped, to garnish

1. Mix the mushrooms with the onion in a bowl.
2. Shake together the mustard, lemon juice and olive oil in a screw-top jar and season to taste.
3. Pour the dressing over the mushrooms and onions and toss well to mix.
4. Just before serving, sprinkle with the snipped chives.

GARLIC TOAST

The garlic purée can be made the previous day and stored in an airtight container.

1 bulb garlic
4 tablespoons olive oil
Salt and freshly ground black pepper
1 ciabatta loaf

1. Pre-heat the oven to 200C/400F/Gas 6 and bake the garlic whole in a small ovenproof dish for 25–30 minutes or until tender.
2. Remove from the oven and, when cool enough to handle, separate the cloves, snip the ends and squeeze the flesh into a bowl. Mix with the olive oil and season to taste.
3. Thinly slice the ciabatta and toast on one side. Spread the garlic purée over the untoasted side and grill until crisp. Serve warm.

SALMON, SCALLOP AND PRAWN KEBABS WITH BASIL AND GINGER BUTTER

The fish can be prepared several hours in advance and stored in the fridge. If you want to make the *Basil and Ginger Butter* in advance, complete stage 3 then store in the fridge for up to 2 days.

Serves 6

675 g (1¹/₂ lb) salmon fillet, skinned
12 queen scallops or 6 large scallops
12 uncooked prawns in shells
4 tablespoons freshly squeezed lime juice
2 tablespoons olive oil
4 basil leaves, shredded
12 fresh bay leaves
Salt and freshly ground black pepper

For the Basil and Ginger Butter
1 teaspoon grated fresh root ginger
1 tablespoon lime juice
12 basil leaves, chopped
100 g (4 oz) unsalted butter, softened
85 ml (3 fl oz) dry white wine
Basil leaves, to garnish

1. To make the kebabs, cut the salmon into 2.5 cm (1 in) chunks and halve the scallops, if they are large. Shell the prawns, leaving on the tail section.

Salmon, Scallop and Prawn Kebabs with Basil and Ginger Butter, Saffron and Chilli Rice (page 58) and Herb Salad (page 58)

Place all the fish in a bowl and mix with the lime juice, oil, basil and seasoning.
2. Thread the salmon, prawns and scallops alternately on to 12 skewers, adding a bay leaf to each skewer, each of which should have at least one scallop and one prawn.
3. To make the *Basil and Ginger Butter*, beat together the ginger, lime juice, basil and butter with a little seasoning until well combined.
4. Cook the kebabs under a medium grill or on a barbecue for about 8–10 minutes, turning occasionally, until evenly cooked and lightly browned on all sides.
5. Meanwhile, boil the wine until it is reduced to 2 tablespoons. Remove from the heat, and gradually whisk into the basil and ginger butter to form a shiny sauce. If the sauce becomes too thick, return to the heat briefly, whisking all the time. Serve the seafood kebabs with the butter accompanied by *Saffron and Chilli Rice* and *Herb Salad* (see page 58).

SAFFRON AND CHILLI RICE

Serves 6

350 g (12 oz) basmati rice
A generous pinch of saffron strands
2 red chillies, seeded and finely chopped
Salt and freshly ground black pepper

1. Wash the rice in several changes of cold water until the water runs clear. Place in a pan with the remaining ingredients and 900 ml (1½ pints) water and bring to the boil. Stir once, then cover and cook gently for 10–12 minutes until the rice is tender.

HERB SALAD

Serves 6

1 lettuce, such as Cos or Webb's
A handful of rocket leaves
A handful of young spinach leaves
A selection of fresh herb sprigs, such as dill, parsley, tarragon, chives and chervil

For the dressing
1 tablespoon freshly squeezed lemon juice
3 tablespoons walnut oil
Salt and freshly ground black pepper

1. Tear the lettuce into large pieces and place in a bowl with the rocket, spinach and herbs.
2. Shake together the dressing ingredients in a screw-top jar. Just before serving, toss the salad in the dressing until the leaves are evenly coated.

LEMON CREAM WITH SUMMER FRUIT

This easy-to-make dessert needs to be started the day before the party so that the lemon cream has time to drain. If you don't have a coeur à la crème mould, use a basket or sieve – it will look just as good.

Serves 6

225 g (8 oz) curd cheese
75 g (3 oz) icing sugar
1 teaspoon finely grated lemon rind

1 tablespoon lemon juice
300 ml (10 fl oz) double cream
675 g (1½ lb) soft summer fruit, such as strawberries, cherries, blackberries, raspberries, redcurrants and blackcurrants
2 tablespoons crème de cassis
Strips of lemon zest, to decorate

1. Beat together the curd cheese, icing sugar, lemon rind and juice. Whip the cream until it just holds its shape and fold into the cheese mixture.
2. Line a sieve, basket or large coeur à la crème mould with muslin. Fill with the cream mixture and smooth the top. Set it over a bowl to catch the drips and leave to drain in the fridge overnight.
3. Turn the cream on to a large plate and remove the muslin. Slice the strawberries and mix with the other fruit and crème de cassis. Spoon around the cream, then decorate with a sprinkling of lemon zest strips.

ALMOND SHORTBREAD

Makes 18 pieces

150 g (5 oz) plain flour
75 g (3 oz) ground almonds
175 g (6 oz) butter
100 g (4 oz) caster sugar
A few drops almond essence
1 egg white, lightly beaten
50 g (2 oz) flaked almonds
Caster sugar, for sprinkling

1. Pre-heat the oven to 160C/325F/Gas 3. Combine the flour and ground almonds in a bowl. Cut the butter into small pieces and rub in to the flour and almonds with your fingertips until the mixture resembles breadcrumbs – you can do this in a food processor, but take care not to over-mix.
2. Stir in the sugar and almond essence, then squeeze the mixture together to form a dough. Place the dough on a buttered 18 x 28 cm (7 x 11 in) shallow oblong baking tin. Press down lightly with the back of a metal spoon to spread the dough to the edges of the tin.
3. Lightly brush the top with egg white and sprinkle over the flaked almonds. Bake for 30–35 minutes until lightly browned. Leave to cool in the tin, then cut into six across the long edge and three down the short. Sprinkle with a little sugar just before serving.

COUNTDOWN

• **Two days before**
Make the *Almond Shortbread* and store in an airtight container.

• **The day before**
Make the *Lemon Cream* and *Basil and Ginger Butter* up to the stage before the adding of the wine; chill both.
Bake the garlic and make the paste for *Garlic Toast*.
Prepare the *Garlicky Plum Tomatoes*.
Make up all the salad dressings.

• **In the morning**
Marinate the fish for the kebabs.
Grill and skin the peppers for *Grilled Peppers and Olives*.

• **In the afternoon**
Make up all the starters.
Prepare the summer fruit and mix with the crème de cassis.

• **Two hours before**
Prepare the leaves for the *Herb Salad*.
Thread the seafood on to the skewers.

• **One hour before**
Toast the ciabatta on one side and spread with garlic purée.
Arrange the starters on large plate.

• **Half an hour before**
Turn out *Lemon Cream* and surround with fruit.

• **Just before serving**
Finish grilling *Garlic Toast*.
Cook *Saffron and Chilli Rice*.
Finish making the *Basil and Ginger Butter*.
Grill or barbecue the kebabs.

Lemon Cream with Summer Fruit
and *Almond Shortbread*

A BALTI SUPPER FOR FRIENDS

BASIC BALTI SAUCE

MEDIUM BALTI CHICKEN

STIR-FRIED BALTI VEGETABLES

SPICY HOT BALTI LAMB

NAAN BREAD WITH VARIATIONS

KEEMA NAAN

PESHWARI NAAN

SPICED NAAN

INDIAN PISTACHIO ICE-CREAM

FRUIT SHRIKAND

LIME SHERBET

SWEET LASSI

MASALA TEA

Balti curries are Indian stir-fries cooked and served in a wok-like bowl known as a karahi or Balti pan. Naan bread is the traditional accompaniment – simply break off a piece and use it to scoop up the food.

BASIC BALTI SAUCE

 Makes about 600 ml (1 pint)

4 tablespoons vegetable oil
2 Spanish onions, chopped
3 garlic cloves, chopped
2 tablespoons finely chopped root ginger
4 green chillies, chopped
15 whole cloves
Seeds from 10 green cardamom pods
1 tablespoon ground coriander
1 tablespoon paprika
1 tablespoon ground cinnamon
1 tablespoon ground turmeric
2 teaspoons ground cumin
1 teaspoon ground fenugreek
1 teaspoon mustard powder
400 g (14 oz) tin chopped tomatoes
600 ml (1 pint) vegetable stock
2 tablespoons lemon juice
Pared rind of 1 lemon

1. Heat the oil in a heavy-based pan and fry the onions, garlic and ginger for 5 minutes. Add the chillies and cook for a further 2 minutes.
2. Add the spices and stir-fry for 30 seconds. Add the tomatoes, stock, lemon juice and rind. Bring to the boil, then simmer uncovered for 30 minutes.
3. Discard the lemon rind. The sauce is now ready to be used or it may be cooled and kept in the fridge for several days.

MEDIUM BALTI CHICKEN

Serves 6

2 tablespoons vegetable oil
900 g (2 lb) chicken breast fillets, skinned and cubed
1 onion, sliced
1 quantity Basic Balti Sauce (see previous recipe)
225 g (8 oz) green beans, cut into 4 cm (1½ in) lengths
350 g (12 oz) firm tomatoes, chopped
15 g (½ oz) fresh basil, roughly torn
Salt and freshly ground black pepper

1. Heat the oil in a large Balti pan or wok and stir-fry the chicken for 5 minutes or until golden. Add the onion and continue to stir-fry for 1 minute. Pour in the *Basic Balti Sauce* and add the beans. Bring to the boil and simmer gently for 8 minutes, stirring occasionally.

2. Stir in the tomatoes and basil and cook for a further 2 minutes or until the chicken is tender. Taste and adjust the seasoning before serving.

STIR-FRIED BALTI VEGETABLES

  Serves 6

3 tablespoons vegetable oil
1 tablespoon black mustard seeds
1 tablespoon fennel seeds
2 cinnamon sticks
1 onion, sliced
225 g (8 oz) cauliflower florets
225 g (8 oz) aubergine, cut into chunks
225 g (8 oz) small new potatoes, cooked and halved
2 red peppers, seeded and cut into 2.5 cm (1 in) squares

175 g (6 oz) okra, trimmed
400 g (14 oz) tin chick peas, rinsed and drained
1 quantity Basic Balti Sauce *(see recipe left)*
150 ml (5 fl oz) vegetable stock
4 tablespoons chopped fresh coriander
Salt and freshly ground black pepper

1. Heat the oil in a large Balti pan or wok, add the mustard seeds, fennel seeds and cinnamon sticks and stir-fry until the seeds start to pop and splutter. Add the onion and stir-fry for a further 2 minutes. Add the remaining vegetables, chick peas, *Basic Balti Sauce* and stock.

2. Bring to the boil, then simmer for 15 minutes or until the vegetables are tender. Stir in 2 tablespoons of the coriander and season to taste. Sprinkle over the remaining coriander to garnish.

From left: *Stir-fried Balti Vegetables, Spicy Hot Balti Lamb (page 62)* and *assorted Naan Breads (page 62)*

SPICY HOT BALTI LAMB

Serves 6

2 tablespoons vegetable oil
1 onion, chopped
900 g (2 lb) boneless lamb steaks, trimmed and cubed
2 tablespoons dried crushed chillies
1 teaspoon ground nutmeg
1 tablespoon fennel seeds
1 teaspoon black onion seeds
2 red peppers, seeded and cut into 2.5 cm (1 in) squares
2 green peppers, seeded and cut into 2.5 cm (1 in) squares
1 quantity Basic Balti Sauce *(see page 60)*
6 tablespoons chopped fresh coriander
2 tablespoons lemon juice
Salt and freshly ground black pepper
Coriander sprigs, to garnish

1. Heat the oil over a high heat in a Balti pan or wok and fry the onion for 2–3 minutes. Add the lamb and cook for 5 minutes.
2. Add the chillies, nutmeg, fennel seeds and black onion seeds and stir-fry for 2 minutes. Add the peppers and *Basic Balti Sauce* and cook for 10 minutes or until the lamb is tender.
3. Just before serving, stir in the coriander and lemon juice. Taste and the adjust seasoning. Garnish with coriander sprigs.

Naan Bread

NAAN BREAD

Makes 6

675 g (1¹/₂ lb) strong white bread flour
1¹/₂ teaspoons salt
75 g (3 oz) butter
25 g (1 oz) caster sugar
1 sachet easy-blend dried yeast
450 ml (15 fl oz) warm milk
15 g (¹/₂ oz) ghee or butter, melted

1. Mix together the flour and salt then rub in the butter. Stir in the sugar and yeast. Make a well in the centre of the flour mixture and pour in the milk. Mix to a dough.
2. Turn out on to a floured surface and knead for 10 minutes or until the dough is smooth and elastic. Place in a bowl, cover with some oiled polythene (a bin liner will do) and leave to rise in a warm place for 1 hour or until doubled in size.
3. Knock back the dough, then divide into 6 equal portions. Roll out each piece into a large, thin, round or teardrop shape, then fork holes all over the dough.
4. Warm a large baking sheet under the grill. Grill the naan for a few minutes on each side until brown patches appear. Remove from the grill, then brush with melted ghee or butter. Wrap in foil until needed. Serve warm.

KEEMA NAAN

Heat 2 teaspoons of vegetable oil and fry 100 g (4 oz) minced lamb for 5 minutes. Add ¹/₂ small chopped onion and cook until softened. Stir in ¹/₂ teaspoon of ground cumin and a pinch of salt and cook for 2 minutes. Leave to cool. Roll out 1 quantity of *Naan Bread* dough into a round as before, then place the lamb mixture in the middle and bring up the sides to the centre to cover the meat. Turn over and roll out to a flat round. Grill as before.

PESHWARI NAAN

Mix together 100 g (4 oz) ground almonds, 25 g (1 oz) desiccated coconut, 25 g (1 oz) caster sugar, 25 g (1 oz) sultanas and 25 g (1 oz) softened butter. Roll out one quantity of *Naan Bread* dough into a round and add the almond and coconut mixture as for *Keema Naan*.

SPICED NAAN

Add 1 teaspoon fennel seeds, 2 teaspoons black onion seeds and 1 teaspoon cumin seeds to the *Naan Bread* dry ingredients. Complete recipe as for *Naan Bread* and roll out to a round. Sprinkle with 1 tablespoon of chopped fresh coriander and pat into dough. Grill as before.

INDIAN PISTACHIO ICE-CREAM

Serves 6

2 x 400 g (14 oz) tins evaporated milk
5 green cardamom pods, split
Pared rind of 1 lemon
75 g (3 oz) caster sugar
100 g (4 oz) shelled pistachio nuts, ground
A few drops green food colouring (optional)

To decorate
Pistachio nuts, chopped
Rose petals

1. Set the freezer to its coldest setting. Warm the evaporated milk in a heavy pan with the cardamom pods, lemon rind and sugar, stirring until the sugar has dissolved. Remove from the heat and cool, stirring continuously.
2. Strain the milk into a bowl and stir in the nuts and colouring (if using). Pour into a container and freeze for $2^{1}/_{2}$ hours. Remove from the freezer and stir until smooth. Pour into yoghurt pots, cover and freeze overnight or until firm.
3. Remove from the freezer to soften for 15 minutes before turning out on to serving plates. Decorate with the pistachios and rose petals.

FRUIT SHRIKAND

Serves 6

450 g (1 lb) curd cheese
600 g ($1^{1}/_{4}$ lb) Greek yoghurt
75 g (3 oz) icing sugar, sifted
$^{1}/_{2}$ teaspoon ground cardamom
50 g (2 oz) blanched almonds, chopped

Peshwari Naan, Indian Pistachio Ice-cream and *Fruit Shrikand*

225 g (8 oz) strawberries, chopped
225 g (8 oz) small seedless grapes, halved
2 small mangoes, chopped

To decorate
Mint sprigs
Strawberries

1. Place the curd cheese and yoghurt in a bowl and beat until smooth. Stir in the icing sugar, ground cardamom and almonds and mix thoroughly.
2. Carefully fold in the fruit, then divide the mixture among 6 serving glasses. Chill for at least 30 minutes before serving. Decorate with the strawberries and mint sprigs.

LIME SHERBET

 Serves 6

8 limes
75 g (3 oz) caster sugar
A small pinch of salt
Ice, to serve

1. Squeeze the limes and pour the juice into a large jug. Add the sugar and salt and stir until dissolved, then pour in 1.5 litres (2¹/₂ pints) cold water and top up with plenty of ice to serve.

SWEET LASSI

 Serves 6

450 g (1 lb) natural yoghurt
75 g (3 oz) caster sugar
600 ml (1 pint) iced water
600 ml (1 pint) cold milk
Ground cinnamon, to sprinkle

1. Whisk all the ingredients except the cinnamon in a large bowl until well-blended and frothy. Pour into 6 tall glasses and sprinkle with cinnamon before serving.

MASALA TEA

 Serves 6

1 cinnamon stick
1 teaspoon ground ginger
8 whole cloves
5 cardamom pods
75 g (3 oz) caster sugar
3 breakfast tea bags
Milk, to taste

1. Place the cinnamon stick, ginger, cloves, cardamom pods and sugar with 1.5 litres (2¹/₂ pints) cold water in a pan and bring to the boil.
2. Cover and simmer for 10 minutes then add the tea bags and allow to infuse for 2–3 minutes. Strain the tea and add milk to taste.

Lime Sherbet, Masala Tea and Sweet Lassi

QUICK PASTA SUPPER

BAKED CHEESE AND HERB FRENCH SLICES
PENNE WITH A CREAMY TOMATO SAUCE

Hugely popular and amazingly versatile, pasta is perfect for casual entertaining. If you want to serve a dessert, choose something light from another menu or simply serve fresh fruit. You could prepare the sauce for the penne before your guests arrive and just warm it gently before adding it to the pasta.

BAKED CHEESE AND HERB FRENCH SLICES

 Serves 4–6

1 French loaf, cut into 12 slices
2 garlic cloves
4–6 tablespoons olive oil
1–2 teaspoons Italian seasoning
2 tablespoons freshly grated Parmesan

1. Pre-heat the oven to 200C/400F/Gas 6. Place the slices of bread on a baking tray and bake for about 10 minutes until they turn golden. Turn over once during the cooking time.
2. Cut the garlic cloves in half and rub over one side of each slice of bread. Brush with the olive oil and sprinkle with the Italian seasoning and Parmesan. Bake for 3–5 minutes until crisp, then serve immediately with the *Penne with a Creamy Tomato Sauce*.

PENNE WITH A CREAMY TOMATO SAUCE

Serves 4

350 g (12 oz) tricolour penne (pasta quills)
1 onion, roughly chopped
3 tablespoons olive oil
225 g (8 oz) lightly smoked bacon, diced
1 teaspoon dried oregano
400 g (14 oz) tin chopped tomatoes with basil
500 g (1¼ lb) carton creamed tomatoes (passata)
4 tablespoons double cream
25 g (1 oz) sun-dried tomatoes in oil, roughly chopped

Penne with a Creamy Tomato Sauce and *Baked Cheese and Herb French Slices*

25 g (1 oz) black olives, stoned and halved
5–6 fresh basil leaves, roughly chopped
Salt and freshly ground black pepper

1. Cook the pasta in a pan of boiling, salted water for 10–12 minutes until just tender.
2. Meanwhile, gently fry the onion in the oil for 5 minutes until soft. Add the bacon and cook quickly for 2–3 minutes. Stir in the oregano and chopped tomatoes and cook for 5 minutes or until the sauce has thickened.
3. Drain the pasta and transfer to a warm serving dish.
4. Add the creamed tomatoes to the pan and heat through for 2–3 minutes. Stir in the cream and seasoning and pour the mixture over the pasta. Toss together and scatter over the sun-dried tomatoes, olives and basil.

QUICK SANDWICH SUPPER

BRIE-TOPPED TOASTED CIABATTA ROLLS

CHOCOLATE ICE-CREAM SANDWICHES

Even the most casual entertaining needs something to inspire you. This menu is ideal as a tasty, late-evening snack.

BRIE-TOPPED TOASTED CIABATTA ROLLS

Serves 6

6 ciabatta rolls
25 g (1 oz) butter
1 tablespoon wholegrain mustard
A large handful of ready-to-serve mixed salad leaves
2 tablespoons French dressing (optional)
175 g (6 oz) wafer-thin ham slices
200 g (7 oz) Brie, rind removed

1. Cut the rolls in half. Toast the bottom halves on both sides and the tops on the cut underside only.
2. Melt the butter in a small pan and stir in the wholegrain mustard. Arrange the toasted bases on a serving dish and liberally brush each one with the melted butter and mustard mixture. Top with the salad leaves and some dressing (if using) then put the slices of ham on top.
3. Pre-heat the grill to high then transfer the ciabatta bases to the grill pan. Cut the Brie into thin slices and place a few on each roll. Place under the grill for about a minute or until the Brie just melts and begins to run. Put a lid on top of each filled base and serve at once.

CHOCOLATE ICE-CREAM SANDWICHES

Serves 6

6 Amaretti biscuits
12 plain chocolate digestive biscuits
475 ml (16 fl oz) vanilla and chocolate chip ice-cream

1. Put the Amaretti biscuits into a food processor or blender and process until they form coarse crumbs or place inside a polythene bag and crush with a rolling pin.
2. Take one of the chocolate biscuits and spread a 2 cm (³/₄ in) layer of ice-cream on its non-chocolate side. Place another biscuit on top, chocolate side uppermost. Squeeze the biscuits gently together and smooth the ice-cream around the edge, then make 5 more.
3. Roll the edges of the biscuit sandwiches in the crushed Amaretti to coat them, then place on a tray in the freezer. Serve straight from the freezer wrapped in a paper napkin.

Brie-topped Toasted Ciabatta Rolls

QUICK STIR-FRY SUPPER

Chicken Stir-fry

Jacket Bananas with

Chocolate Marshmallow Sauce

Healthy and amazingly fast to cook, stir-fries are full of fabulous ingredients and make the perfect quick supper for a relaxed evening with friends or family.

CHICKEN STIR-FRY

Almost any vegetable will do for a stir-fry, but halved baby carrots, mini sweetcorn, tiny broccoli florets, asparagus spears and mangetout are particularly good.

Serves 4

4 tablespoons sunflower oil
450 g (1 lb) chicken breasts cut into thin strips
50 g (2 oz) unsalted cashew nuts
6 spring onions, sliced diagonally
1 garlic clove, crushed
1 cm (1/2 in) piece root ginger, peeled and finely grated
450 g (1 lb) fresh mixed vegetables cut into 2.5 cm (1 in) pieces
2 tablespoons light soy sauce
1 tablespoon hoisin sauce
1 tablespoon rice or sherry vinegar
1 tablespoon tomato purée
1 teaspoon light muscovado sugar
2 teaspoons grated orange rind
175 g (6 oz) Chinese rice noodles

1. Heat 2 tablespoons of oil in a wok or large frying pan. Add the chicken and stir-fry for 2–3 minutes. Add the nuts and cook for a minute or until golden. Transfer the chicken and nuts to a plate and keep them warm.
2. Heat the remaining oil in the pan, add the spring onions, garlic and ginger and stir-fry briefly to flavour the oil. Add the vegetables and stir-fry for 3–4 minutes until tender but still crisp.
3. Return the chicken and nuts to the pan. Mix together the remaining ingredients, except the noodles, and stir into the pan, then heat for 2–3

minutes. Meanwhile, cook the noodles according to packet instructions, drain and stir into the pan.

JACKET BANANAS WITH CHOCOLATE MARSHMALLOW SAUCE

Serves 4

4 medium bananas, slightly unripe
50 g (2 oz) chocolate polka dots
24 mini or 4 large marshmallows
Cream or ice-cream, to serve

1. Pre-heat the oven to 160C/325F/Gas 3. Trim the ends off the bananas, leaving on the skins. Using a sharp knife, make a lengthways slit in each one.
2. Gently prise open each banana and fill with chocolate polka dots and marshmallows (if using large marshmallows snip into 6 with dampened scissors), then wrap each one in foil. Bake for 15–20 minutes. Serve hot with cream or ice-cream.

Chicken Stir-fry

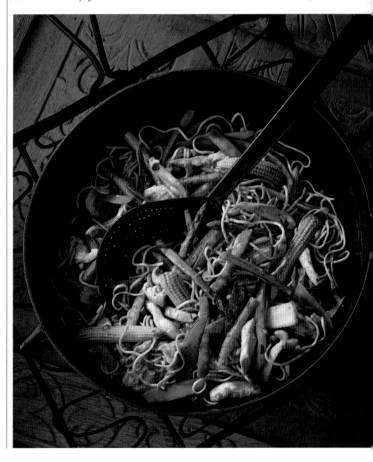

STYLISH VEGETARIAN DINNER

LEEK AND TARRAGON SOUP

MIXED GREEN SALAD WITH WALNUT VINAIGRETTE

GOAT'S CHEESE FILO PIE

TOMATO AND ORANGE SALAD

ALMOND SHAPES

RHUBARB AND GINGER FOOL

A wonderful vegetarian dinner party menu to welcome in the spring.

LEEK AND TARRAGON SOUP

 Serves 4

50 g (2 oz) butter
1 onion, finely chopped
450 g (1 lb) leeks, finely chopped
1 carrot, diced
900 ml (1½ pints) vegetable stock
1 tablespoon fresh tarragon, chopped
A little lemon juice (optional)
Salt and freshly ground black pepper

Leek and Tarragon Soup

To garnish
2 tablespoons single cream (optional)
Sprigs of tarragon

1. Melt the butter in a large pan and gently fry the onion for 5 minutes, then add the leeks and carrot. Cook for 10–15 minutes until soft, stirring occasionally.
2. Add the stock and tarragon and bring to the boil. Cover and simmer for 25 minutes. Cool, then liquidise until smooth. Strain through a fine sieve.
3. To serve, return the soup to the pan and re-heat gently. Season, then, if desired, add the lemon juice to sharpen the flavour. Garnish each bowl with single cream, if using, and a tarragon sprig.

MIXED GREEN SALAD WITH WALNUT VINAIGRETTE

 Makes 150 ml (5 fl oz) dressing

A selection of mixed salad leaves (e.g. endive, frisée, lamb's lettuce, watercress, radicchio)

For the vinaigrette
3 tablespoons walnut oil
3 tablespoons olive oil
50 g (2 oz) walnuts, lightly toasted
2 tablespoons wine vinegar
1 clove garlic
½ teaspoon cumin seeds
2 tablespoons fresh coriander, chopped
Salt and freshly ground black pepper

1. Mix together the walnut and olive oils. Grind the walnuts in a food processor with the vinegar, garlic, cumin and coriander. Add the oil a little at a time, blending it in until smooth then season.
2. Place the salad leaves in a bowl then, just before serving, toss in the vinaigrette.

Goat's Cheese Filo Pie (page 70), Tomato and Orange Salad (page 70) and Mixed Green Salad with Walnut Vinaigrette

GOAT'S CHEESE FILO PIE

 Serves 4

3 tablespoons olive oil
1 onion, finely chopped
2 cloves garlic
1 aubergine, diced
1 red pepper, diced
2 teaspoons fresh oregano, chopped
225 g (8 oz) soft goat's cheese
225 g (8 oz) ricotta
2 eggs
8 sheets filo pastry
Melted butter and olive oil, mixed
Salt and freshly ground black pepper

1. Pre-heat the oven to 200C/400F/Gas 6. Heat the olive oil in a large pan and fry the onion and garlic until quite soft. Add the aubergine and red pepper and fry over a moderate heat for several minutes until very soft. Mix in the oregano and season to taste.
2. In a separate bowl, or food processor, blend the goat's cheese with the ricotta and eggs until smooth. Season well.
3. Line a 23 cm x 18 cm (9 x 7 in) shallow dish with one sheet of filo pastry, then brush liberally with the mixed melted butter and olive oil. Put another sheet on top and brush again. Repeat twice more (4 sheets in total).
4. Spoon in the cooked aubergine mixture, then pour over the goat's cheese mix. Cover with a sheet of filo and brush with the melted butter and olive oil. Then repeat with 2 more sheets. Crumple the last one attractively over the top of the pie. Make several diagonal slices through the top of the pie to allow the steam to escape. Bake for 35–40 minutes until the pastry is golden and the filling just set. Serve hot or warm.

TOMATO AND ORANGE SALAD

 Serves 4

450 g (1 lb) tomatoes, sliced
1 orange, peeled and thinly sliced
50–75 g (2–3 oz) stoned black olives
1–2 teaspoons olive oil
Freshly ground black pepper
Snipped chives, to garnish

1. Arrange the tomato and orange slices on a plate. Scatter over the olives. Sprinkle the salad with olive oil and black pepper. Garnish with snipped chives.

ALMOND SHAPES

 Makes about 20

50 g (2 oz) butter
50g (2 oz) light muscovado sugar
1 egg
1 egg yolk
100 g (4 oz) wholemeal flour
1 teaspoon baking powder
75 g (3 oz) ground almonds
A pinch of salt
25 g (1 oz) blanched almonds, chopped
1 teaspoon orange zest, to decorate

1. Pre-heat the oven to 190C/375F/Gas 5. Beat the butter and sugar together until pale and creamy. Gradually add the whole egg and egg yolk.
2. Fold in the flour, baking powder, ground almonds and salt and mix to a soft dough. Handling as lightly as possible, roll out on a lightly floured board to a thickness of 5 mm ($^1/_4$ in) and cut into tiny shapes (stars, crescents, circles, etc.) using decorative pastry cutters. Scatter over the chopped almonds.
3. Transfer the shapes to a greased baking sheet and bake for 15–18 minutes or until just pale brown. Remove to a wire rack, sprinkle with the orange zest and allow to cool.

RHUBARB AND GINGER FOOL

 Serves 4

450–675 g (1–1$^1/_2$ lb) rhubarb
65 g (2$^1/_2$ oz) light muscovado sugar
$^1/_2$ teaspoon ground ginger, mixed with a little water
1–2 teaspoons chopped preserved ginger
150 ml (5 fl oz) double cream

1. Wipe the rhubarb then trim and cut into 1–2.5 cm ($^1/_2$–1 in) pieces. Put in a heavy-based pan with 50 g (2 oz) of the sugar and cook over a very gentle heat so that the sugar dissolves in the rhubarb's own juice. (If you're using a lightweight pan, add a tablespoon or so of water.)
2. Add both the ground ginger and most of the

preserved ginger (reserve a little for decoration) to the pan. Cook until the rhubarb is tender. Remove from heat and allow to cool.

3. Blend the rhubarb purée until smooth. You should have between 450–600 ml (15–20 fl oz) of purée.

4. Whip the double cream with the remaining sugar until stiff, then fold into the purée. Spoon into serving dishes and chill. Decorate with the reserved ginger and serve with *Almond Shapes*.

Rhubarb and Ginger Fool and *Almond Shapes*

VEGETARIAN ITALIAN-STYLE

BRAISED CURLY ENDIVE

WILD MUSHROOM RISOTTO

VERY SPECIAL TIRAMISÚ

This simple supper menu is perfect for casual entertaining. Quick to prepare, it is particularly suited as an after-work supper with friends.

BRAISED CURLY ENDIVE

Serves 4

500 g (1¼ lb) curly endive
6 tablespoons olive oil
2 garlic cloves, crushed
2 ripe tomatoes, roughly chopped
1 small red chilli, seeded and chopped

20 capers
Salt and freshly ground black pepper

To serve
Country-style bread
Garlic
Olive oil

1. Wash the endive and pat dry, then cut into short lengths. Heat the oil in a large pan, add the garlic and tomatoes and cook over a gentle heat for 3 minutes. Increase the heat, add the endive, chilli and capers and stir-fry for 1 minute.
2. Add 600 ml (1 pint) of water to the pan and bring to the boil. Cover and simmer gently for 20–30 minutes or until the endive is tender and most of the liquid has evaporated. Season to taste and serve with toasted country-style bread rubbed with garlic and brushed with olive oil.

Braised Curly Endive, Wild Mushroom Risotto and *Mixed Green Salad with Walnut Vinaigrette (page 68)*

WILD MUSHROOM RISOTTO

Dried porcini mushrooms can be found in most good Italian delicatessens. They are expensive, but just a few add a wonderfully intense flavour to this classic dish.

  Serves 4

25 g (1 oz) dried porcini mushrooms
120 ml (4 fl oz) boiling water
2 tablespoons olive oil
1 small onion, finely chopped
350 g (12 oz) button mushrooms, halved if large
350 g (12 oz) arborio or risotto rice
1.2 litres (2 pints) vegetable stock
15 g (¹/₂ oz) butter
50 g (2 oz) vegetarian Parmesan, grated
Salt and freshly ground black pepper

1. Soak the porcini in the boiling water for 15 minutes then drain, reserving the liquid. Chop the porcini.
2. Heat the oil in a large frying pan, add the onion and fry gently for 5 minutes or until golden. Add the button mushrooms and chopped porcini and cook over a medium heat for 3 minutes. Add the rice and cook for a further 1 minute stirring continuously to avoid the rice sticking.
3. Add 150 ml (5 fl oz) of the stock and cook, stirring frequently, until it has been absorbed. Add the remaining stock and reserved porcini liquid a little at a time, stirring frequently, for 30 minutes or until the rice is just tender but still firm.
4. Remove the pan from the heat, stir in the butter and vegetarian Parmesan, season to taste and serve at once, with a crisp salad of mixed leaves.

VERY SPECIAL TIRAMISÚ

  Serves 4

6 egg yolks
75 g (3 oz) sugar
120 ml (4 fl oz) sweet dessert wine (such as Moscato Passito di Pantelleria or Beaumes de Venise)
175 ml (6 fl oz) strong black coffee
1 tablespoon coffee liqueur
10–12 boudoir biscuits or sponge fingers
2 tablespoons cocoa powder, to decorate

Very Special Tiramisú

1. Place the egg yolks and sugar in a bowl and beat together until pale and creamy. Beat in the sweet dessert wine. Sit the bowl over a pan of gently simmering water and continue beating for about 10 minutes or until thickened.
2. Combine the coffee and coffee liqueur in a bowl and dip in the biscuits until they absorb the liquid but do not fall apart.
3. Layer the biscuits and egg mixture in 4 individual bowls, finishing with a layer of egg mixture. Dust with cocoa powder and chill for 2 hours until firm.

AL FRESCO

When the sun shines there's nothing like eating
outdoors to give your guests an appetite.
So whether it's lunch on the patio, a grand
picnic at an open-air music concert or a
barbecue, these recipes are bound to inspire
you to entertain *al fresco*

Clockwise from the left: *Nectarine and Raspberry Torte (page 80),
Rocket and Green Bean Salad with Garlic and Chilli Croûtons (page 79),
Chicken, Spinach and Apricot Pie (page 77), Layered Cream Cheese and
Smoked Salmon Ring (page 77), Stuffed Pesto Peppers (page 78), Spiced
New Potato and Carrot Salad (page 78), Artichoke Purée with Crudités
(page 76)* and *Romesco Sauce (page 76)*

SPLENDID PICNIC

ROMESCO SAUCE

ARTICHOKE PURÉE

LAYERED CREAM CHEESE AND

SMOKED SALMON RING

CHICKEN, SPINACH AND APRICOT PIE

SPICED NEW POTATO AND CARROT SALAD

STUFFED PESTO PEPPERS

TOMATO AND OLIVE LOAF

FLAVOURED BUTTERS

ROCKET AND GREEN BEAN SALAD WITH GARLIC

AND CHILLI CROÛTONS

NECTARINE AND RASPBERRY TORTE

The food for this meal is more sophisticated than the usual picnic fare as it's intended for a special occasion, like an open-air classical music concert. It is surprisingly easy to prepare and many of the dishes can be made in advance or frozen.

When you start preparing for the picnic, ask friends to help, dividing the tasks fairly. Non-cooks can supply drinks or nibbles. Follow our countdown on page 81 to help you plan ahead.

ROMESCO SAUCE

This Spanish sauce is often served with fish, but it also goes well with raw vegetables or breadsticks.

 Serves 6

1 large red pepper
1 large ripe tomato
100 ml (3¹/₂ fl oz) olive oil
4 garlic cloves, peeled
1 red chilli, seeded and finely chopped
1 slice day-old bread
25 g (1 oz) blanched almonds, toasted
25 g (1 oz) blanched hazelnuts, toasted
1 tablespoon chopped fresh parsley
2 tablespoons red wine vinegar
Salt and freshly ground black pepper

1. Quarter and seed the pepper, then place under a hot grill, skin side up, for 6–8 minutes or until the skin is charred. Grill the tomato, turning once, until softened. Cool the vegetables slightly, then peel the skin from the pepper and chop the flesh. Peel, halve and scoop out the seeds from the tomato, then chop the flesh.
2. Heat 3 tablespoons of the oil in a pan, add the pepper, tomato, garlic and chilli and fry gently for 5 minutes. Break up the bread and add to the pan, turning it in the oil until lightly browned.
3. Put the mixture into a blender or food processor and whizz briefly. Add the nuts, parsley, vinegar and seasoning and blend to a rough purée. With the machine running, pour in the remaining oil in a steady stream until it forms a thick sauce. Taste and adjust seasoning, if necessary.

ARTICHOKE PURÉE

 Serves 6

400 g (14 oz) tin artichokes in brine, drained
2 garlic cloves, finely chopped
6 tablespoons extra virgin olive oil
Salt and freshly ground black pepper

To serve
Breadsticks or raw vegetable crudités, such as radishes, spring onions, courgettes, carrots, cherry tomatoes or asparagus,

1. Cut the artichokes into quarters, then place in a food processor or blender with the garlic, oil and seasoning. Blend to a rough purée. Serve with the breadsticks or raw vegetables as a dip.

Layered Cream Cheese and Smoked Salmon Ring

LAYERED CREAM CHEESE AND SMOKED SALMON RING

This dish travels well if wrapped in foil.

Serves 6–8

1 ring or cob loaf
350 g (12 oz) low-fat soft cheese
2 tablespoons lemon juice
1 avocado, mashed
1 teaspoon poppy seeds
3 tablespoons snipped fresh chives
1 tablespoon chopped fresh tarragon
225 g (8 oz) smoked salmon
Salt and freshly ground black pepper

To garnish
Lime wedges
Fresh dill sprigs

1. Cut the loaf into three layers. Blend the soft cheese with the lemon juice and seasoning. Reserve one third, mix another third with the avocado and poppy seeds, then mix the remaining third with the chives and tarragon.
2. Place the base portion of the loaf on a board and spread the cut side with the herb cheese. Place the centre portion on top and spread with the avocado cheese, then cover with the top piece of bread.
3. Spread the remaining unflavoured cheese thinly over the crust. Drape the salmon over the top to completely cover it. Garnish with lime wedges and dill sprigs.

CHICKEN, SPINACH AND APRICOT PIE

The best way to transport this pie is in the cake tin overwrapped with foil. The pie can be frozen for up to 1 month.

Serves 6–8

For the pastry
450 g (1 lb) plain flour
1 tablespoon dried Italian herbs
150 g (5 oz) butter
1 egg, beaten, to glaze

For the filling
450 g (1 lb) spinach

Freshly grated nutmeg
450 g (1 lb) boneless chicken breasts, skinned
225 g (8 oz) sausagemeat
1 bunch spring onions, chopped
25 g (1 oz) chopped fresh parsley
4 fresh apricots, stoned and chopped
1 teaspoon grated lemon rind
1 egg, beaten
Salt and freshly ground black pepper
Fresh parsley sprigs, to garnish

To serve
Spring onions
Radishes

Chicken, Spinach and Apricot Pie

1. Pre-heat the oven to 200C/400F/Gas 6. Grease a 23 cm (9 in) round loose-bottomed cake tin.
2. Mix together the flour, herbs and seasoning. Melt the butter in a pan with 250 ml (8 fl oz) water, then bring to the boil. Quickly stir into the flour, mixing to a soft dough. Cool slightly, then turn out and knead briefly on a lightly floured surface. Wrap in cling film and leave to cool.
3. Meanwhile, make the filling. Wash the spinach in several changes of water, then place in a large pan with no water and cook covered for 4–5 minutes until the spinach is wilted and tender. Drain well, pressing out any excess liquid. Chop, then season with nutmeg, salt and pepper.
4. Chop the chicken into small cubes and place in a bowl with the sausagemeat, spring onions, parsley, apricots, lemon rind and egg. Combine thoroughly with your hands. Add the spinach and seasoning and mix well.

SPICED NEW POTATO AND CARROT SALAD

  Serves 6-8

900 g (2 lb) new potatoes
3 tablespoons olive oil
2 teaspoons cumin seeds
2 teaspoons mustard seeds
2 carrots, grated
2 tablespoons red wine vinegar
Salt and freshly ground black pepper
Fresh coriander sprigs, to garnish

1. Cut any large potatoes in half. Boil or steam the potatoes in their skins for about 15–20 minutes until just tender.
2. Heat the oil in a pan, add the cumin and mustard seeds and fry until they start to pop. Add the carrots and stir-fry quickly. Remove from the heat and stir in the vinegar and seasoning. Pour over the potatoes and mix well, then garnish with the coriander.

STUFFED PESTO PEPPERS

  Serves 6

3 orange peppers
4 spring onions, finely chopped
100 g (4 oz) button mushrooms, sliced
3 tablespoons ready-made pesto
6 tomato slices

1. Pre-heat the oven to 200C/400F/Gas 6. Halve the peppers, slicing through the stalks but leaving them on, and remove the seeds.
2. Mix together the onions, mushrooms and pesto and pile into the pepper halves, then place a slice of tomato on top of each. Arrange in a shallow oven-proof dish and bake for 20 minutes until tender. Leave to cool.

Spiced New Potato and Carrot Salad

5. Roll out two-thirds of the pastry and line the greased cake tin, taking care to press the pastry well into the tin. Fill the pastry case with the chicken mixture. Press down and smooth over the top to make it level.
6. Dampen the pastry edges, then roll out the remaining pastry to cover the pie. Trim off any excess and reserve, then pinch the edges together to seal the pie.
7. Roll out the pastry trimmings; cut into spinach and herb leaf shapes and one thin strip. Brush the pie with some beaten egg, then decorate the top with the leaves tied with the strip of pastry. Brush the trimmings with beaten egg.
8. Bake for 1–1$^1/_4$ hours until golden. Cool in the tin for 20 minutes, then remove and cool completely. Serve with spring onions and radishes, garnished with parsley.

TOMATO AND OLIVE LOAF

To transport the loaf, slice it before leaving, then reassemble, spread with *Flavoured Butter* and wrap in foil.

 Makes 1 large loaf

1 x 280g pack white bread mix
100 g (4 oz) sun-dried tomatoes in oil, drained
100 g (4 oz) stoned black olives
1 beaten egg, to glaze
Coarse sea salt, for sprinkling
Flavoured Butter, to serve (see following recipe)

1. Grease a baking sheet and make up the bread mix according to the packet then divide the dough in two. Chop the tomatoes, reserving a few pieces for decoration, then knead the remainder into one half of the bread mix. Reserve a few olives for decoration, then chop the remainder and knead into the other half of the dough.
2. Shape each piece of dough into a 25 cm (10in long sausage shape. Pinch the ends together, then twist the pieces together to form a rope. Pinch the ends to seal. Transfer to the baking sheet.
3. Cover the dough with oiled cling film and leave to rise for about 30–40 minutes until doubled in size. Pre-heat the oven to 220C/425F/Gas 7.
4. When risen, brush the top with egg, sprinkle with salt and press in the reserved tomatoes and olives. Bake for 30–35 minutes until it turns golden and sounds hollow when tapped on the base. Remove from the baking sheet and leave to cool on a wire rack.

Stuffed Pesto Peppers

FLAVOURED BUTTERS

Choose any one of the flavourings to mix with the butter.

 Serves 6-8

100 g (4 oz) butter, softened

For the flavouring
3 tablespoons chopped fresh herbs, such as dill, chives and tarragon
8 basil leaves, shredded
2 teaspoons wholegrain mustard
1 teaspoon paprika and a good pinch of chilli powder
1 tablespoon sun-dried tomato paste

1. Beat any of the flavourings into the softened butter then chill until required.

ROCKET AND GREEN BEAN SALAD WITH GARLIC AND CHILLI CROÛTONS

Pack the salad leaves and croûtons in separate polythene bags and put the dressing in a small sealable container or screw-top jar.

 Serves 6-8

4 tablespoons olive oil
2 garlic cloves, peeled
1 teaspoon dried crushed chillies
2 thick slices bread, cubed
250 g (8 oz) green beans, lightly cooked
75 g (3 oz) rocket leaves
Selection of salad leaves

For the dressing
3 tablespoons low-fat natural yoghurt
1 teaspoon clear honey
1 teaspoon wholegrain mustard
1 tablespoon lemon juice
Salt and freshly ground black pepper

1. Heat half the oil in a pan and add the garlic and chillies. Fry gently for a few minutes, then stir in the bread and fry quickly, turning until crisp and golden. Drain the bread on kitchen paper and discard the garlic.
2. Place the remaining oil in a screw-top jar with the dressing ingredients and shake well. Cut the

beans into short lengths and mix with the rocket and salad leaves.

3. Just before serving, arrange the salad in a bowl and sprinkle with the croûtons. Drizzle over the dressing and serve.

NECTARINE AND RASPBERRY TORTE

Transport the *Torte* in its tin and decorate just before serving.
The *Torte* can be frozen for up to one month.

 Serves 6–8

175 g (6 oz) self-raising flour
1 teaspoon baking powder
1 teaspoon ground cinnamon
50 g (2 oz) ground almonds
175 g (6 oz) butter or margarine, softened
175 g (6 oz) light muscovado sugar
3 eggs
Juice and grated rind of 1 orange
3 nectarines, halved, stoned and sliced
225 g (8 oz) raspberries
100 g (4 oz) redcurrants (optional)
25 g (1 oz) flaked almonds

225 g (8 oz) mascarpone or cream cheese
Icing sugar, for dusting

1. Pre-heat the oven to 180C/350F/Gas 4. Grease and line the base of a 20 cm (8 in) round cake tin.
2. In a bowl, mix together the flour, baking powder, cinnamon, ground almonds, butter or margarine, sugar, eggs, orange rind and 2 tablespoons of the juice. Beat for 3–4 minutes until light and fluffy.
3. Put half the mixture in the tin and smooth. Arrange half the nectarine slices and half the raspberries and redcurrants (if using) on top. Spread remaining cake mixture over top and sprinkle with the almonds.
4. Bake for 45–50 minutes until golden and firm to the touch. Cool in the tin for 10 minutes, then remove and cool on a wire rack.
5. Spread mascarpone or cream cheese on top to within 2.5 cm (1 in) of the edge of the cake. Decorate with the remaining nectarines, raspberries and redcurrants, if using, then dust the top carefully with icing sugar.

Nectarine and Raspberry Torte

COUNTDOWN

There is a choice as to when you make some recipes, depending on whether you freeze them or not, so some will be listed more than once.

Up to one month before
• Make and freeze *Tomato and Olive Loaf*, *Flavoured Butter*, *Chicken, Spinach and Apricot Pie* and *Nectarine and Raspberry Torte*.

Up to one week before
• Make *Romesco Sauce* and *Flavoured Butter*; chill.

Up to two days before
• Make *Nectarine and Raspberry Torte* and store in a cool place, in a rigid container or wrapped in foil.
• Make *Artichoke Purée*, chill.
• Buy drinks and chill.
• Put cool packs in freezer.
• Gather containers, plates, bowls, cutlery, glasses, cups, napkins, rugs and cool box.
• Make *Chicken, Spinach and Apricot Pie*, cool and chill.

The day before
• Buy vegetables for the crudités and breadsticks for the dips.
• Make *Tomato and Olive Loaf*; cool, slice, spread with *Flavoured Butter*, reassemble and wrap in foil.
• Make *Stuffed Pesto Peppers*.
• Make *Layered Cream Cheese and Smoked Salmon Ring*, wrap in foil; chill.
• Make *Spiced New Potato and Carrot Salad*; chill.
• Make *Garlic and Chilli Croûtons* for the *Rocket and Green Bean Salad* and store in a polythene bag.
• Cook green beans and make dressing for *Rocket and Green Bean Salad*; chill.
• Defrost *Tomato and Olive Loaf, Flavoured Butter, Chicken, Spinach and Apricot Pie* and *Nectarine and Raspberry Torte*; chill.

On the day
• Prepare and pack fruit for garnishing and mascarpone or cream cheese to spread on the *Nectarine and Raspberry Torte*.
• Prepare vegetables for the *Artichoke Purée* dip; store in a polythene bag.
• Wash the salad leaves, store in a polythene bag; chill.
• Put dressing for *Rocket and Green Bean Salad* in a small screw-top container.
• Return *Chicken, Spinach and Apricot Pie* to cake tin, overwrap with foil; chill.

Packing a Perfect Picnic
• Keep perishable foods, especially meat, poultry or fish, well chilled by packing with frozen ice packs.
• Dress leafy salads at the last moment – take the dressing to the picnic in a screw-top jar.
• Don't keep dry and moist foods in the same container.
• Cut cold meat, cakes and bread into slices before you go.
• Pour hot and cold drinks into vacuum flasks.
• Pack juicy foods into a container with a tight seal.
• Keep any squashable items in rigid containers.
• Don't leave litter behind – take a bag to fill so that you can take it home with you.
• Don't forget crockery, cutlery, napkins, paper or plastic cups and any sauces, chutneys/pickles and salt and pepper you may require.

LAMB CUTLETS WITH SPANISH TOMATO BREAD

Use a large, coarse-textured loaf for the best results

Serves 6

6 lamb cutlets
2 teaspoons chopped fresh rosemary
3 fat garlic cloves, peeled
Olive oil
1 large crusty loaf
3–4 tomatoes
Salt and freshly ground black pepper

1. Wipe the cutlets and place in a shallow dish. Sprinkle over the rosemary, chop 1 garlic clove and sprinkle over. Drizzle with 1 tablespoon of olive oil and seasoning.
2. Heat the barbecue or the grill and cook the chops for 5–6 minutes on each side or until browned but still pink in the centre. Cut the bread into thick slices and toast lightly.
3. Rub one side of each slice of bread with the remaining garlic cloves. Cut the tomatoes in half and squeeze the pulp on top. Drizzle with the olive oil and serve with the lamb.

 ## BARBECUE MARINADES

Blend 2 tablespoons of orange juice, ketchup, soy sauce, demerara sugar and vinegar. Add 2 teaspoons of grainy mustard. Use for chops, sausages and burgers.
Blend 150 ml (5 fl oz) wine, 2 tablespoons of oil and lemon juice, 2 teaspoons of chopped fresh oregano and seasoning. Use for chicken and vegetables.

Sweet and Chilli Chicken, Burgers Parmigiano, Lamb Cutlets with Spanish Tomato Bread and *Grilled Vegetables*

GRILLED VEGETABLES

Serves 6

You can grill all kinds of vegetables. If you use vegetables which normally take time to cook – boil or steam them a little first.

6 large new potatoes, parboiled and thickly sliced
18 asparagus spears, woody ends trimmed
6 courgettes, thickly sliced diagonally
2 ears sweetcorn, thickly sliced
Olive oil
Salt and freshly ground black pepper

1. Brush all the vegetables liberally with oil and season generously. Grill for a few minutes on each side until lightly charred. Serve at once.

BURGERS PARMIGIANO

Serves 6

675 g (1½ lb) lean minced beef or lamb
1 shallot, finely chopped

75 g (3 oz) sun-dried tomatoes in oil, drained and chopped
25 g (1 oz) Parmesan, grated
3 tablespoons chopped fresh basil
Salt and freshly ground black pepper

To serve
1 red pepper
1 yellow pepper
4 ciabatta rolls
Lettuce leaves

1. Mix the meat, shallot, tomatoes, cheese, basil and seasoning. Divide into 6 and shape into thick rounds.
2. Halve and seed the peppers, then cut the flesh into thick strips. Place on a baking tray, season and grill under a high heat for about 5 minutes until just charred.
3. Cook the burgers on the barbecue for 12–15 minutes, turning once, until browned. Fill the rolls with the burgers, peppers and lettuce.

SWEET AND CHILLI CHICKEN

Serves 6

6 chicken wings
6 chicken drumsticks

For the marinade
6 tablespoons mango chutney
2 garlic cloves, crushed
2 shallots, chopped
4 tablespoons paprika
1 teaspoon turmeric
½ teaspoon dried crushed red chillies
Grated rind and juice of 1 orange
Salt and freshly ground black pepper

1. Make a couple of deep cuts in each chicken piece and place in a shallow, non-metallic dish,
2. Place all of the marinade ingredients in a food processor and blend to a coarse purée. Pour over the chicken pieces, turning to ensure that they are evenly coated, and leave in the fridge for at least 1 hour, or overnight if possible.
3. Grill or barbecue the chicken pieces for about 15 minutes, turning occasionally, until they are golden brown and the juices run clear when the flesh is pierced with a fork. Serve hot or cold with plenty of paper napkins.

SPICY INDIAN BARBECUE

SPICED CHICKEN, LAMB, VEGETABLES, PRAWNS
OR FISH ON THE GRILL
SAFFRON RICE SALAD
YOGHURT AND CUCUMBER DRESSING
CORIANDER CHUTNEY
MINTED SUMMER FRUIT
FRUIT AND NUT TORTE
ICED PEACH TEA

SPICED CHICKEN ON THE GRILL

You can buy chicken supremes (boneless breast portions with wings attached) from a speciality butcher. Alternatively, use skinned chicken legs or part-boned breasts.

Serves 8

8 chicken supremes, skinned

For the marinade
500 g (1¼ lb) Greek yoghurt
2 garlic cloves, crushed
2.5 cm (1 in) piece fresh root ginger, peeled and grated
1 red or green chilli, seeded and chopped
1 tablespoon ground cumin
1 tablespoon ground coriander
2 teaspoons curry or tandoori paste
A few drops of yellow or red food colouring (optional)
Melted ghee, butter or oil, to baste
Fresh lemon juice, to serve

1. Slash each chicken portion two or three times with a sharp knife. Mix together all of the marinade ingredients, except the last two, in a large shallow dish, add the chicken pieces and coat well, rubbing the marinade into the slashes. Cover and leave to marinate in the fridge for at least 1 hour or, preferably, overnight.
2. Cook the chicken on a hot barbecue or under a hot grill for about 15–20 minutes on each side, basting with ghee, butter or oil as it cooks. Keep turning to ensure it cooks evenly.
3. To serve, arrange the chicken around a mound of *Saffron Rice Salad* (see page 85) and sprinkle with

lemon juice. Accompany with mango chutney, olives, cocktail pittas and *Yoghurt and Cucumber Dressing* (see page 86).

SPICED LAMB OR VEGETABLES

Omit the food colouring from the marinade and add 1 tablespoon of crushed coriander seeds and 3 tablespoons of chopped fresh coriander. Replace the chicken with 1.25 kg (2½ lb) lean, boneless lamb cut into large cubes, or 1 kg (2 lb) chunky vegetables such as onion wedges and chunks of pepper, courgette and sweetcorn. Thread the marinated meat or vegetables on to skewers and cook as before for about 15 minutes. Serve garnished with fresh mint.

SPICED PRAWNS OR FISH

Omit the food colouring from the marinade and substitute 2 teaspoons of ground turmeric, 2 tablespoons of dessicated coconut, the juice and grated rind of 1 lime and 2 finely chopped spring

onions. Replace the chicken with king prawns, small whole fish or cubes of firm-fleshed fish. Thread the prawns or fish on to skewers and cook as before for 10–20 minutes, depending on their size. Serve garnished with lime wedges.

SAFFRON RICE SALAD

Present a dramatic mound of this aromatic salad as a centre-piece for the *Spiced Chicken on the Grill* (see page 84).

 Serves 8

1 teaspoon saffron strands
6 green cardamom pods
6 cloves
1 cinnamon stick
450 g (1 lb) basmati rice
2 tablespoons olive oil
Squeeze of fresh lemon juice
Salt and freshly ground black pepper
50 g (2 oz) flaked almonds, toasted, to garnish

1. Place the saffron in a small bowl with 3 tablespoons of boiling water and leave to infuse while the rice is cooking.
2. Pour 1 litre (1¾ pints) water into a pan, season with salt and bring to the boil. Add the spices and rice. Return to the boil, stir with a fork, lower the heat, cover and simmer for 10 minutes.
3. Stir the rice again, then pour in the saffron liquid without stirring – the aim is for only some of the rice to be flavoured and coloured. Cook for a further 5–10 minutes until all of the liquid is absorbed and the rice is tender – be careful not to overcook it. Drain off any excess liquid.
4. Transfer the rice to a bowl and fluff up with a fork. Stir in the oil and lemon juice and leave to cool. Pile the rice on to a serving platter, season with black pepper and sprinkle over the toasted almonds to garnish.

From the left: *Coriander Chutney (page 86), Saffron Rice Salad, Spiced Chicken on the Grill, Spiced Prawns, Yoghurt and Cucumber Dressing (page 86)* and *Spiced Lamb*

Minted Summer Fruit, Fruit and Nut Torte and Iced Peach Tea

YOGHURT AND CUCUMBER DRESSING

Make quantity required

Serves 8

225 g (8 oz) natural yoghurt
½ cucumber, diced
A small bunch of fresh mint, to garnish

1. Mix the yoghurt with the cucumber and spoon into a serving bowl.
2. Garnish with a sprig of mint and serve cool.

CORIANDER CHUTNEY

Serves 8

1 onion
1 garlic clove
1–2 green chillies
1 large bunch of fresh coriander, trimmed
2 tablespoons ground almonds, toasted
3 tablespoons lime or lemon juice
3 tablespoons vegetable oil
2 teaspoons sugar
1 teaspoon salt

1. Place all of the ingredients in a food processor and whizz until well mixed but still retaining some texture. Transfer to a bowl, cover and leave for 1 hour for the flavours to develop.

MINTED SUMMER FRUIT

Try different mixtures of seasonal fruit, such
as mangoes, strawberries, raspberries and
blackcurrants. As a variation, use just two or
three fruits, such as papayas and
cape gooseberries.

 Serves 8

75 g (3 oz) caster sugar
Juice and finely grated rind of 2 limes
1 kg (2 lb) mixed fresh fruit
A large handful of fresh mint

To serve
Whipped cream
A pinch of cinnamon

1. Place the sugar in a small pan with 300 ml
(10 fl oz) water. Heat gently, stirring occasionally,
until the sugar has dissolved. Bring to the boil and
boil rapidly without stirring for 2 minutes. Stir in
the lime juice and rind. Remove from the heat and
leave to cool.
2. Prepare the fruit, leaving it whole or cutting into
large chunks as you prefer. Stir carefully into the
cooled syrup with half of the mint. Chill for at least
1 hour.
3. Sprinkle with the remaining mint and serve with
the whipped cream sprinkled with cinnamon.

FRUIT AND NUT TORTE

Choose a soft nougat, either a bar or individual
sweets, for this delicious torte. You can use a
bought lemon sponge or Madeira cake.

 Serves 8

75 g (3 oz) caster sugar
450 g (1 lb) lemon sponge or Madeira cake
500 g (1¼ lb) ricotta cheese
100 g (4 oz) plain chocolate-coated almonds,
finely chopped
75 g (3 oz) soft nougat, finely chopped
50 g (2 oz) candied peel, finely chopped
Finely grated rind of 1 orange
Finely grated rind of 1 lemon
75 g (3 oz) sultanas or raisins
2 tablespoons Amaretto or orange liqueur

175 g (6 oz) shredded or flaked almonds, toasted
Icing sugar, for sifting
Cape gooseberries, to decorate

1. Place the caster sugar in a large pan with 150 ml
(5 fl oz) water. Heat gently, stirring occasionally,
until the sugar has dissolved. Bring to the boil and
boil rapidly without stirring for 10 minutes until
syrupy. Leave to cool.
2. Meanwhile, line a 24 cm (9½ in) spring-release
cake tin with foil or greaseproof paper. Cut the
cake into very thin slices and use it to line the base
and sides of the tin.
3. Beat the cheese in a bowl then gradually add
150 ml (5 fl oz) of the sugar syrup, stirring
constantly.
4. Stir in the almonds, nougat, candied peel, orange
and lemon rinds, sultanas or raisins and liqueur.
Beat thoroughly, then spoon into the sponge-lined
tin. Sprinkle with toasted almonds. Cover with
clear plastic film and chill overnight or until firm.
5. To serve, transfer the torte to a large flat plate
and sift over icing sugar. Decorate with the
gooseberries.

ICED PEACH TEA

 Serves 8

6 ripe peaches
2 tablespoons Darjeeling tea
4 tablespoons caster sugar
Ice cubes, to serve

1. Halve, stone and slice 4 of the peaches. Place in a
large heatproof jug or bowl with the tea and sugar.
2. Pour over 1.75 litres (3 pints) boiling water, cover
and leave to infuse for at least 1–2 hours.
3. Strain the tea mixture into a jug. Halve, stone
and slice the remaining peaches and add to the tea
with some ice cubes.

EVENING PARTY AL FRESCO

BARBECUED VEGETABLES

GRILLED PORK AND PRUNES

HERBY AND SOY SAUCE MARINADES

OYSTER MUSHROOM AND TOMATO SALAD

SPINACH SALAD WITH LENTILS AND YOGHURT

SMOKED HADDOCK WITH

AVOCADO, LIME AND CHILLI

PARSLEYED HAM AND TONGUE

SUMMER FRUIT ICE BOWL

Barbecued Vegetables, Grilled Pork and Prunes and Soy Sauce Marinade

 ## BARBECUED VEGETABLES

Use a variety of fresh vegetables such as:
Peppers, red, green or yellow, quartered lengthways
Whole baby carrots
Whole baby turnips
Whole baby beetroot, simmered in boiling water until tender
Whole pattypan squashes
Aubergines, thickly sliced
Whole mushrooms
Courgettes, halved lengthways
Beefsteak tomatoes, halved
Chicory, thickly sliced

For the marinade
Olive oil
1 or 2 crushed garlic cloves, to taste
A variety of fresh herbs, chopped
Salt and freshly ground black pepper

1. Marinate the prepared vegetables in the combined marinade ingredients for at least 2 hours.
2. Oil the barbecue rack to prevent the vegetables from sticking and grill the vegetables for about 10 minutes, turning them and brushing with the marinade every few minutes until they are tender.
3. Season the vegetables to taste, brush with a little more oil and serve immediately.

GRILLED PORK AND PRUNES

Serves 6

750 g (1³/₄ lb) pork fillet, cut into cubes
18 dried prunes stoned
Soy Sauce Marinade *(see right)*

1. Place the pork fillet into a glass or china dish and add the prunes. (Ready-to-eat prunes can be used, but don't add them to the marinade until just before cooking or they will become too soft.) Pour the *Soy Sauce Marinade* over the pork and prunes, cover and leave in a cool place for at least 3 hours, or leave overnight in the fridge.
2. Drain off the marinade and set aside. Pat the pork and prunes dry with kitchen paper and then thread on to the skewers. Grill on barbecue until meat is sealed on all sides and then continue to cook until it is quite well done, basting occasionally with the reserved marinade. Serve hot.

MARINADES

Marinades add flavour and also tenderise meat and fish. The quantities below are for 450 g (1 lb) food. Marinate fish for 20 minutes only; meat or poultry benefit from 1–2 hours or overnight in the fridge. Always place in a glass or china dish. Never cover with foil as foil can dissolve on long contact with a marinade.

HERBY MARINADE

5 tablespoons olive oil
150 ml (5 fl oz) dry white wine
Juice of $\frac{1}{2}$ lemon or lime
2 tablespoons fresh mixed herbs, finely chopped
Freshly ground black pepper

1. Shake together all the ingredients in a screw-top jar.

SOY SAUCE MARINADE

6 tablespoons soy sauce
6 tablespoons sweet sherry
1 teaspoon root ginger, grated
1 teaspoon soft brown sugar
1 garlic clove, crushed

1. Shake all the ingredients together in a screw-top jar.

OYSTER MUSHROOM AND TOMATO SALAD

Serves 6

225 g (8 oz) oyster mushrooms
450 g (1 lb) tomatoes, sliced
2 tablespoons chopped fresh parsley

For the dressing
10 tablespoons sunflower oil
8 tablespoons white wine vinegar
1 red pepper
A squeeze of lemon juice
A pinch of ground cumin
2 tablespoons olive oil
Salt and freshly ground black pepper

1. Put the mushrooms, tomatoes and parsley in a medium salad bowl. Mix together the sunflower oil and 4 tablespoons of the vinegar, season and pour over the salad. Toss and leave to marinate for 1 hour, gently tossing from time to time.
2. Meanwhile, halve and seed the pepper and char under the grill. Place the pepper in a polythene bag for about 10 minutes. Peel off the blackened skin and cut the pepper into chunks.
3. Whizz the pepper in a blender with the remaining dressing ingredients. Spoon over the salad and serve at once.

Marinades and *Flavoured Butters (page 79)*

SPINACH SALAD WITH LENTILS AND YOGHURT

 Serves 6

225 g (8 oz) green lentils
225 g (8 oz) red lentils
225 g (8 oz) young spinach leaves
150 g (5 oz) natural yoghurt
Juice of 1 lemon
Salt and freshly ground black pepper

1. Wash the lentils separately, removing any grit or discoloured lentils.
2. Place in separate pans of cold water and bring to the boil. Simmer the red lentils for about 15 minutes and the green for about 45 minutes until they are tender, yet still holding their shape. Drain and cool.
3. Wash the spinach leaves and trim off any thick stalks. Place in a salad bowl. Scatter the lentils on top. Mix the yoghurt, lemon juice and seasoning, pour over the salad and serve.

SMOKED HADDOCK WITH AVOCADO, LIME AND CHILLI

Serves 6

450 g (1 lb) smoked haddock, very thinly sliced
1 avocado

For the dressing
10 tablespoons olive oil
3 tablespoons lime juice
2 red chillies, finely sliced
Salt and freshly ground black pepper

1. Lay the haddock in a china or glass dish. Mix the dressing ingredients and pour over the fish. Leave to marinate in the fridge for several hours.
2. Halve, peel, stone and slice the avocado. Lay the avocado on top of the fish and spoon over the dressing in the dish.

From the left: *Summer Fruit Ice Bowl, Oyster Mushroom and Tomato Salad (page 89), Smoked Haddock with Avocado, Lime and Chilli, Parsleyed Ham and Tongue* and *Spinach Salad with Lentils and Yoghurt*

PARSLEYED HAM AND TONGUE

A whole tongue weighs about 1.5 kg (3 lb).
Cook it all and use the excess for cold cuts.

Serves 6-8

750 g (1¾ lb) piece of gammon
750 g (1¾ lb) beef tongue
1 bay leaf
A few sprigs each of fresh parsley, thyme and sage
1 teaspoon black peppercorns
1 bottle (750 ml/1¼ pints) dry white wine
3 sachets powdered gelatine
2 teaspoons white wine vinegar
1 large bunch flatleaf parsley, stems removed and coarsely chopped

1. Soak the gammon in cold water for several hours. Drain and place in a pan filled with fresh water. Add the tongue and slowly bring to the boil. Reduce the heat and simmer for 45 minutes.
2. Remove the gammon and tongue and rinse out the pan. Return to the pan and add the herb sprigs, peppercorns, wine and 450 ml (15 fl oz) water.

Bring to the boil, reduce the heat and simmer for 1½–2 hours or until tender.
3. Once the gammon and tongue have cooked, dissolve the gelatine in a little of the meat stock. Strain the remaining stock through a muslin cloth. Stir the gelatine and the wine vinegar into the stock and chill until it begins to set.
4. Cut the gammon and tongue into rough bite-sized chunks and stir into the partially set jelly with the flatleaf parsley.
5. Wet the inside of a 1.75 litre (3 pint) loaf tin and pour in the partially set jelly. Once again leave the jelly to chill for several hours until it has set firmly.
6. Finally, dip the tin briefly in boiling water to loosen the terrine, then turn it out carefully on to a plate and serve.

 ## SUMMER FRUIT ICE BOWL

This can be frozen for up to 3 months.

Sprigs of herbs (e.g. mint, lemon balm, feverfew or thyme)
Edible flowers (e.g. pansies, primulas, violets, rose petals and borage flowers)
Seasonal fruits (e.g. passion fruit, papaya, star fruit, plums, nectarines, peaches, strawberries, grapes)

1. Make the ice bowl first. Half-fill a mixing bowl with cooled, boiled water (boiled water makes clearer ice). Float a slightly smaller bowl inside, then weigh it down (using food cans or old-fashioned scale weights) until the space between the bowls is about 1–2 cm (½–¾ in) all round. Secure the bowls together with tape. Top up with more water, if necessary.
2. Push the herbs and flowers into the water, then place in the freezer and leave overnight or until thoroughly frozen.
3. Remove from the freezer and leave for 5 minutes. Remove the inner bowl. Run some cold water over the outside bowl until it can be removed easily. Wrap the ice bowl in foil or polythene and freeze until needed.
4. When ready to serve, prepare the fruit as necessary and pile into the ice bowl. Place the bowl on a large plate (to catch the drips) and serve at once. It will last for about 1 hour.

BUFFETS AND DRINKS PARTIES

Finger food, a fork buffet, a hot help-yourself
spread or canapés; whatever your choice of food,
there are recipes here that will be sure to make
your party go with a swing.

From the left:*Party Sausage Patties (page 94)*,
Goat's Cheese, Pimiento and Pine Nut Pizzas (page 94)
and *Mini Oatcakes with Smoked Salmon Rillettes (page 94)*

FABULOUS FINGER BUFFET

PARTY SAUSAGE PATTIES
GOAT'S CHEESE, PIMIENTO AND PINE NUT PIZZAS
MINI OATCAKES WITH SMOKED SALMON RILLETTES
CHICKEN AND MANGO KEBABS
MUSHROOM AND WALNUT CROSTINI
TOMATO AND MOZZARELLA CROSTINI
PARTY PALMIERS

PARTY SAUSAGE PATTIES

Once cooked, these delicious bites can be frozen for up to 1 month and re-heated when required.

Makes about 24

6 slices mixed grain bread
6 spicy butcher's sausages
10–12 tablespoons sweetcorn relish
Oil, for shallow frying
Shredded radicchio

To garnish
Mustard and cress
Sliced onion

1. Lightly toast the bread. Using a 5 cm (2 in) plain round cutter, stamp out 4 rounds from each slice.
2. Squeeze the sausages from their skins and knead with 3 tablespoons of relish. Divide into 24 equal pieces and roll each one into a ball with wetted hands. Lightly flatten each ball with the palm of your hand.
3. Heat a little oil and fry the patties for 2 minutes on each side. Drain on kitchen paper.
4. Place a little of the radicchio on top of each of the toasts and top with a scant teaspoon of relish. Place a sausage patty on top of each one, garnish with the mustard and cress and sliced onion and serve immediately.

GOAT'S CHEESE, PIMIENTO AND PINE NUT PIZZAS

If you don't want to use goat's cheese – Mozzarella, Lancashire or feta also work well. These can be made and frozen, before baking, for up to 1 month.

 Makes 40

1 packet pizza base mix
4 tablespoons black olive paste
225 g (8 oz) soft goat's cheese
2–3 tinned pimientos, drained and rinsed
2 tablespoons pine nuts
Freshly ground black pepper
Fresh thyme sprigs, to garnish

1. Pre-heat the oven to 200C/400F/Gas 6. Prepare the pizza dough according to the instructions on the packet. Roll out the dough thinly on a floured surface and cut out 5 cm (2 in) rounds. Place on a greased baking sheet.
2. Spread a thin layer of olive paste on each of the rounds and crumble over the goat's cheese. Cut the pimientos into thin strips and pile on top of the cheese. Sprinkle each one with pine nuts and grind over some black pepper.
3. Bake for 10–15 minutes until the edges are browned. Top each one with a thyme sprig and serve warm.

MINI OATCAKES WITH SMOKED SALMON RILLETTES

Both the oatcake biscuits and salmon can be made a month in advance. Store the biscuits in an airtight tin and freeze the salmon mixture.

Makes 20–25

For the oatcakes
225 g (8 oz) medium oatmeal
100 g (4 oz) plain flour
½ teaspoon salt
1 teaspoon baking powder
100 g (4 oz) butter, melted

For the rillettes
225 g (8 oz) fresh salmon tail
65 ml (2½ fl oz) white wine

1 bay leaf
A few black peppercorns
175 g (6 oz) unsalted butter, softened
175 g (6 oz) smoked salmon trimmings
A squeeze of lemon juice
Cayenne pepper
Salt and freshly ground black pepper

To garnish
Snipped fresh chives
Sliced tomato

1. Pre-heat the oven to 150C/300F/Gas 2. Place the oatmeal, flour, salt and baking powder in a bowl. Add the melted butter and enough water to mix to a stiff dough.
2. Roll out to a thickness of 3 mm ($^1/_8$ in) on a lightly floured surface. Using a pastry cutter, cut out 9 cm ($3^1/_2$ in) rounds then cut into quarters. Place on a baking sheet and bake for 30 minutes. Leave to cool.
3. To make the rillettes, put the salmon tail in a pan with the wine, bay leaf and peppercorns. Add enough water to cover and simmer for about 20 minutes, then leave to cool in the liquid.
4. Melt 50 g (2 oz) of the butter and cook the smoked salmon until it turns pale pink. Set aside and leave to cool.
5. Skin the salmon tail and flake the flesh. Break up the smoked salmon trimmings and add to the salmon tail. Beat in the remaining butter and season with lemon juice, cayenne pepper, salt and pepper.
6. Just before serving, pile the salmon mixture on to each oatcake and garnish with chives and sliced tomato.

Party Sausage Patties

From the top: *Goat's Cheese, Pimiento and Pine Nut Pizzas* and *Mini Oatcakes with Smoked Salmon Rillettes*

CHICKEN AND MANGO KEBABS

Makes 50

5 x 225 g (8 oz) boneless, skinless chicken breasts
4 tablespoons lime juice
4 tablespoons chopped fresh mint
1 teaspoon dried chilli flakes
3 spring onions, finely chopped
1 tablespoon sunflower oil
4 mangoes
50 mint leaves, to garnish

1. Cut each chicken breast into 10 cubes. Place in a bowl with the lime juice, chopped mint, chilli flakes and spring onions. Mix together well and leave to marinate in the fridge for at least 1 hour.
2. Heat the oil in a large pan and fry the chicken and marinade for 10 minutes until tender.
3. Peel and stone the mangoes and cut the flesh into 50 pieces. Thread the chicken and mango on to wooden skewers with a mint leaf between each piece, and serve.

MUSHROOM AND WALNUT CROSTINI

Makes about 30

1 thin French baguette
4–5 tablespoons olive oil
25 g (1 oz) dried ceps, soaked in warm water for 30 minutes
250 g (9 oz) packet mixed fresh mushrooms
1 tablespoon coriander seeds, roughly crushed
6 spring onions, trimmed and sliced
100 g (4 oz) walnut pieces, toasted
Salt and freshly ground black pepper
Snipped fresh chives, to garnish

1. Pre-heat the oven to 200C/400F/Gas 6. Cut the French baguette into 1 cm ($^1/_2$ in) slices. Reserve 2 tablespoons of oil then brush both sides of each slice of bread with a little olive oil.
Bake for 8–10 minutes, turning once until golden. Cool on a wire rack.
2. Drain the ceps then chop them finely. Slice the mixed mushrooms.
3. Heat the reserved 2 tablespoons of olive oil in a frying pan and add the crushed coriander seeds. Fry for 30 seconds to release the flavour, then add the spring onions and cook for 1 minute. Add the dried and fresh mushrooms and cook over a high heat for 2 minutes until they are browned but still firm but don't overcook them. Stir in the toasted walnuts and seasoning.
4. Pile on to the toasts and garnish with chives. Serve hot or cold.

TOMATO AND MOZZARELLA CROSTINI

If fresh basil is unavailable, mix 1 tablespoon of pesto with the olive oil.

Makes about 30

1 thin French baguette
5–6 tablespoons extra virgin olive oil
300 g (10 oz) Mozzarella
A few drops Tabasco sauce
2 tablespoons chopped fresh basil or chives
4 ripe tomatoes

From the top: *Party Palmiers, Mushroom and Walnut Crostini, Tomato and Mozzarella Crostini* and *Chicken and Mango Kebabs (page 95)*

Salt and freshly ground black pepper
Shredded basil, to garnish

1. Pre-heat the oven to 200C/400F/Gas 6. Cut the French baguette into 1 cm (1/2 in) thick slices. Reserve 3 tablespoons of the olive oil, then brush both sides of each slice of bread with the remaining oil. Bake for 8–10 minutes, turning once until golden. Cool on a wire rack.
2. Cut the Mozzarella into small cubes. Mix the reserved olive oil with the Tabasco sauce, basil or chives and seasoning. Stir in the Mozzarella. Leave for 10 minutes to absorb the oil.
3. Slice the tomatoes thickly to give 4 good slices from each one. Halve each slice.
4. Place a tomato slice on each toast and top with a pile of Mozzarella. Garnish with basil and serve hot or cold.

PARTY PALMIERS

These delicious crispy biscuits can be made in minutes. Store
them uncooked in the freezer ready to pop into the oven at a moment's notice. They can be frozen for up to 1 month.

  Makes about 40

2 x 20 cm (8 in) squares frozen puff pastry, thawed
3 tablespoons pesto, olive or sun-dried tomato paste
3 tablespoons freshly grated Parmesan
Coarse salt crystals

1. Pre-heat the oven to 220C/425F/Gas 7. Spread the pastry squares with your chosen paste and sprinkle with Parmesan. Roll each square from opposite edges towards the centre to form two rolls which meet in the middle.
2. Flatten the rolls lightly with the palm of your hand where the two rolls meet. Cut each roll into 20 slices.
3. Place the slices on baking sheets and sprinkle with a little coarse salt. Lightly roll the salt into the palmiers with a rolling pin.
4. Bake for about 4 minutes on each side until risen and golden brown. Transfer to a wire rack to cool.

COUNTDOWN

Where there is a choice as to when some recipes can be made, they may appear twice.

Up to a month before
• Make and freeze the *Mini Oatcakes*, and their accompanying *Smoked Salmon Rillettes*, *Goat's Cheese, Pimiento and Pine Nut Pizzas*, *Party Palmiers* and *Party Sausage Patties*.

The week before
• Check that there are enough plates and glasses.
• Sort through and launder tablecloths and napkins or buy paper ones.
• Decide how to arrange the room.

Two days before
• Make the *Mini Oatcake* bases and store in an airtight container.

The day before
• Make the *Smoked Salmon Rillettes* for the oatcakes and store in the fridge.

On the day
• Shape *Party Sausage Patties*; chill. Toast bread and stamp out rounds.
• Make *Goat's Cheese, Pimiento and Pine Nut Pizzas*, ready to cook.
• Bake bread for *Mushroom and Walnut* and *Tomato and Mozzarella Crostinis*.
• Marinate chicken for *Chicken and Mango Kebabs*.
• Decorate the table.
• Chill the white wine.

1–2 hours before
• Cook *Party Sausage Patties*.
• Cook *Goat's Cheese, Pimiento and Pine Nut Pizzas*.
• Make *Mushroom and Walnut* and *Tomato and Mozzarella Crostini* toppings.
• Assemble *Mini Oatcakes with Smoked Salmon Rillettes*.
• Cook *Chicken and Mango Kebabs*.
• Bake the *Party Palmiers*.

Hot Buffet

CHESTNUT SOUP

BRAISED BEEF WITH CRANBERRY, WALNUT AND
BULGAR WHEAT STUFFING

MIXED BEAN, MUSHROOM AND GRUYÈRE SALAD

SMOKED HAM AND LEEK PIE

SEAFOOD AND MELON SALAD WITH GINGER
AND LIME DRESSING

ORANGE, DATE AND CARROT SALAD

FENNEL, PEAR AND POPPY SEED SALAD WITH
STILTON DRESSING

POTATO SALAD WITH HORSERADISH AND
DILL PICKLES

TURKISH DELIGHT ICE-CREAM WITH
PISTACHIO MERINGUES

TANGERINE AND CHOCOLATE CHEESECAKE

BRANDIED CLEMENTINES WITH ROSEMARY AND
RATAFIA CREAM

In order to cater for 25 guests, you will need to double up on some of these recipes.

CHESTNUT SOUP

Tinned chestnuts save time and have an excellent flavour. They should be added to the soup after 15 minutes. You could try a ready-made stock available in large supermarkets. Or use half canned consommé and half water to give the soup a really rich flavour. A stock cube will not be the same.
To freeze the soup, before adding the cream and sherry. Pour into containers, leaving at least 25 cm (1 in) for expansion, or line a container with a freezer bag and freeze until solid, then remove the bag, seal and label. Store for up to 1 month.

Serves 12–15

450 g (1 lb) dried chestnuts
50 g (2 oz) butter
2 large onions, chopped

Chestnut Soup

2 medium potatoes, diced
6 celery sticks, sliced
2.75 litres (5 pints) fresh chicken or turkey stock
2 juniper berries, crushed
1/2 teaspoon freshly grated nutmeg
1 teaspoon light muscovado sugar
600 ml (1 pint) double cream
4 tablespoons medium sherry
Salt and freshly ground black pepper

To garnish
Chopped fresh parsley
Croûtons

1. Soak the chestnuts in cold water overnight; drain and chop roughly. Melt the butter in a large pan and gently fry the onions until soft but not coloured. Add the chestnuts, potatoes, celery, stock, juniper berries, nutmeg and sugar. Bring to the boil and simmer half-covered for 25 minutes until the potatoes and chestnuts are tender.
2. Remove from the heat, pour into a food processor and blend until smooth. Sieve, then return to the pan. Stir in the cream and seasoning and reheat gently. Just before serving, stir in the sherry, then garnish with the chopped parsley and croûtons.

Mixed Bean, Mushroom and Gruyère Salad

BRAISED BEEF WITH CRANBERRY, WALNUT AND BULGAR WHEAT STUFFING

To freeze: cool, then wrap in double thickness of foil, taking care to exclude as much air as possible. Store for up to 1 month.

Serves 12

1.5 kg (3 lb) boned rolled brisket of beef
50 g (2 oz) bulgar wheat
25 g (1 oz) butter
1 bunch spring onions, sliced
A generous pinch of ground allspice
50 g (2 oz) walnut pieces, chopped
100 g (4 oz) fresh cranberries
2 tablespoons oil
450 ml (15 fl oz) brown ale
Salt and freshly ground black pepper
Flatleaf parsley, to garnish

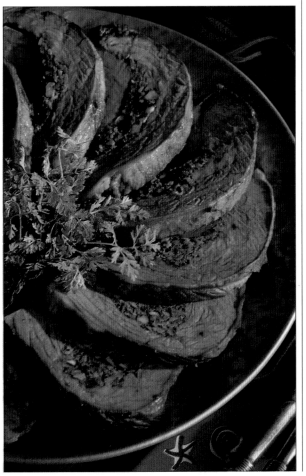

1. Untie the brisket and lay it flat on a board. Cover and set aside. Cover the bulgar wheat with boiling water and leave to soak.
2. Melt the butter in a pan and gently fry the spring onions until they are just softening. Stir in the allspice, walnuts and cranberries. Cook for a few minutes until the cranberries have burst their skins, then remove from the heat.
3. Drain the bulgar wheat and squeeze dry with your hands. Stir into the cranberry mixture and season well. Spread the stuffing evenly over the beef, then roll up and tie with string to secure.
4. Pre-heat the oven to 160C/325F/Gas 3. Heat the oil in a large flameproof casserole and brown the rolled beef all over. Pour in the brown ale, cover tightly and cook for $2^1/_2$–3 hours, basting occasionally, until tender. Cool, then chill and serve thinly sliced, or serve hot, thickly sliced with the juices. Garnish with parsley.

MIXED BEAN, MUSHROOM AND GRUYÈRE SALAD

Serves 20–25

225 g (8 oz) French beans or runner beans
225 g (8 oz) frozen broad beans
3 x 400 g (14 oz) tins mixed pulses, drained
225 g (8 oz) button mushrooms, sliced
225 g (8 oz) Gruyère, coarsely grated

For the dressing
175 ml (6 fl oz) olive oil
50 ml (2 fl oz) red wine vinegar
4 tablespoons wholegrain mustard
4 tablespoons chopped fresh parsley
Salt and freshly ground black pepper

1. Trim and cut the French beans in half. Cook in boiling, salted water for 3–4 minutes then refresh under cold running water and drain well. Cook the broad beans according to instructions on the packet. Refresh under cold water and drain well.
2. Mix the cooked French beans and broad beans with the pulses, mushrooms and cheese.
3. To make the dressing, shake together all the ingredients in a screw-top jar. Pour over the salad and toss gently.

Braised Beef with Cranberry, Walnut and Bulgar Wheat Stuffing

Smoked Ham and Leek Pie

The pastry can be made the day before and stored in the fridge. If you don't want to make your own, you can use 450 g (1 lb) frozen puff pastry instead. To freeze, open freeze the pie uncooked, then wrap it in foil and store in a freezer for up to 1 month. Leave to thaw in the fridge overnight, then bake as you would normally.

Serves 12

For the pastry
500 g (1¼ lb) plain flour
½ teaspoon salt
400 g (14 oz) butter, softened
4 egg yolks

For the filling
100 g (4 oz) butter
450 g (1 lb) leeks, thinly sliced
100 g (4 oz) Gruyère, grated
50 g (2 oz) freshly grated Parmesan
225 g (8 oz) chestnut mushrooms, sliced
450 g (1 lb) sliced oak-smoked cooked ham, diced

Smoked Ham and Leek Pie and *Fennel, Pear and Poppy Seed Salad with Stilton Dressing (page 102)*

4 tablespoons wholegrain mustard
300 ml (10 fl oz) fromage frais
Freshly ground black pepper
1 beaten egg, to glaze

1. To make the pastry, sift together the flour and salt. Blend together the butter and egg yolks in a food processor until pale. Add the flour and process for 1 minute or until the mixture is just coming together. Add about 3 tablespoons of iced water and continue to mix for a few more seconds. Tip out on to a floured surface and knead lightly until the dough comes together – it will be quite soft. Wrap in greaseproof paper and chill for at least 30 minutes.
2. Pre-heat the oven to 200C/400F/Gas 6. Divide the dough into 2 pieces, making 1 piece slightly larger than the other. Roll out the smaller piece to fit a baking sheet measuring approximately 28 x 33 cm (11 x 13 in). Reserve any trimmings. Prick the pastry base all over with a fork, then bake for 15 minutes. Leave to cool.
3. To make the filling, melt the butter in a frying pan and fry the leeks until they begin to soften, then stir in the Gruyère and Parmesan. Spread half of the mixture over the cooked base to within 2.5 cm (1 in) of the edges. Cover with half the mushrooms, then the ham. Mix the mustard with the fromage frais and spread over the ham. Season

with some freshly ground black pepper. Top with the remaining mushroom and leek mixture.

4. Roll out the larger piece of pastry on a lightly floured surface, making it large enough to cover the filling. Moisten the edges of the cooked pastry and cover with the uncooked pastry, pressing the edges to seal. Trim the edges and brush all over with beaten egg.

5. Roll together the pastry trimmings and cut out holly leaves using a cutter or template. Arrange over the pie and brush with the beaten egg. Bake the pie for about 30 minutes until it is golden and crisp. Serve either hot or cold, cut into square portions.

SEAFOOD AND MELON SALAD WITH GINGER AND LIME DRESSING

The dressing stores well in the fridge for up to three days.

Serves 20–25

For the dressing
150 ml (5 fl oz) sunflower or peanut oil
Juice of 8 limes
Finely grated rind of 2 limes
75 g (3 oz) root ginger, peeled and cut into matchsticks
4 fresh red chillies, seeded and very thinly sliced
1 teaspoon salt
4 tablespoons chopped fresh coriander

For the salad
2 kg (4¼ lb) seafood salad (including prawns, mussels and squid), defrosted if frozen
4 ripe melons, each weighing about 675 g (1½ lb), such as Ogen, Cantaloupe or Honeydew
8 ripe tomatoes
2 red onions, thinly sliced
Salad leaves, to garnish

1. To make the dressing, shake together the oil and lime juice in a screw-top jar until they are thoroughly combined. Add the lime rind, root ginger, chillies, salt and coriander. Shake again to mix.

2. Put the seafood in a shallow dish in an even layer and pour over the dressing. Mix gently to make sure that the seafood is evenly coated. Cover and leave to marinate for 1–2 hours.

3. Halve the melons, remove and discard the seeds. Using a melon baller, scoop out as many balls from

Orange, Date and Carrot Salad

the flesh as possible, reserving any juice.

4. Place the tomatoes in a bowl, pour over boiling water and leave for 30 seconds. Drain and plunge into cold water and peel off the skins. Cut the tomatoes into quarters and remove the seeds, then cut into strips.

5. Add the melon balls with any reserved juice, the tomatoes and onions to the marinated seafood and mix gently. Arrange on a serving platter and garnish with mixed salad leaves.

ORANGE, DATE AND CARROT SALAD

Fresh dates are not as sweet and sticky as the boxed ones, but do remember to peel off the tough skin.

 Serves 20–25

8 oranges
900 g (2 lb) carrots, grated
450 g (1 lb) fresh dates, stoned, quartered and peeled
100 g (4 oz) blanched almonds, toasted and chopped
4 tablespoons lemon juice
2 teaspoons golden caster sugar
1 teaspoon salt

1. Using a sharp knife, cut all the pith and membrane off the oranges, then carefully cut into segments between the membranes.

2. Combine the grated carrot, oranges and dates in a large bowl. Add 75 g (3 oz) of the toasted almonds.

3. Mix together the lemon juice, sugar and salt, then pour over the salad and mix gently.

4. Transfer to a serving dish, then sprinkle with the remaining almonds and serve.

Seafood and Melon Salad with Ginger and Lime Dressing (page 101)

FENNEL, PEAR AND POPPY SEED SALAD WITH STILTON DRESSING

 Serves 20–25

6 medium bulbs fennel
6 Conference pears
3 bunches of watercress, trimmed
15 g (½ oz) poppy seeds

For the dressing
175 g (6 oz) Stilton, crumbled
350 g (12 oz) natural yoghurt
3 tablespoons lemon juice
Salt and freshly ground black pepper

1. Trim the fennel and cut the bulbs in half lengthways, then cut into thin slices.
2. Peel and core the pears and cut them into chunks. Mix together the fennel, watercress, pears and poppy seeds.
3. To make the dressing, put all the ingredients in a bowl and lightly beat together, retaining the texture of the cheese.
4. Pour the dressing over the salad and toss gently.

POTATO SALAD WITH HORSERADISH AND DILL PICKLES

Firm, waxy potatoes such as Charlotte, Pink Fir Apple, Romano or Désirée are best for potato salad. They will absorb the flavours better if they are still slightly warm when the dressing is added.

 Serves 20–25

2 kg (4¼ lb) potatoes
3 large dill pickled cucumbers
300 ml (10 fl oz) horseradish sauce
275 ml (9 fl oz) whipping cream
Salt and freshly ground black pepper
Fresh dill sprigs, to garnish

1. Boil the potatoes in salted water until tender. Drain and leave to cool slightly. Peel off the skins, then cut into chunks.
2. Cut 2 pickled cucumbers into matchsticks and mix with the potatoes. Spoon over the horseradish and cream, season and mix well.
3. Transfer the salad to a serving bowl. Cut the remaining dill pickle into strips or slices and use to garnish the salad along with the fresh dill sprigs.

Fennel, Pear and Poppy Seed Salad with Stilton Dressing

Potato Salad with Horseradish and Dill Pickles

TURKISH DELIGHT ICE-CREAM WITH PISTACHIO MERINGUES

To crystallise rose petals, separate the petals from a scented pink rose. Brush each petal with lightly beaten egg white, then toss in caster sugar, shaking off the excess. Leave on a wire rack for 4 hours. The meringues can be made up to two weeks in advance and stored in an airtight container, or frozen. The meringues and the ice-cream can be stored frozen for up to 1 month.

 Serves 12

350 g (12 oz) rose-flavoured (pink) Turkish delight with almonds
700 ml (1¼ pints) ready-to-serve fresh custard
300 ml (10 fl oz) double cream
2–3 tablespoons rosewater

For the meringues
2 egg whites
120 g (4½ oz) caster sugar

120 g (4½ oz) shelled pistachio nuts, chopped
Crystallised rose petals, to decorate

1. Cut the Turkish delight into small pieces. Place in a pan with 4–6 tablespoons of water and cook over a low heat, stirring, until the mixture has almost melted but still has small lumps. Stir the mixture into the custard.
2. Lightly whip the cream until it forms soft peaks, then fold gently into the custard. Stir in the rosewater to taste.
3. Pour the mixture into a 1.2 litre (2 pint) loaf tin lined with clear film and freeze for at least 3 hours until firm.
4. Pre-heat the oven to 120C/250F/Gas ½. Whisk the egg whites until stiff but not dry. Add 1 tablespoon of the sugar and continue whisking until stiff and shiny. Fold in the remaining sugar and 50 g (2 oz) of the pistachio nuts.
5. Place teaspoonfuls of the meringue on a baking sheet lined with non-stick baking paper. Sprinkle with the rest of the nuts. Bake for about 2 hours until the meringues are dry and lift easily from the paper.
6. Remove the ice-cream from the freezer 30 minutes before serving. Turn out on to a serving plate and peel off the clear film. Decorate the top with some of the meringues and scatter with crystallised rose petals. Arrange the remaining meringues and crystallised rose petals around the base of the ice-cream.

Turkish Delight Ice-cream with Pistachio Meringues

TANGERINE AND CHOCOLATE CHEESECAKE

For extra punch, try using tangerines in liqueur and sugar syrup, on sale in delicatessens and major supermarkets.
This cheesecake can be open frozen, undecorated, until firm, then wrapped in freezer film and stored for up to 1 month. To serve, thaw in the fridge overnight and decorate the cake on the day it is to be eaten.

Serves 12

For the base
100 g (4 oz) butter
225 g (8 oz) chocolate digestive biscuits, crushed

For the filling
8 tangerines
25 g (1 oz) powdered gelatine
450 g (1 lb) Mascarpone or another full-fat soft cheese
4 eggs, separated
175 g (6 oz) caster sugar
300 ml (10 fl oz) crème fraîche or soured cream
3 tablespoons Cointreau or Grand Marnier

To decorate
Whipped cream
Piped chocolate
Matchsticks of pared orange or tangerine rind, blanched

Tangerine and Chocolate Cheesecake

1. Line a 25 cm (10 in) spring-release cake tin with non-stick baking paper and lightly grease the sides. Melt the butter and mix in the biscuit crumbs. Press into the base of the tin and chill for 30 minutes.
2. Finely grate the zest of 2 tangerines and set aside. Squeeze the juice from 4 tangerines into a small pan, sprinkle over the gelatine and leave to soak. Remove the flesh from the membranes of the remaining tangerines, then roughly chop.
3. Place the Mascarpone, egg yolks, 100 g (4 oz) of the caster sugar, crème fraîche or soured cream and liqueur in a bowl and beat until smooth. Heat the gelatine slowly until it has dissolved, cool slightly, then stir into the cheese mixture. Fold in the tangerine zest and the chopped tangerines.
4. Whisk the egg whites until stiff, then whisk in the remaining caster sugar. Gently fold into the cheese mixture, pour into the tin, level the surface and chill for 3–4 hours until set.
5. Carefully remove the cheesecake from the tin and decorate with swirls of whipped cream, topped with the chocolate and strips of orange or tangerine.

BRANDIED CLEMENTINES WITH ROSEMARY AND RATAFIA CREAM

 Serves 10

20 clementines
225 g (8 oz) caster sugar
5 tablespoons brandy

For the cream
6 large rosemary sprigs
450 ml (15 fl oz) double cream
75 g (3 oz) ratafia or Amaretti biscuits, crushed
Rosemary sprigs, to decorate

1. Peel the clementines and prick all over with a fork. Place in a dish.
2. Place the sugar in a small, heavy-based pan with 3 tablespoons of water. Heat gently, stirring, until the sugar dissolves. Bring to the boil and then boil rapidly until deep golden.
3. Remove from the heat and add 75 ml (3 fl oz) water (stand back – it will splutter). Return to the hob and heat gently until smooth. Stir in the brandy and pour it over the oranges. Cool, cover and chill overnight.

4. To make the cream, place the rosemary and 150 ml (5 fl oz) of the cream in a small pan. Bring to the boil, then cool. Strain, discard the rosemary and chill the cream.

5. Stir in the remaining cream and whip until peaking. Fold in the biscuits and turn into a serving dish. Decorate the oranges with the sprigs of rosemary and serve with the cream.

Brandied Clementines with Rosemary and Ratafia Cream

COUNTDOWN

Up to a month before
• Make and freeze the *Turkish Delight Ice-cream*. Turn out of the tin, wrap in double thickness freezer wrap and return to the freezer immediately.

The week before
• Check that there are enough plates, serving plates, glasses and cutlery.
• Launder tablecloths and napkins, or buy paper ones.
• Make plans to and/or rearrange the furniture to accommodate guests.

Two days before
• Clear the decks in the kitchen, making space in the fridge and freezer for all your party food.
• Order or buy the party drinks; don't forget the soft drinks for children and drivers.
• Make the *Tangerine and Chocolate Cheesecake* and store in the fridge, undecorated.
• Cook the beef, cool, wrap in foil and store in the fridge. Reserve its juices for re-heating if you plan to serve it hot.
• Make the *Smoked Ham and Leek Pie*; bake if serving cold, or store uncooked in the fridge.
• Prepare the *Stilton Dressing* and the dressings for the *Seafood and Melon Salad* and *Mixed Bean, Mushroom and Gruyère Salad*, then chill.

The day before
• Soak the dried chestnuts.
• Make the fresh stock for the *Chestnut Soup*; cool and chill.

On the day
• Make the *Potato Salad with Horseradish and Dill Pickles*, chill.
• Decorate the *Tangerine and Chocolate Cheesecake*.
• Make the *Chestnut Soup*.
• Assemble the *Seafood and Melon Salad* and the *Mixed Bean, Mushroom and Gruyère Salad*.
• Chill the white wine.

One hour before
• Bake the *Smoked Ham and Leek Pie* if you are serving it hot.
• Slice the *Braised Beef with Cranberry, Walnut and Bulgar Wheat Stuffing*, or heat in its juices if serving hot.
• Assemble the *Fennel, Pear and Poppy Seed Salad* and the *Orange, Date and Carrot Salad*.
• Heat the *Chestnut Soup*.
• Uncork the red wine.
• Take the *Turkish Delight Ice-cream* out of the freezer to soften 30 minutes before serving.

COCKTAIL CANAPÉS

PIZZA TOASTS

CHEESE SABLÉS

GOAT'S CHEESE CROUSTADES

OPEN SANDWICHES

SMOKED MUSSELS IN BACON

CHOUX PASTRY

STILTON PUFFS

AVOCADO AND TOMATO CHOUX BUNS

BACON COCKTAIL SAUSAGES

CORN AND PEPPER SPIRALS

TOMATO PARMESAN TWISTS

ROAST BEEF AND MUSTARD CANAPÉS

PRAWN AND ALFALFA SPROUT CANAPÉS

CAMEMBERT AND BACON CANAPÉS

CREAMY HORSERADISH AND SALMON CANAPÉS

FRUIT CANAPÉS

CITRUS PUFFS

RASPBERRY AND FROMAGE FRAIS CHOUX BUNS

CHOCOLATE FRUITS

SPICED FRUIT WARMER

All canapés should be prepared on the day of the party although the *Cheese Sablés* and basic *Choux Pastry* can be made up to 1 week in advance.

PIZZA TOASTS

Makes about 20

1 ready-to-bake mini baguette
2 tablespoons olive oil
400 g (14 oz) tin chopped tomatoes
1 onion, finely chopped
2 tablespoons tomato purée
1 teaspoon caster sugar
1 orange or red pepper, seeded and chopped
2 garlic cloves, crushed
$1/2$ tin anchovies, chopped

Salt and freshly ground black pepper
Parsley sprigs, to garnish

1. Cut 20 thin slices from the baquette and toast on both sides. Place the remaining ingredients (except the garnish) in a pan and cook for 10 minutes until pulpy.
2. Spoon on to the toasts and serve warm or cold, garnished with parsley.

CHEESE SABLÉS

Makes about 40

50 g (2 oz) plain flour
50 g (2 oz) butter
50 g (2 oz) mature Cheddar, grated
Sesame seeds, to sprinkle

1. Pre-heat the oven to 200C/400F/Gas 6. Lightly grease a large baking sheet. Sift the flour into a bowl. Rub the butter into the flour. Add the cheese and mix to a firm dough. Chill for 30 minutes.
2. Roll out thinly on a floured surface. Cut out the shapes, 2.5 cm (1 in) in diameter.
3. Place on a baking sheet and sprinkle with the seeds. Bake for 7 minutes until golden. Transfer to a wire rack to cool. Store for up to 1 week in a cake tin.

GOAT'S CHEESE CROUSTADES

The bases for these can be made and cooked the day before your party.

Makes about 24

6 thin slices bread
40 g (1$1/2$ oz) butter, melted
150 g (5 oz) mild goat's cheese
A dash of milk
Paprika, to sprinkle

1. Pre-heat the oven to 200C/400F/Gas 6. Stamp out about 24 rounds from the bread, using a 4 cm (1$1/2$ in) plain or fluted cutter.
2. Dip one side of each round into melted butter and press, buttered side up, into mini tartlet tins (or lay flat on a baking sheet). Bake for 7 minutes until deep golden around the edges. Cool.
3. Whip the cheese with the milk and spoon or pipe into the cases. Dust with paprika.

OPEN SANDWICHES

Make quantity required

A selection of breads, sliced
Butter, to spread
A variety of toppings such as smoked salmon, olives,
prawns, ham, cheese, exotic fruits, radishes, green pep-
per, mustard and cress, parsley
Aspic powder or powdered gelatine

1. Cut the bread into small squares, triangles or
rectangles and spread with the butter.
2. Arrange the toppings on the bread as required.
3. Prepare either the aspic or the gelatine according
to the manufacturer's instructions and make up to
450 ml (15 fl oz) with water. When nearly set brush
this over the canapés to glaze and retain moisture.

SMOKED MUSSELS IN BACON

Makes about 24

225 g (8 oz) thinly cut streaky bacon, rinded
100 g (4 oz) tin smoked mussels
75 g (3 oz) ready-to-eat dried apricots, halved

1. Halve the bacon rashers crossways. Drain the
mussels. Wrap a mussel and a halved apricot in a
piece of bacon. Pack into a shallow heatproof dish
with the bacon ends tucked underneath.
2. Grill the wrapped mussels for about 5 minutes,
turning once until the bacon starts to crisp. Serve
warm or cold.

CHOUX PASTRY

If you are making all four of the savoury and sweet
choux pastry canapés, make a double quantity of
this and divide accordingly. Make sure the choux
puffs, and all choux pastries, are quite crisp before
removing them from the oven. They can be made
3–4 days in advance. Store in a cake tin or freeze,
and recrisp in the oven before filling.

40 g (1½ oz) butter
65 g (2½ oz) plain flour
2 eggs

1. Pre-heat the oven to 220C/425F/Gas 7. Lightly
grease 2 baking sheets.
2. Melt the butter in a pan with 150 ml (5 fl oz) of
water. Bring to the boil. Remove the pan from the
heat, add the flour all at once and beat until the
mixture leaves the sides of the pan.
3. Cool slightly, then gradually beat in the eggs
until the mixture is glossy.

From the left: *Smoked Mussels in Bacon, Open
Sandwiches, Goat's Cheese Croustades, Cheese Sablés,
Stilton Puffs (page 108)* and *Pizza Toasts*

STILTON PUFFS

Makes about 30

¹/₂ quantity Choux Pastry *(see page 107)*
100 g (4 oz) Stilton
4 tablespoons Greek yoghurt

1. Pre-heat the oven to 220C/425F/Gas 7. Lightly grease a baking sheet.
2. Pipe rounds of *Choux Pastry* about 1 cm (¹/₂ in) in diameter on to the baking sheet. Bake for 10 minutes until puffed and golden. Cut vertical slits through the pastries.
3. Blend the Stilton with the yoghurt until smooth. Spoon or pipe the mixture into the pastries.

From the left: *Prawn and Alfalfa Sprout Canapés (page 110), Camembert and Bacon Canapés (page 110), Creamy Horseradish and Salmon Canapés (page 110)* and *Avocado and Tomato Choux Buns; Bacon Cocktail Sausages, Corn and Pepper Spirals* and *Tomato Parmesan Twists; Raspberry and Fromage Frais Choux Buns (page 111)*

AVOCADO AND TOMATO CHOUX BUNS

Makes about 30

¹/₂ quantity Choux Pastry *dough (see page 107)*
1 small avocado, halved, stoned and peeled
1 tablespoon French dressing
Fresh basil, finely chopped
Tomato, seeded and finely chopped

To garnish
Paprika
Sprigs of basil

1. Pre-heat the oven to 200C/425F/Gas 7. Lightly grease a baking sheet.
2. Spoon 1 cm (¹/₂ in) dollops of *Choux Pastry* on to the baking sheet, keeping them well spaced. Bake for 8 minutes until puffed, crisp and golden. Cool on a wire rack, then slit each bun.
3. Finely dice the avocado and mix with the French dressing, basil and tomato.
4. Spoon the avocado mixture into the buns, sprinkle with paprika and garnish with sprigs of basil.

BACON COCKTAIL SAUSAGES

These can be prepared the day before and
served hot or cold.

Makes 40

20 rashers streaky bacon
Herb mustard, for spreading
40 cocktail sausages

1. Stretch the bacon rashers with the back of a
knife. Spread with a little herb mustard and cut in
half.
2. Grill the sausages and allow to cool a little before
wrapping bacon around each one.
3. Grill for 5–10 minutes, turning occasionally
until the bacon is crisp and the sausages are
cooked through.

CORN AND PEPPER SPIRALS

Keep the uncooked spirals in the freezer, or make
to the end of step 3 and store in the fridge.

 Makes about 25

150 g (5 oz) tinned creamed sweetcorn
1 tablespoon chopped fresh parsley
25 g (1 oz) fresh bread, diced
2 tablespoons olive oil
1 garlic clove, crushed
175 g (6 oz) red pepper, seeded and finely chopped
25 g (1 oz) dried breadcrumbs
4 sheets filo pastry, thawed if frozen
25–50 g (1–2 oz) melted butter

1. Pre-heat the oven to 200C/400F/Gas 6. Mix the
sweetcorn, parsley and diced bread.
2. Heat the oil and fry the garlic and red pepper
until soft, then mix in the dried breadcrumbs.
3. Take 1 sheet of filo pastry, brush with a little
melted butter, then place another 3 sheets on top,
brushing each one with melted butter. Leaving a
4 cm (1¹/₂ in) border, spread the corn mixture
lengthways over half of the pastry, then cover the
remaining half with the pepper mixture. Roll up
the pastry tightly, starting with the corn side,
brush lightly with a little melted butter and chill
for at least 1 hour.

4. Cut into 1 cm (¹/₂ in) thick slices and place on a
baking sheet. Bake for about 15 minutes until crisp,
then leave to cool on a wire rack.

TOMATO PARMESAN TWISTS

These can be stored for up to 3–4 days in a cake tin
once made.

 Makes about 40

375 g (13 oz) ready-made puff pastry
3 tablespoons tomato purée
Freshly ground black pepper
Milk, for brushing
3 tablespoons freshly grated Parmesan

1. Pre-heat the oven to 200C/400F/Gas 6.
2. Roll out the pastry into a 35 x 40 cm (14 x 16 in)
rectangle and trim the edges.
3. Spread the tomato purée on top and season with
black pepper.
4. Fold the pastry in half widthways, brush with
milk and sprinkle with the Parmesan.
5. Cut the pastry into 1 cm (¹/₂ in) wide strips.
Gently twist each one and cut in half lengthways.
6. Place on baking sheets and bake for 10 minutes
until crisp and golden. Cool on a wire rack.

ROAST BEEF AND MUSTARD CANAPÉS

Makes 12

3 slices crustless bread
2 teaspoons mild mustard
1 teaspoon butter
3–4 slices rare roast beef
1 tablespoon chopped gherkins

1. Toast the bread. Blend the mustard with the
butter and spread over the toast.
2. Cut the slices into 12 4 cm (1¹/₂ in) equal-side
triangles.
3. Top each toast triangle with a 2.5 cm (1 in)
square slice of beef.
4. Divide the gherkins among the toasts and serve.

PRAWN AND ALFALFA SPROUT CANAPÉS

Makes 10

2 tablespoons cottage cheese
2 tablespoons curd cheese
25 g (1 oz) tinned pimientos, chopped
Cayenne pepper
A dash of lemon juice
10 small crackers
10 prawns
Alfalfa sprouts

1. Mix together the cottage and curd cheeses. Stir in the pimientos and season with the cayenne pepper. Add a dash of lemon juice.
2. Spread the mixture on the crackers and top with a prawn before sprinkling on a few alfalfa sprouts.

CAMEMBERT AND BACON CANAPÉS

Makes 12

3 slices rye bread
Butter, to spread
Lamb's lettuce leaves
100 g (4 oz) Camembert
100 g (4 oz) grilled back bacon, finely chopped
Fresh chives, snipped, to garnish

1. Butter the bread and cut into quarters.
2. Arrange the lettuce leaves so that they overlap the edges of the square.
3. Thinly slice the Camembert and arrange on the lettuce leaves.
4. Divide the bacon among the squares and garnish with chives.

CREAMY HORSERADISH AND SALMON CANAPÉS

Makes 10

Pumpernickel bread
2 tablespoons Greek yoghurt
2 teaspoons horseradish sauce
1 slice smoked salmon
Sprigs of dill, to garnish

1. Using a 4 cm (1½ in) round cutter, stamp out rounds from the bread.
2. Mix the yoghurt and horseradish and divide the mixture among the rounds.
3. Cut the smoked salmon into 10 thin strips. Place on the bread and garnish with the dill.

FRUIT CANAPÉS

Makes about 30

350 g (12 oz) puff pastry
225 g (8 oz) white almond paste
2 tablespoons apricot jam
1 small mango
2 kiwi fruit, sliced
225 g (8 oz) strawberries, sliced
1 star fruit, sliced
A small bunch of seedless black grapes
3 tangerines, segmented
Cranberries
1 sachet powdered gelatine
2 tablespoons caster sugar

1. Pre-heat the oven to 220C/425F/Gas 7. Roll out the pastry very thinly and stamp out 30 x 6 cm (2¼ in) rounds. Prick with a fork and bake for 8–10 minutes until crisp. Press lightly if the pastry puffs up. Cool.
2. Roll out the almond paste and cut out rounds, slightly smaller than the pastry. Stick on top of the pastries with jam.
3. Slice through the mango, both sides of the flat stone, and remove small balls with a melon baller. Use a variety of the fruits to decorate the pastries.

Fruit Canapés

Chill whilst making the gelatine.

4. Dissolve the gelatine and sugar in 300 ml (10 fl oz) of water to make a glaze. Brush over the fruits. Keep cool.

CITRUS PUFFS

Makes about 30

½ quantity Choux Pastry *(see page 107)*
150 ml (5 fl oz) double cream
Finely grated rind of 1 lemon
Finely grated rind of 1 lime
2 tablespoons lemon juice
2 tablespoons lime juice
25 g (1 oz) icing sugar

1. Pre-heat the oven to 220C/425F/Gas 7. Lightly grease a baking sheet.
2. Pipe small stars of *Choux Pastry* on to a baking sheet. Bake for 10 minutes until puffed and golden. Cut vertical slits through the pastries.
3. Whip the cream with the rinds, juices and icing sugar. Use this mixture to sandwich together the pastries. Serve dusted with a little icing sugar.

RASPBERRY AND FROMAGE FRAIS CHOUX BUNS

Makes about 30

½ quantity Choux Pastry *(see page 107)*
150 g (5 oz) raspberries, chopped and 30 whole, to decorate
1½ tablespoons fromage frais
3 tablespoons whipped double cream
3 teaspoons crème de cassis
1½ teaspoons golden caster sugar
1½ teaspoons fresh mint, chopped

1. Pre-heat the oven to 220C/425F/Gas 7. Lightly grease a baking sheet.
2. Spoon 1 cm (½ in) dollops of *Choux Pastry* on to the baking sheet, keeping them well spaced. Bake for 8 minutes until puffed, crisp and golden. Cool on a wire rack and then slit each bun.
3. Mix all the other ingredients together (except the whole raspberries). Spoon into the buns and decorate with the whole raspberries.

Raspberry and Fromage Frais Choux Buns

CHOCOLATE FRUITS

Makes 10

50 g (2 oz) plain chocolate
10 strawberries
Waxed paper

1. Melt the chocolate in a heatproof bowl set over a pan of barely simmering water.
2. Holding the stalks firmly, dip the strawberries into the chocolate.
3. Place on waxed paper, leave to cool and chill until set.

SPICED FRUIT WARMER

Makes about 30 glasses

450 ml (15 fl oz) water
2 cinnamon sticks
10 cloves
100 g (4 oz) light muscovado sugar
4 tablespoons clear honey
1.75 litres (3 pints) fresh orange juice
1.75 litres (3 pints) fresh apple juice
Slices of orange, lemon and apple, to garnish

1. Place the water, cinnamon sticks, cloves and sugar into a pan and bring to the boil.
2. Simmer for 5 minutes until the sugar has dissolved, then stir in the clear honey.
3. Add the orange and apple juices and heat through thoroughly.
4. Strain the liquid and then add the fruit slices. Serve hot.

SAVOURY PLATTER

DOUGH TRAY WITH:
LEEK SODA SCONES WITH CREAMY SMOKED TROUT
PARMESAN STARS
YEASTED SAUSAGE ROLLS
DOLCELATTE PANCAKE ROLLS
BLACK PUDDING ON TOAST WITH CARROT AND CUMIN PURÉE

MIDDLE-EASTERN BITES

WHOLEMEAL TRAY WITH:
YELLOW PEPPER AND MINT DIP
RED TOMATO AND AUBERGINE CHUTNEY
AVOCADO AND SOURED CREAM DIP
MINCED LAMB KEBABS
CHICKEN BITES
GARLIC PITTA BREAD

THAI CANAPÉS

TREACLE POPPY SEED TRAY WITH:
THAI SPICED CHILLI AND COCONUT DIP
CRAB CAKES WITH LEMON GRASS
NOODLE WRAPPED PRAWNS
CREAMY MUSHROOM DIP
PASTRY TWISTS

SWEET MELTING MOUTHFULS

SCRUNCHED FILO TRAY WITH:
ORANGE SABLÉS WITH WHISKY CREAM
BUTTERSCOTCH PEAR BISCUITS
TUILES WITH MANGO FOOL
FROZEN CHERRY RIPPLES

DOUGH TRAY

To freeze, place the cooked tray in an airtight bag, seal and freeze for up to 1 month.

 Makes 1 tray

280 g (10½ oz) pack white bread mix
1 beaten egg, to glaze

1. Make up the dough following the pack instructions. Reserve one third of the dough and roll out the remainder to a 30 cm (12 in) round. Carefully transfer to a greased baking sheet.
2. Reserve a quarter of the remaining dough, then divide the larger piece in half. Roll each half to a strip long enough to fit around the edge of the dough base. Twist the strips of dough together, then brush the dough base with beaten egg and fix the twist of dough around the edge, joining the ends neatly.
3. Using half the remaining dough, make two handles using short strips of dough twisted together. Attach to the edges of the tray. Roll out the remaining dough and cut into holly leaves using a cutter or the point of a sharp knife. Make berries with trimmings. (Other seasonal leaves or flowers can be used here, too.) Attach to the edge of the dough.
4. Pre-heat the oven to 200C/400F/Gas 6. Brush the tray with egg and leave to rise for 15 minutes. Bake for 20–25 minutes, until golden brown. Cool on a wire rack.
5. To use, set on a board or tray and arrange nibbles on top.

From the top right clockwise: *Yeasted Sausage Rolls (page 115), Leek Soda Scones with Creamy Smoked Trout (page 114), Parmesan Stars (page 114), Dolcelatte Pancake Rolls (page 115), Black Pudding on Toast with Carrot and Cumin Purée (page 116)* on a *Dough Tray*

Parmesan Stars and *Leek Soda Scones with Creamy Smoked Trout*

LEEK SODA SCONES WITH CREAMY SMOKED TROUT

To freeze, cool the cooked scones quickly, place in an airtight bag, seal and freeze for up to 1 month. To serve, defrost, then continue from step 4.

Makes 24 scones

For the dough
25 g (1 oz) butter
1 leek, finely chopped
225 g (8 oz) plain flour
225 g (8 oz) wholemeal self-raising flour
$\frac{1}{2}$ teaspoon salt
$\frac{1}{2}$ teaspoon bicarbonate of soda
300 ml (10 fl oz) buttermilk or low-fat natural yoghurt

For the topping
150 g (5 oz) smoked trout fillet, flaked
1 tablespoon lemon juice
225 g (8 oz) light soft cheese
Salt and freshly ground black pepper
Parsley or chervil sprigs, to garnish
Paprika, for dusting

1. Pre-heat the oven to 200C/400F/Gas 6. Melt the butter in a small pan, add the leek and fry gently for about 5 minutes, until softened. Cool slightly.
2. Mix together the flours in a bowl. Add the salt and bicarbonate of soda and rub into the flour to mix evenly. Make a well in the centre and add the leek and its juices and the buttermilk or yoghurt. Mix quickly and lightly to a soft dough.
3. Knead the dough briefly on a lightly floured

surface. Roll out to 1 cm ($\frac{1}{2}$ in) thickness and cut into 2.5 cm (1 in) rounds with a cutter or sherry glass. Gather up the trimmings, roll again and cut out more rounds.
4. Arrange the scones a little apart on a baking sheet dusted with flour. Bake for 15–18 minutes, until risen and golden. Cool on a wire rack.
5. Flake the fish into a bowl, add the lemon juice, soft cheese and seasoning and mix well. Split the scones in half and either sandwich together with the trout mixture, or pile a little of the mixture on to each scone half. Garnish with sprigs of chervil or parsley and dust with paprika.

PARMESAN STARS

To freeze, cool the biscuits quickly, place in an airtight bag, seal and freeze for up to 1 month.

Makes 40

For the dough
175 g (6 oz) plain flour
100 g (4 oz) butter
A pinch of cayenne pepper
40 g ($1\frac{1}{2}$ oz) Parmesan, finely grated
75 g (3 oz) mature Cheddar, finely grated
1 egg, beaten, to glaze

For the topping
25 g (1 oz) stoned black olives
50 g (2 oz) tin anchovies, drained
75 g (3 oz) sun-dried tomatoes

1. Pre-heat the oven to 190C/375F/Gas 5. Measure the flour into a bowl. Cut the butter into small pieces, then rub into the flour until the mixture resembles fine breadcrumbs.
2. Stir in the cayenne pepper and cheeses, then sprinkle in 1 tablespoon of cold water and mix to a firm dough. Turn out on to a lightly floured surface and knead briefly.
3. Halve the olives, cut the anchovies in half down their length and chop the tomatoes into small pieces. Roll out the dough thinly and cut into small star shapes with a cutter. Transfer to a baking sheet, brush with a little beaten egg and press olives on to one third, anchovies on to another third and tomatoes on to the remainder.
4. Bake for 12–15 minutes until crisp and lightly browned.

YEASTED SAUSAGE ROLLS

To freeze, open freeze after step 5 until firm, pack in airtight bags and freeze for up to 1 month. To serve, remove from freezer, cover with oiled polythene and defrost on greased baking sheets. Continue from the beginning of step 6.

Makes about 40

8 thick herb or spicy sausages

For the dough
250 g (9 oz) white bread flour
1/2 teaspoon salt
50 g (2 oz) butter
1/2 teaspoon powdered saffron
1 teaspoon sugar
2 teaspoons easy-blend dried yeast
1 egg, beaten
150 ml (5 fl oz) warm milk
1 egg beaten, to glaze
2 teaspoons sesame seeds

1. To make the dough, measure the flour and salt into a bowl, add the butter cut into small pieces and rub in with the fingertips until the mixture resembles fine breadcrumbs. Stir in the saffron, sugar and yeast.
2. Make a well in the centre of the mixture and add the egg and milk. Mix to a soft dough, then turn out on to a lightly floured surface and knead for 5 minutes, until the dough feels smooth and silky and is no longer sticky.
3. Place the dough in a large oiled polythene bag or a bowl covered with cling film and leave to rise for 1–1 1/4 hours, until doubled in size.
4. Knead the dough again briefly to knock out any large air bubbles. Roll out to an oblong 40 x 20 cm (16 x 8 in). Remove the skins from the sausages. Cut the dough in half lengthways, then place 4 sausages down each piece of dough, butting up against each other. Position the sausages to one side of the dough.
5. Brush the edges of the dough with egg or water and fold it over to enclose the sausages, pressing the edges to seal. Cut each strip of dough into about 20 slices, then transfer them, a little apart, to greased baking sheets.
6. Cover with oiled polythene and leave to rise for 30 minutes.
7. Pre-heat the oven to 200C/400F/Gas 6. Brush the sausage rolls with egg and sprinkle with sesame seeds. Bake them for 20–25 minutes, until risen and golden brown. Serve warm or cold.

DOLCELATTE PANCAKE ROLLS

To freeze, cool quickly after step 4, pack into a rigid container, seal and freeze for up to 1 month.
To serve, defrost on a greased baking sheet and cook as in step 5.

 Makes about 24

For the batter
125 g (4 1/2 oz) plain flour
2 teaspoons dried mixed herbs
2 tablespoons snipped chives
1 egg
300 ml (10 fl oz) semi-skimmed milk
Salt and freshly ground black pepper
A little oil, for frying

1 long leek, cut into thin strips
175 g (6 oz) Dolcelatte

1. Mix together the flour, herbs and seasoning. Make a well in the centre and add the egg and a little milk. Stir the flour gradually into the egg and milk, adding the milk a little at a time to form a smooth batter.
2. Blanch the leek strips in boiling salted water for 2 minutes, until they are just softened, then cool under running cold water and drain.
3. Heat a little oil in a heavy pancake or frying pan. Add tablespoonfuls of the batter, well apart to allow for spreading. Cook until the undersides are golden, then turn over and cook on the other side. Remove to a plate and continue cooking the pancakes until all the batter is used up.
4. Pre-heat the oven to 190C/375F/Gas 5. Cut the Dolcelatte into sticks slightly shorter than the pancakes. Place a piece of cheese on each pancake and roll up to enclose it. Tie a strip of leek around to secure and make the remaining pancakes in the same way.
5. Just before serving arrange the pancakes over a greased baking sheet, a little apart and bake for 7–8 minutes, until the pancakes are hot and the cheese just melted. Serve warm.

BLACK PUDDING ON TOAST WITH CARROT AND CUMIN PURÉE

To freeze the purée, cool quickly after step 1, place in an airtight container, seal and freeze for up to 1 month. To serve, defrost, then re-heat in the microwave for 2–3 minutes or in a small pan over a moderate heat, stirring well.

Makes 24

For the purée
225 g (8 oz) carrots
1 tablespoon olive oil
1 teaspoon cumin seeds
A pinch of sugar
3 tablespoons fresh orange juice

From the left clockwise: *Avocado and Soured Cream Dip (page 118), Garlic Pitta Bread (page 119), Red Tomato and Aubergine Chutney, Minced Lamb Kebabs (page 118) and Yellow Pepper and Mint Dip* on a *Wholemeal Tray*

2 tablespoons Greek yoghurt
225 g (8 oz) black pudding
6 large slices wholemeal bread
Butter for spreading
Salt and freshly ground black pepper

1. Chop the carrots and place in a pan with the oil, cumin, sugar and orange juice. Bring the the boil, stir then cover and cook for 12–15 minutes, until the carrots are tender. Turn the carrots and pan juices into a food processor or blender and blend until smooth.
2. Add the yoghurt and mix well. Return to the pan and keep warm (or re-heat in a microwave just before you need them.
3. Cut the black pudding into 24 slices, then arrange over a grill pan and grill on both sides for 5–6 minutes until cooked. Toast the bread, then butter lightly and stamp each slice into 4 rounds using a small cutter.
4. To assemble, place a piece of black pudding on to each round of bread and top with carrot and cumin purée. Sprinkle with black pepper and serve warm.

WHOLEMEAL TRAY

To freeze, place the cooked tray in an airtight bag, seal and freeze for up to 1 month.

Makes 1

175 g (6 oz) plain flour
50 g (2 oz) oatmeal
100 g (4 oz) butter or margarine

1. Pre-heat the oven to 200C/400F/Gas 6. Mix the flour and cereal in a bowl, then rub in the fat until the mixture resembles fine breadcrumbs. Add 3–4 tablespoons of cold water and mix to a firm dough.
2. Knead briefly on a lightly floured surface. Reserve a quarter of the dough and roll out the remainder to a 35 cm (14 in) round. Transfer to a large greased baking sheet.
3. Roll out the reserved dough and cut into leaf shapes. Dampen the underside of the leaves and attach them to the edge of the pastry round. Bake at 200C/400F/Gas 6 for 20–25 minutes, until crisp and lightly browned. Cool on a wire rack. To use, place the pastry on a tray or board and arrange the nibbles on top.

Yellow Pepper and Mint Dip

For serving this dish, select two peppers which will stand up on their own.
To freeze, cool quickly after step 2, place in a rigid container, seal and freeze. To serve, defrost and continue with step 3.

 Makes enough for 10-12 portions

4 large yellow peppers, seeded and quartered
4 garlic cloves, crushed
150 ml (5 fl oz) vegetable stock
A bunch of fresh mint, chopped
2 tablespoons Greek yoghurt
Salt and freshly ground black pepper
2 large yellow peppers, to serve

1. Place the seeded and quartered peppers skin side uppermost on a baking tray. Cook under a pre-heated grill until the skin is charred. Remove from the grill then place in a polythene bag for 5 minutes before peeling off the skins.
2. Chop the skinned peppers and place in a pan with the garlic and stock, bring to the boil, reduce the heat and simmer for 10 minutes. Season and allow to cool, then liquidise. The sauce can be frozen for several weeks at this stage.
3. To finish the dip, defrost (if frozen) then fold in the mint and yoghurt. To make the serving container cut the stalk end from the peppers, remove the seeds and the white pith and fill with the dip. Serve with *Minced Lamb Kebabs* (see page 118).

Red Tomato and Aubergine Chutney

To freeze, cool quickly after step 3, place in a rigid container, seal and freeze for up to 1 month. To serve, defrost for several hours or overnight and continue at step 4.

 Makes enough for 10-12 portions

1 aubergine, diced
1 tablespoon olive oil
1 red onion, chopped
1 red pepper, seeded and diced
1 tablespoon tomato purée
450 g (1 lb) tomatoes, skinned, seeded and roughly chopped
25 ml (1 fl oz) white wine vinegar
40 g (1½ oz) soft light brown sugar
1 teaspoon cumin seeds
1 teaspoon mustard seed
6 black peppercorns
2 teaspoons salt
1 bay leaf
1 sprig thyme
4 garlic cloves, crushed
1 tablespoon chopped parsley
2 large red peppers, to serve

1. Place the aubergine in a colander and sprinkle with salt. Set aside for 15 minutes or until the juices begin to run.
2. Heat the oil in a large pan, add the onion and diced pepper, cover and cook gently for 10 minutes. Rinse the aubergine and drain thoroughly, add to the pan and cook for a further 5 minutes. Add the tomato purée and fry for 1 minute.
3. Add the tomatoes, vinegar and sugar to the pan. Lightly crush the spices and add to the pan with the salt, herbs and garlic. Cover and simmer for 30 minutes or until the vegetables are softened. The mixture can now be cooled and frozen or stored in the fridge for several days.
4. Defrost (if frozen) and stir in the parsley. Serve in red pepper cups (see step 3 of *Yellow Pepper and Mint Dip*, left) with *Garlic Pitta Bread* (see page 119).

Yellow Pepper and Mint Dip

AVOCADO AND SOURED CREAM DIP

Although this dip cannot be frozen, it is very quick to make and can be made a few hours before the party and is delicious with *Chicken Bites* (see right).

Makes enough for 10-12 portions

2 ripe avocados
Juice of 1 lemon
150 ml (5 fl oz) soured cream
1 tablespoon snipped chives
Salt and freshly ground black pepper
2 green peppers, to serve

1. Halve the avocados, remove the stones and scoop the flesh into a bowl. Mash with a fork and add lemon juice to taste, the soured cream and the chives. Season.
2. Squeeze a little lemon juice over the surface, cover with cling film, pressing down on to the avocado mixture to prevent any air getting in. Chill for up to 3 hours. Stir well and spoon into the green pepper cups (see step 3 of *Yellow Pepper and Mint Dip* on page 117).

MINCED LAMB KEBABS

To freeze, cool quickly after step 1, place in airtight bags, seal and freeze for up to 1 month. To serve, defrost for several hours or overnight in the fridge then heat through just before serving.

Makes about 35

450 g (1 lb) minced lamb
1 teaspoon ground coriander
1 teaspoon ground cumin
A large pinch of chilli powder
1 tablespoon tomato purée
1 tablespoon coriander leaves
Pared rind of 1 lemon
Oil, for frying
Salt and freshly ground black pepper

1. Process all the ingredients, except the oil, in a food processor until well blended. Take teaspoons of the mixture and shape with your hands into small rounds or ovals.
2. Heat the oil in a large pan or deep fat fryer. Fry

the meatballs in batches for 3–4 minutes or until golden. Leave to cool, then store in the fridge for up to 1 day.
3. Pre-heat the oven to 200C/400F/Gas 6. Place the meatballs on a lightly greased baking tray and heat through for 10–12 minutes. Serve on small skewers.

CHICKEN BITES

To freeze, pack the chicken in airtight bags after step 2, seal and freeze for up to 1 month. Freeze the breadcrumb mixture after step 3. To serve, defrost both in the fridge overnight and continue with step 4.

Makes about 24

4 x 100 g (4 oz) boned and skinned chicken breasts
200 g (7 oz) jar sun-dried tomatoes in oil
1 chilli, seeded and chopped
2 garlic cloves
A small bunch of fresh basil
2 tablespoons olive oil
25 g (1 oz) Parmesan cheese, grated
25 g (1 oz) fresh breadcrumbs
1 tablespoon chopped parsley
Olive oil
Salt and freshly ground black pepper

1. Cut the chicken breasts into 1 cm ($^1/_2$ in) cubes and lay in a shallow dish.
2. Process the tomatoes, their oil, the chilli, garlic and basil in a food processor until finely chopped and combined. Spoon on to the chicken pieces with the olive oil and season. Stir and leave to marinate for at least 2 hours.
3. Mix together the cheese, breadcrumbs and parsley. Season.
4. Pre-heat the oven to 190C/375F/Gas 5. Thread 2 chicken pieces on to each of 24 skewers and brush with the marinade. Lay the chicken sticks on a lightly oiled baking tray and sprinkle with the breadcrumbs. Drizzle with a little oil and bake for 10–12 minutes. Serve hot or cold.

Minced Lamb Kebabs

GARLIC PITTA BREAD

Pitta bread can be bought well in advance and frozen, an ideal standby as it takes little time to defrost.

 Makes about 48

75 g (3 oz) butter
4 cloves garlic, crushed
1 tablespoon chopped fresh herbs, such as parsley, coriander, basil
8 pitta breads

1. Melt the butter and add the garlic and herbs. Lay the pitta breads on a grill rack and grill on one side. Turn over and brush with the flavoured butter, then grill for 1–2 minutes, until warmed through.
2. Cut into strips and serve warm with dips (see pages 117–18).

TREACLE POPPY SEED TRAY

To freeze, place the cooked tray in an airtight bag, seal and freeze for up to 1 month.

 Makes 1 tray

350 g (12 oz) wholemeal flour
75 g (3 oz) butter or margarine
2 tablespoons black treacle
150 ml (5 fl oz) water
2 teaspoons poppy seeds

1. Pre-heat the oven to 200C/400F/Gas 6. Measure the flour into a bowl. Heat together the fat, treacle and water until the fat has melted. Bring to the boil, then stir quickly into the flour to form a soft dough.
2. Reserve a quarter of the dough, then roll out the remainder to a 30 cm (12 in) square, trimming the edges. Transfer to a greased baking sheet.
3. Roll out the reserved dough and cut into thin strips. Brush the edges of the large square of dough with water and arrange pastry strips around the edge in a wavy line. Sprinkle poppy seeds around the edge.
4. Bake for 15–18 minutes, until the pastry is crisp and lightly coloured. Place on a tray and set nibbles on top to serve.

From the top right clockwise: *Thai Spiced Chilli and Coconut Dip, Pastry Twists (page 121), Creamy Mushroom Dip (page 121), Crab Cakes with Lemon Grass (page 120)* and *Noodle Wrapped Prawns (page 120)*

THAI SPICED CHILLI AND COCONUT DIP

If you prefer your food less hot, use fewer chillies. If you need to pep up the taste later add a little chilli powder or Tabasco sauce.
To freeze, cool the dip quickly, then freeze for up to 1 month in a rigid container. To serve, defrost the sauce overnight in the fridge, then re-heat slowly, stirring well. A little extra stock or water may be needed if the sauce has thickened.

2 teaspoons coriander seeds, roughly crushed
2 teaspoons cumin seeds, roughly crushed
4 garlic cloves, peeled
Juice and grated rind of 1 lime

2 stalks lemon grass, chopped
5 cm (2 in) piece root ginger, peeled and chopped
6–8 red chillies, seeded and chopped
A small bunch of coriander, roughly chopped
1 tablespoon sesame oil
10 spring onions, chopped
2 teaspoons shrimp paste (optional)
350 ml (12 fl oz) chicken stock
350 ml (12 fl oz) tinned coconut milk
2 tablespoons fish sauce (nam pla)
Salt and freshly ground black pepper
1 coconut, to serve

1. Grind the coriander and cumin seeds together in a clean coffee mill, pestle and mortar or food processor. Add the garlic, lime zest, lemon grass, ginger and 1/2 teaspoon of salt and grind to a smooth paste.
2. Add the chillies, coriander and lime juice and blend until smooth. This paste can be stored in a screw-top jar in the fridge for several days.
3. Heat the sesame oil in a heavy-based pan, add the spring onions and fry briefly. Add the shrimp paste (if using) and the curry paste and fry over a moderate heat for 1 minute, stirring to ensure the mixture does not burn. Add the chicken stock and coconut milk, bring to the boil and simmer for 10 minutes. Add the fish sauce and black pepper. Taste and add more salt if needed.
4. To serve, drain the juice from the coconut and break in half as evenly as possible. Set the coconut halves on the serving tray and fill with the sauce. Serve with *Crab Cakes with Lemon Grass* and *Noodle Wrapped Prawns* (see below).

CRAB CAKES WITH LEMON GRASS

White crab meat is available vacuum-packed or frozen from fishmongers or larger supermarkets. To freeze, place the cooled cakes in a rigid container, separating the layers with non stick paper. Seal and freeze for up to 1 month. To serve, defrost overnight in the fridge, then arrange on a baking sheet and cook at 200/400F/Gas 6 for 8–10 minutes.

Makes 25–30

15 g (1/2 oz) butter
15 g (1/2 oz) plain flour
100 ml (4 fl oz) hot milk
450 g (1 lb) white crab meat, defrosted if frozen

1 stalk lemon grass, finely chopped
2 green chillies, seeded and chopped
A small bunch of fresh coriander, chopped
2.5 cm (1 in) piece root ginger, peeled and grated
Salt and freshly ground black pepper
1 egg white
Oil, for deep frying

1. Melt the butter in a small pan, add the flour and cook for 1 minute, stirring. Add the milk, a little at a time, stirring until the sauce is thickened, smooth and glossy. Cook for 2 minutes, stirring occasionally. You need 2 tablespoons of the sauce for this dish and the remainder can be poured over vegetables or used in another dish.
2. Place the defrosted crab meat in a sieve and press out as much water as possible using the back of a wooden spoon. Place in a food processor or blender with the lemon grass, chillies, coriander, ginger and seasoning. Process in bursts so all the ingredients are finely chopped but not puréed. Add 2 tablespoonsful of the sauce and the egg white and mix briefly.
3. Shape the mixture into walnut-sized balls, place on a tray and chill for 15 minutes. Heat the oil to 180C/350F/Gas 4 or until a cube of bread browns in 30 seconds. Add the crab cakes in batches and fry until golden brown and crisp. Drain on kitchen paper. Serve warm with *Thai Spiced Chilli and Coconut Dip* (see page 119).

NOODLE WRAPPED PRAWNS

These easy-to-make prawns cannot be frozen but are perfect for dipping.

Makes about 40

900 g (2 lb) large prawns in shells, preferably uncooked
6 cloves garlic, crushed
2 tablespoons chopped fresh coriander
2 green chillies, seeded and finely chopped
Juice and grated rind of 2 limes
25 g (1 oz) dried egg noodles
Salt and freshly ground black pepper

1. Defrost the prawns and peel away the shells, leaving the tail sections intact. Place the garlic, coriander, chillies, grated rind and juice of the lime, and seasoning in a large shallow bowl. Add the prawns and mix well. Leave in the fridge to marinade for about 2 hours.

2. Cook the noodles in boiling salted water for 1 minute, until just tender, then drain and refresh under cold water. Wrap each prawn with a noodle.
3. Place prawns on a lightly greased baking sheet. Grill for 4–5 minutes, turning once. Serve hot with *Thai Spiced Chilli and Coconut Dip* (see page 119).

CREAMY MUSHROOM DIP

To freeze, cool the dip quickly, then freeze in a rigid container for up to 1 month. Defrost overnight in the fridge, then re-heat gently in a large pan, stirring occasionally.

 Makes enough for 10-12 portions

*900 g (2 lb) mushrooms, a mixture of button,
wild and chestnut
50 g (2 oz) butter
4 shallots, chopped finely
2 cloves garlic, crushed
2 tablespoons lemon juice
120 ml (4 fl oz) dry white wine
300 ml (10 fl oz) double cream
2 tablespoons chopped fresh parsley
Salt and freshly ground black pepper
2 acorn squash, to serve*

1. Wipe the mushrooms with damp kitchen paper and roughly chop any large ones. Heat the butter in a large frying pan, add the shallots and cook over a moderate heat for about 5 minutes until softened but not coloured.
2. Add the mushrooms and garlic to the pan, stir well, then add the lemon juice and seasoning. Cook for 5 minutes, until the mushrooms start to exude their juices.
3. Pour in the wine and cook gently for about 15 minutes or until the liquid is reduced by half. Add the cream and parsley and cook for about 5 minutes until the sauce is thick and creamy.
4. Process the sauce briefly in a food processor or blender, until it is finely chopped.
5. To serve, cut the top off the squash and trim the base if necessary to make it stand upright. Scoop out the seeds and remove as much of the flesh as possible using a spoon. Fill with the hot mushroom mixture and serve with *Pastry Twists* (see right).

Creamy Mushroom Dip

PASTRY TWISTS

To freeze, cool the twists quickly, then pack into a rigid container and freeze for up to 3 months. To serve, defrost and serve cold or warm through for a few minutes in a moderate oven.

 Makes 60

*225 g (8 oz) puff pastry, defrosted if frozen
1 egg
Salt
2 teaspoons pesto
2 teaspoons tapenade
20 sage leaves, chopped
50 g (2 oz) Parmesan or Pecorino, finely grated*

1. Pre-heat the oven to 200C/400F/Gas 6. Roll out the pastry to a large oblong about 3 mm (1/8 in) thick. Cut into 3 equal portions. Beat the egg with a little salt, then brush thinly over the pastry. Spread 1 portion of pastry with pesto, another with tapenade and sprinkle a third with sage. Sprinkle the cheese over all the portions.
2. Fold each portion of pastry in half to conceal the filling, press down well to seal the filling, then carefully roll out each to a 20 cm (8 in) square. Brush with a little egg, then trim the edges. Cut each square into 5 mm (1/4 in) wide strips.
3. Twist the strips, then lay them, a little apart, on to lightly greased baking sheets. Chill for 30 minutes, then bake for 12–15 minutes or until puffed up and golden. Serve warm or cold.

SCRUNCHED FILO TRAY

To freeze, place the cooked tray in an airtight bag, seal and freeze for up to 1 month.

Makes 1 tray

8 sheets filo pastry
Oil, for brushing
Icing sugar, for dusting

1. Pre-heat the oven to 200C/400F/Gas 6. Layer 6 sheets of the filo pastry on a greased baking sheet, brushing oil between the layers. Trim to a square if necessary.
2. Cut the remaining filo into strips and arrange around the edge of the pastry square, scrunching them to form a frill. Secure in place with a little oil. Bake for 12–15 minutes or until golden brown and crisp. Cool, then dust lightly with icing sugar. Set on a board and arrange the sweet nibbles on top.

ORANGE SABLÉS WITH WHISKY CREAM

To freeze the cooked pastry cases, cool quickly, pack into a rigid container, seal and freeze for up to 1 month. Store the oat praline in a screw-topped jar.

Makes 24

For the dough
225 g (8 oz) plain flour
A pinch of salt
25 g (1 oz) ground almonds
50 g (2 oz) icing sugar, sifted
120 g (4¹/₂ oz) butter, diced
Pared rind of 1 orange
2 egg yolks
1 teaspoon orange flower water

For the filling
75 g (3 oz) granulated sugar
75 g (3 oz) porridge oats, lightly toasted
300 ml (10 fl oz) double cream
50 g (2 oz) icing sugar

50 ml (2 fl oz) whisky
Juice of 1 orange

For decoration
Juice and pared rind of 1 orange
25 g (1 oz) granulated sugar

1. To make the dough, sift the flour and salt into the bowl of a food processor, add the almonds and sifted icing sugar. Add the butter and pared orange rind, process until the mixture resembles fine breadcrumbs.
2. Add the egg yolks and 1 dessertspoon of cold water along with the orange flower water. Process to a smooth dough. Do not overwork or the dough will be tough. Wrap in clear plastic film and chill for 1 hour or freeze until required.
3. Pre-heat the oven to 190C/375F/Gas 5. Roll the dough out on a lightly floured surface to 3 mm (¹/₈ in) thick and line 24 tartlet tins. Prick the bases and chill for 15 minutes.
4. Line the tartlets with kitchen paper and baking beans and bake blind for 10 minutes. Remove the beans and paper and return to the oven for a further 5 minutes until golden. Cool slightly before removing from the tins and placing on a wire rack. The tartlets can be frozen at this stage.
5. To make the filling, place the sugar in a small pan with 1 tablespoon of water. Cook over a low heat until the sugar has dissolved. Increase the heat and cook to a golden caramel. Watch carefully as you will find it suddenly turns. Add the oats, stir once then turn on to a lightly oiled tray. Leave to set then crush lightly in a pestle and mortar or with a rolling pin until you have some powder and larger chunks.
6. To make the decoration, cut the pared orange rind into tiny strips. Place in a small pan with the orange juice and sugar and cook over a low heat until the strips become candied. Transfer to a plate to cool.
7. Whip the cream to soft peaks, fold in the oat praline with the icing sugar, whisky and orange juice. If the mixture thickens, add a little extra un-whipped cream to loosen. Divide between the tartlet cases, decorate with the candied zests and serve.

From the top left: *Frozen Cherry Ripples (page 125), Butterscotch Pear Biscuits (page 124), Orange Sablés with Whisky Cream and Tuiles with Mango Fool (page 124)*

Tuiles with Mango Fool

BUTTERSCOTCH PEAR BISCUITS

To freeze the cooked biscuits and pear topping, place in separate containers, seal and freeze for up to 1 month. To serve, defrost, then assemble and sprinkle with nuts just before serving.

  Makes 25–30 biscuits

For the dough
100 g (4 oz) plain flour
A pinch of salt
25 g (1 oz) hazelnuts, toasted and ground
25 g (1 oz) icing sugar
50 g (2 oz) butter, diced
1 egg yolk

For the topping
2 tablespoons raisins
1 tablespoon rum
450 g (1 lb) pears
Juice of 1 lemon
50 g (2 oz) butter
50 g (2 oz) soft brown sugar
Pared rind of ½ lemon
2 tablespoons toasted chopped hazelnuts, to serve

1. Make the dough: sift the flour and salt into the bowl of a food processor, add the hazelnuts and icing sugar. Add the butter and process until the mixture resembles fine breadcrumbs. Add the egg yolk and 1–2 teaspoons of cold water. Process to a smooth dough. Do not overwork or the pastry will

be tough. Wrap in clear plastic film and chill for 1 hour. Alternatively freeze until required.
2. Roll out the dough on a lightly floured surface to 3 mm (⅛ in) thick. Using a fluted round pastry cutter stamp out 1 cm (½ in) rounds. Place slightly apart on large baking sheets, prick with a fork and chill for 15 minutes.
3. Pre-heat the oven to 190C/375F/Gas 5. Bake the biscuits for 8–10 minutes until golden. Cool on a wire rack. The biscuits can be kept in an airtight tin for 3–4 days or frozen until required. Defrost for 2–3 hours before using.
4. To make the topping, soak the raisins in 2 tablespoons of water mixed with the rum. Peel, core, cut into small slices and dip the pears in the lemon juice. Melt the butter and sugar in a large frying pan. Add the pear slices with the lemon rind and fry over a medium heat until the pear slices are soft and the butter and sugar are just starting to caramelise. Stir in the raisins, cook for 30 seconds and remove from the heat. Using a slotted spoon remove the pears and raisins from the pan. Boil the syrup until it is thickened and coats the back of a spoon. Allow to cool.
5. Top each biscuit with a little of the pear mixture and sprinkle with the chopped hazelnuts.

TUILES WITH MANGO FOOL

The filling can be frozen after step 4. The cooked tuiles are not suitable for freezing, but the mixture can be frozen or made and baked up to 1 week in advance and stored in a tin.

Makes 20–25

For the dough
2 egg whites
50 g (2 oz) butter, melted and cooled
50 g (2 oz) plain flour
65 g (2½ oz) caster sugar

For the filling
2 mangoes, peeled and roughly chopped
Rind and juice of 1 lime
25–50 g (1–2 oz) icing sugar
150 ml (5 fl oz) double cream, whipped
Oil, for greasing
1 dessertspoon gelatine for setting, if desired

1. Place the egg whites in a bowl and lightly whisk with a fork. Stir in the cooled melted butter. Fold in the flour and sugar. Work quickly to form a smooth dough. This batter will freeze well.

2. Pre-heat the oven to 190C/375F/Gas 5. Lightly grease 2 baking trays and spread teaspoonfuls of the mixture into 7.5 cm (3 in) rounds, spacing them well apart. Cook for 4–5 minutes, until golden.

3. While still hot, slide a palette knife under each biscuit to loosen then carefully press it into a small muffin tin so it forms a cup. Alternatively shape over small spice jars. Allow the biscuits to set in shape before cooling on a wire rack. Keep the tuiles in an airtight container for up to 1 week.

4. To make the filling, place the mango flesh in a blender with the lime juice and zest. Process until smooth and add icing sugar to taste. The purée can be frozen at this stage.

5. To finish the fool fold the cream into the mango purée and spoon a little into each tuile just before serving to avoid the bases going soggy.

6. If you want to set the *Mango Fool* with gelatine, soak 1 dessertspoon of gelatine in 1 tablespoon of water, heat to dissolve and whisk into the defrosted purée before adding the cream. Do not freeze after adding the gelatine or cream.

FROZEN CHERRY RIPPLES

If fresh cherries are not available use a 200 g (7 oz) tin of stoned black cherries in syrup. Strain the juice reserving 1 tablespoon. Cook the cherries, reserved syrup and 1 tablespoon of kirsch for 3 minutes then liquidise and continue as for fresh cherries.

Substitute a good-quality bought ice-cream if you do not have time to make your own.

To freeze, place the cherry ripples in one layer in a shallow rigid container and freeze for up to 1 month.

 Makes 20–25

100 g (4 oz) plain chocolate, broken into pieces
100 g (4 oz) black cherries, pitted and chopped
15 g (½ oz) caster sugar
1 tablespoon kirsch

For the ice-cream
250 ml (8 fl oz) milk
1 vanilla pod, split
3 egg yolks
50 g (2 oz) caster sugar
200 ml (7 fl oz) double cream

1. Slowly melt the chocolate in a heatproof bowl over a pan of barely simmering water. Allow to melt slowly. Using your index finger spread a thin layer of chocolate on the insides of waxed mini paper cases. Stand the cases on a tray and leave in a cool place until set hard. When set spread an extra layer of chocolate around the sides of each case to make removing the paper easier.

2. Place the cherries in a pan with the sugar, kirsch and 1 tablespoon of water. Cook over a low heat until the sugar dissolves. Turn up the heat and simmer for 5 minutes until the cherries are soft and the liquid syrupy. Place in a processor or blender and liquidise until smooth. Cool and put in the freezer for 15 minutes before using.

3. To make the ice-cream, place the milk and vanilla pod in a saucepan and bring to the boil. Whisk the egg yolks and sugar until thick and light. Stir in a little of the milk, stir, then add the egg mixture to the pan. Cook, stirring, until the custard thickens. Cool and remove the vanilla pod.

4. Pour into an ice-cream machine and churn until thick. Add the cream and continue churning until frozen. Remove from the ice-cream machine and lightly fold in the cherry mixture, leaving it streaky. Transfer to a freezerproof container and freeze for 3 hours until quite firm. If you do not have an ice-cream machine freeze the mixture until it is set 2.5 cm (1 in) in from the edges, then whisk to break down the large ice crystals and whisk in the cream. Freeze until just firm, then stir in the cherry mixture, leaving it streaky.

5. Carefully peel the paper cases away from the set chocolate and place on a chilled tray. Spoon a little ice-cream into each. Freeze until firm, cover and store until required. These are best eaten within a week of being made.

Frozen Cherry Ripples

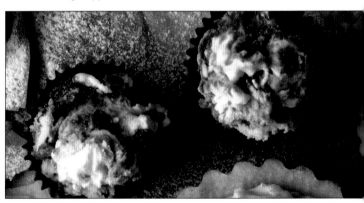

CHILDREN'S PARTIES

Preparing for a children's party can be time-consuming but it is always good fun. Our clever cakes will enchant any child, and the food is as simple as ABC!

From the left: *Traffic Light Biscuits, Liquorice Locomotive (page 128)*, with *Sausage Biplanes, Jelly Sail Boats* and *Chattanooga Chew-chew (all page 129)*

CHILDREN'S PARTIES

Giving a children's party a fun theme adds plenty of extra excitement – and solves the problem of how to provide entertainment. You can create a real sense of occasion by getting the kids to turn up in fancy dress, with appropriate food, decorations and games to match the mood.
Let all the guests know the theme well in advance. That way, they can have a rummage through their dressing-up boxes for suitable outfits. Colourful, home-made invitations are a fun way of setting the scene – make them from card or paper and send out at least 2 weeks in advance.
The party preparation is all part of the fun and can involve the kids too.
Rather than using expensive, shop-bought decorations let children have a free hand in designing party hats, masks, streamers, take-home goody bags and pictures.
Here are 4 fantastic party settings to choose from. If you plan to create one of the theme cakes, you can save yourself an awful lot of trouble by making it in advance. Decorated cakes will keep for up to 2 weeks if they are stored in a cool, dry place. You can even use shop-bought cake bases to save time – simply cut them to fit.
Come up with as many amusing party games as you can. It involves a bit of extra work, but is guaranteed to give those small VIPs the party of a lifetime.

TRAINS, PLANES AND AUTOMOBILES PARTY

LIQUORICE LOCOMOTIVE

SAUSAGE BIPLANES

CHATTANOOGA CHEW-CHEW

TRAFFIC LIGHT BISCUITS

JELLY SAIL BOATS

LIQUORICE LOCOMOTIVE

Makes 1 cake/serves 8

900 g (2 lb) ready-to-roll Sugar Paste *(see page 212)*
Concentrated paste food colouring: red, blue, yellow and black
35 x 25 cm (14 x 10 in) rectangular cake board or tray
Cornflour, for dusting
15–18 cm (6–7 in) ready-made Swiss roll
15 x 7.5 cm (6 x 3 in) ready-made Madeira or slab cake
50 g (2 oz) icing sugar
6 liquorice Catherine wheels

To decorate
12 liquorice 'jelly' sweets,
Several plain liquorice sweets,
Assortment of small jellies, wine gums, Smarties or

liquorice sweets
Chocolate Matchmakers

1. Colour 225 g (8 oz) of the *Sugar Paste* red. Roll out thinly on a surface dusted with cornflour. Lightly dampen the cake board and cover with *Sugar Paste*. Trim off excess. Cut 3 x 2.5 cm (1 in) slices off the Swiss roll for trucks. Cut a 10 cm (4 in) piece from the slab cake and stand on one end. Cut out a small wedge for the back of the cabin.
2. Colour all but 50 g (2 oz) of the remaining *Sugar Paste* blue and use a quarter to cover the large piece of Swiss roll. Place on the cake board. Use more *Sugar Paste* to cover the rectangular cake, icing one side at a time. Secure behind the Swiss roll, using a dampened paintbrush.
3. Cover the trucks with the remaining blue *Sugar Paste* and arrange in a curved line on the cake board. Colour the remaining *Sugar Paste* yellow and use to shape cabin windows and the front of the train. Secure in place. Blend the icing sugar with a little water to make a thick paste. Half unroll the liquorice Catherine wheels to make the train wheels. Attach them to the train engine with the icing paste.
4. Wrap liquorice jelly sweets in the icing trimmings and secure to the trucks. Secure sweets or wine gums to the trucks with more icing. Use more liquorice strips to link the train. Chop plain liquorice and secure to the back of the engine. Use a whole liquorice for the funnel. Paint the edges of the windows with black food colouring and tuck the Matchmakers under the train for the track.

SAUSAGE BIPLANES

Serves 1

1 ice-cream wafer
2 Hula Hoops
Cheese spread, to decorate
1 small sausage, cooked
Pieces of yellow pepper or processed cheese, to decorate

1. Cut the wafer biscuit into 2 long wings and tail fins.
2. On a serving plate, position 2 Hula Hoops for wheels. Using the cheese spread, secure the wafer to the Hula Hoops.
3. Rest the sausage over the wafer and then position the second wafer on the top and attach the tail fins with cheese spread. Decorate with pieces of yellow pepper or processed cheese.

CHATTANOOGA CHEW-CHEW

Serves 8

5 eggs, hard boiled and finely chopped
4–5 tablespoons mayonnaise, or to taste
10 slices bread
Butter, to spread

To garnish
Twiglets
Hula Hoops

1. Mix the eggs with the mayonnaise and spread the butter on the bread. Using the egg mayonnaise as the filling, make up 5 rounds of sandwiches.
2. Cut 4 sandwiches into 4 cm (1¹/₂ in) squares and trim off the crusts. These form the trucks of the train.
3. Cut the remaining sandwich in half lengthways. Then cut one of the halves in half across the middle and stack these two small sandwiches on end of the other half. This forms the train's engine.
4. Make a winding track of Twiglets to run among the party plates on the table and position the engine and the trucks on the top. Use the Hula Hoops for the wheels.

Liquorice Locomotive, Spiders and Webs (page 132)
and Ladybird Buns (page 132)

TRAFFIC LIGHT BISCUITS

 Makes 8

8 rectangular sweet biscuits
Strawberry or raspberry jam, to spread
225 g (8 oz) ready-to-roll Sugar Paste (see page 212)
8 each of red, yellow and green Smarties

1. Spread the biscuits with a generous coating of jam.
2. Thinly roll out the *Sugar Paste* and cut out rectangles the same size as the biscuits. Cut out 3 rounds, slightly smaller than the Smarties, from the centre of each rectangle using the end of a piping nozzle.
3. Lay the icing over the biscuits and press the Smarties into the holes to form the traffic lights.

JELLY SAIL BOATS

 Makes 12

1 packet orange jelly
2 oranges
Coloured paper or foil
Cocktail sticks

1. Make up the jelly as directed on the packet but using 150 ml (5 fl oz) less water than stated. Allow to cool.
2. Halve the oranges and scoop out the centres. Fill the skins with jelly and allow to set.
3. To serve, cut each orange half into three wedges, using a warm, dampened knife.
4. Cut sails out of the foil or coloured paper and thread on to cocktail sticks before pressing gently into the jelly boats.

BUMBLE BEE TEA

BUMBLE BEE CAKE

UGGY BUGGY SALAD

WIGGLY WORMS

CRUDITE CENTIPEDE

SNAIL TRAIL

LADYBIRD BUNS

SPIDERS AND WEBS

BEASTLY DRINKS

BUMBLE BEE CAKE

 Makes 1 cake/serves 10–12

225 g (8 oz) soft margarine
225 g (8 oz) golden caster sugar
5 eggs
275 g (10 oz) self-raising flour
1/2 teaspoon baking powder
Grated rind of 1 orange
900 g (2lb) ready-to-roll Sugar Paste *(see page 212)*
Concentrated paste food colouring: green, violet, yellow and red
30 cm (12 in) round cake board
Cornflour, for dusting

4 tablespoons clear honey
Chocolate vermicelli
Rice paper
2 Smarties
2 white candy sticks

1. Pre-heat the oven to 160C/325F/Gas 3. Grease a 1.5 litre (2¹/₂ pint) and a 600 ml (1 pint) pudding basin. Line the bases of both containers with greaseproof paper.
2. Beat together the margarine, sugar, eggs, flour, baking powder and orange rind. Divide the mixture between the basins and level the surfaces. Bake in the centre of the oven, allowing 1 hour for the small basin and 1 hour 10 minutes for the large one. Turn out the cakes and leave to cool on wire racks.
3. Colour 175 g (6 oz) of the *Sugar Paste* green. Brush the edges of the board with water. Roll out the green *Sugar Paste* on a surface dusted with cornflour and use to cover the board, trimming off any excess.
4. Colour 175 g (6 oz) of the *Sugar Paste* violet. Roll out and cut out large petal shapes. Arrange them in a flower pattern on the board.
5. Trim about a third off the small cake, so that it fits neatly against the large cake as a head. Spread both cakes with the honey. Reserve a small ball of white *Sugar Paste* and colour the remainder yellow. Use it to cover the cakes. Position them on the board.
6. Brush 2.5 cm (1 in) bands of the yellow *Sugar*

Paste with water and sprinkle with chocolate vermicelli. Cut out two large and two small petal-shaped wings from rice paper and tuck between the body and head (prop up with cocktail sticks). Use the remaining *Sugar Paste*, Smarties and candy sticks to make eyes, mouth (use red colouring) and antennae.

UGGY BUGGY SALAD

Serves 1

Lettuce leaves
1 pitta bread
1 beefburger, cooked to taste
2 cherry tomatoes
Cheese spread
2 raisins
1/4 red pepper, cut into strips

1. Arrange the lettuce leaves on a pitta bread and top with the beef burger.
2. Secure the cherry tomatoes to the burger with cheese spread from a tube.
3. Add a further dollop of cheese spread on top of the tomatoes and place a raisin on each for the centres of the Uggy Buggy's eyes.
4. Garnish with the 4 strips of red pepper for the legs.

WIGGLY WORMS

Serves 8

100 g (4 oz) butter or margarine
225 g (8 oz) plain flour
50 g (2 oz) Cheddar, grated
1 egg, beaten
Sesame seeds

1. Pre-heat the oven to 200C/400F/Gas 6.
2. Rub the butter or margarine into the flour. Add the Cheddar and mix to form a dough.
3. Roll out thinly and cut into strips about 15 cm (6 in) long and 1 cm (1/2 in) wide. Place the strips on to a lightly greased baking sheet and bend into wiggly worms.
4. Brush with the egg and sprinkle with sesame seeds before baking for about 10 minutes. Leave to cool before serving.

CRUDITÉ CENTIPEDE

Serves 8

1 slice processed cheese
1 large tomato
Twiglets
225 g (8 oz) cherry tomatoes
1/4 cucumber
2 carrots
1 green pepper, to decorate

1. Cut out 2 eyes and a mouth from the processed cheese and press on to the large tomato to form a face. (Use small pieces of the green pepper for the centres of the eyes.)
2. Use 2 of the Twiglets for antennae, piercing the skin of the tomato to hold them into position.
3. Position the 'head' on the party table and arrange the cherry tomatoes in a curved line behind it forming the 'body'.
4. Cut the cucumber and carrots into matchstick pieces and use these along with the Twiglets to form the centipede's legs.

From the left: *Wiggly Worms, Uggy Buggy Salad, Spiders and Webs (page 132), Beastly Drinks (page 132), Crudité Centipede, Bumble Bee Cake, Snail Trail (page 132)* and *Ladybird Buns (page 132)*

SNAIL TRAIL

Serves 8

225 g (8 oz) ready-made puff pastry
100 g (4 oz) sausagemeat
2 tablespoons tomato ketchup
Cheese spread, to decorate
2 tomatoes, quartered

1. Pre-heat the oven to 200C/400F/Gas 6.
2. Thinly roll out the pastry and trim the edges.
3. Mix the sausagemeat with the tomato ketchup and spread the mixture over the pastry, leaving one edge free of filling.
4. Roll up the pastry, leaving the unfilled edge of pastry free, then cut into 5 mm (¹/₄ in) thick slices.
5. Place the 'snails' on a baking sheet and bake for 10–15 minutes or until slightly puffed and golden.
6. Once cool, arrange the snails on to plates and, using the cheese spread, secure the raisins as eyes and the pieces of tomato as hats.

LADYBIRD BUNS

 Makes 12

50 g (2 oz) self-raising flour
¹/₄ teaspoon baking powder
50 g (2 oz) golden caster sugar
50 g (2 oz) soft margarine
1 egg
350 g (12 oz) ready-to-roll Sugar Paste (see page 212)
Concentrated paste food colouring: red, and brown or black
Chocolate polka dots

1. Pre-heat the oven to 180C/350F/Gas 4.
2. Mix together the flour, baking powder, caster sugar, margarine and egg and beat until smooth.
3. Spoon into 12 paper cake cases and bake for about 15 minutes. Allow to cool before peeling away the paper cases.
4. Cut 2 thin slices from the sides of the cakes to form oval-shaped buns.
5. Colour the *Sugar Paste* red and divide it into 12. Roll each segment out thinly and use it to cover the buns, tucking the edges under.
6. Paint the central line and head with the brown or black food colouring. Press the chocolate polka dots into the *Sugar Paste* to form the spots.

SPIDERS AND WEBS

 Makes 8

200 g (7 oz) margarine
275 g (10 oz) plain flour
100 g (4 oz) light muscovado sugar
100 g (4 oz) icing sugar
Concentrated paste food colouring: blue
2 liquorice Catherine wheels
8 chocolate mallow snowballs

1. Pre-heat the oven to 190C/375F/Gas 5.
2. Rub together the margarine and flour. Stir in the muscovado sugar and knead to form a dough.
3. Roll the dough out thinly and cut into 8 x 14 cm (5¹/₂ in) rounds. Bake for about 12 minutes until turning golden and then allow to cool.
4. Beat the icing sugar with a little blue food colouring and water to make a thin paste. Place the paste in a piping bag fitted with a small plain nozzle and pipe webs on to each biscuit. (Pipe the lines from the centre to the edge first, then pipe the curved lines.) Leave the icing to set.
5. Unroll the Catherine wheels and cut into 3 cm (1¹/₄ in) lengths. Press 8 liquorice legs into each chocolate mallow snowball and rest 1 'spider' on each biscuit.

Ladybird Buns

BEASTLY DRINKS

 Make quantity required

Limeade
Mint-flavoured milkshake or ice-cream soda
Apple or pineapple juice

1. Serve any of the above in tall glasses and well chilled, with straws.

AMERICAN FOOTBALLER PARTY

AMERICAN FOOTBALLER CAKE

POM-POM STICKS AND CREAMY DIP

BARBECUED SPARE RIBS

BAKED FRIES

CHOCOLATE POPCORN SUNDAES

STRIPY ICE WEDGES

CRANBERRY SPRITZERS

AMERICAN FOOTBALLER CAKE

The protective mesh on this cake is made from floristry wire which is available from florists and cake decorating shops. Remove it before serving as it's not edible.

Ⓥ   Makes 1 cake /Serves 10-12

275 g (10 oz) butter or margarine, softened
275 g (10 oz) caster sugar
5 eggs
350 g (12 oz) self-raising flour
Grated rind of 2 oranges

To decorate
30 cm (12 in) round silver cake board
3 tablespoons apricot jam
1.25 kg (2$^1/_2$ lb) ready-to-roll Sugar Paste (see page 212)
Concentrated paste food colouring: red, brown, blue, green and black
Icing sugar, for dusting
3 x 33 cm (13 in) lengths floristry wire
Concentrated paste food colouring: silver

From the left: *Pom-Pom Sticks and Creamy Dip (page 134), Chocolate Popcorn Sundaes (page 135), Barbecued Spare Ribs (page 135), Stripy Ice Wedges (page 135), Cranberry Spritzers (page 135), American Footballer Cake and Baked Fries (page 135)*

1. Pre-heat the oven to 160C/325F/Gas 3. Grease a 3.25 litre (6 pint) ovenproof glass mixing bowl then line the base with greaseproof paper.

2. Beat together the butter or margarine, sugar, eggs, flour and orange rind. Turn into the bowl and level the surface. Bake for 1 hour 10 minutes until just firm. Loosen from the bowl with a knife, then turn out and leave to cool on a wire rack.

3. Transfer the cake to the cake board and place flat side down, slicing off the dome if it doesn't sit flat. Melt the jam with 1 tablespoon of water, then press through a sieve. Brush the mixture over the cake.

4. Colour 450 g (1 lb) *Sugar Paste* a pale flesh colour with a little of the red and brown food colouring. Roll out a small sausage of *Sugar Paste* and place on the cake board, against the side of the cake to shape a chin. Roll a smaller piece to make the nose and position a third of the way up the cake.

5. Roll out the remaining flesh-coloured icing on a surface dusted with icing sugar and use to cover the entire cake, smoothing the *Sugar Paste* down the sides and around the chin extension. Trim off the excess around the base and mark the nostrils with the end of a paintbrush.

6. Colour another 450 g (1 lb) *Sugar Paste* blue. Roll out 350 g (12 oz) to a semi-circle and dampen the helmet area of the cake. Lay a semi-circle over the cake so the inside edge rests about 2.5 cm (1 in) above the nose. Divide the remaining blue paste and roll out both pieces for the sides of the helmet, then position on the cake. Using a sharp knife, cut a neat edge around the blue paste to frame the face. Trim off the excess blue paste around the base and smooth out the joins between the top and sides.

7. Colour a little more icing green. Roll out to 2 long strips. Dampen the cake board, then use strips to cover the board, one side at a time.

8. Using a small cutter, mark ear areas on sides of helmet. Use a little white icing to shape the chin protector and score the chin piece with a knife before positioning on the cake.

9. Use a wide strip of white *Sugar Paste* for the centre of the helmet and two small pieces for the eyes.

10. Colour some *Sugar Paste* red and use to shape the red stripe, mouth and tongue. Paint on the eyes and 'warpaint' with brown and black colouring. Bend the floristry wire to fit the helmet, pressing ends into the cutter marks. Roll some white *Sugar Paste* into thin strips, 5 mm ($^1/_4$ in) wide. Dampen the undersides, then press into position over the wire. Leave to harden for several hours or overnight, then paint the guard silver.

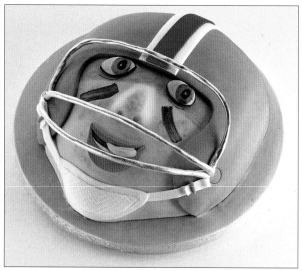

American Footballer Cake (page 133)

POM-POM STICKS AND CREAMY DIP

Serves 8

300 ml (10 fl oz) mayonnaise
2 tablespoons tomato purée
A pinch of chilli powder
2 large carrots, peeled and quartered lengthways
6 celery sticks
6 spring onions
Salt and freshly ground black pepper

1. Mix the mayonnaise with the tomato purée and chilli powder. Season to taste and then pour into a serving dish.

2. Using a sharp knife, make 6 cm ($2^1/_2$ in) deep cuts, 3 mm ($^1/_8$ in) apart, down the end of each carrot stick. Turn the carrot and make cuts on the opposite side.

3. Place the carrots in a bowl of iced water until they fan out.

4. Repeat this process with the celery sticks and spring onions before arranging on a plate with the bowl of dip.

BARBECUED SPARE RIBS

Serves 8

1.75 kg (4 lb) pork spare ribs
6 tablespoons tomato ketchup
3 tablespoons clear honey
2 tablespoons red wine vinegar
2 tablespoons mustard
Salt and freshly ground black pepper
Lettuce, to serve
Tomatoes, cut into wedges, to garnish

1. Pre-heat the oven to 200C/400F/Gas 6.
2. Line a roasting tin with foil and arrange the ribs in a single layer.
3. Mix the tomato ketchup, honey, vinegar and mustard before seasoning to taste.
4. Brush the mixture over the ribs and bake for 1 hour, turning occasionally and basting with any remaining sauce.
5. When cooked, arrange the ribs on a bed of lettuce and garnish with tomato wedges.

BAKED FRIES

Serves 8

1.5 kg (3 lb) small baking potatoes
4 tablespoons vegetable oil
A pinch of chilli powder or paprika
Salt

1. Pre-heat the oven to 200C/400F/Gas 6.
2. Prick the potatoes and bake for 15–20 minutes or until softened.
3. Cut the potatoes into wedges and place in a large ovenproof dish or tray.
4. Brush with vegetable oil and sprinkle with a little chilli powder or paprika. Bake for 45 minutes until golden. Season with salt before serving.

CHOCOLATE POPCORN SUNDAES

Serves 8

100 g (4 oz) plain chocolate
1 packet of toffee popcorn
1 small tub of toffee, peanut or maple syrup ice-cream
1 packet dessert biscuits

1 bottle chocolate dessert sauce

1. Melt the chocolate and spread it on to a sheet of baking parchment. Leave to set.
2. Using a small cutter, carefully cut star shapes out of chocolate.
3. Spoon a little of the popcorn into each of 8 tall glasses and then top with scoops of ice-cream.
4. Sprinkle the sundaes with more popcorn and then decorate with the biscuits, chocolate stars and chocolate sauce.

STRIPY ICE WEDGES

Makes 12

2 rectangular ginger or syrup cakes
50 g (2 oz) ground almonds
40 g (1½ oz) softened butter
1 tablespoon caster sugar
225 g (8 oz) Almond Paste *or* Sugar Paste
(see page 211 and 212)
Concentrated paste food colouring: red and blue

1. Trim the tops off the cakes to flatten them.
2. Beat together the almonds, butter and sugar before spreading the mixture over the cakes.
3. Divide the *Almond Paste* or *Sugar Paste* into 3 bowls. Colour 1 red and 1 blue, and leave the remainder white.
4. Roll out long strips of icing and lay across the cakes, alternating the colours.
5. When iced, cut the cake into wedges.

CRANBERRY SPRITZERS

Make quantity required

Cranberry juice
Sparkling apple juice or mineral water

1. Half fill tall glasses with the cranberry juice before topping with either the apple juice or water. Serve well chilled.

FAIRY CASTLE TEA

FAIRY CASTLE CAKE

HEART-SHAPED SANDWICHES

BEJEWELLED CRISPS

MARSHMALLOW NECKLACES

CHOCOLATE-COVERED STRAWBERRIES

PINK DRINKS

From the left: *Heart-shaped Sandwiches, Chocolate-covered Strawberries, Bejewelled Crisps, Pink Drinks, Fairy Castle Cake* and *Marshmallow Necklaces*

FAIRY CASTLE CAKE

Makes 1 cake/serves 10–12

900 g (2 lb) ready-to-roll Sugar Paste (see page 212)
Icing sugar, for dusting
30 cm (12 in) round cake board
15 x 7.5 cm (6 x 3 in) ready-made Madeira or slab cake
13 cm (5 in) round ready-made sandwich cake
4 mini Swiss rolls
Rice paper
Marshmallows, pink and white
2 meringue nests
Handful of Mint Imperials
75 g (3 oz) icing sugar, sifted
Concentrated paste food colouring: pink and black

To decorate
Silver edible balls
Sugar 'confetti' or small shop-bought sugared flowers

1. Roll out 225 g (8 oz) of the *Sugar Paste* very thinly on a surface dusted with icing sugar. Lightly dampen the cake board and cover with icing, trimming off any excess. Halve the slab cake to make 2 squares and stack on top of each other towards the back of the board. Halve the sandwich cake vertically to make 2 half moons. Place one half, cut side down, against the right-hand side of the slab cake. Slide layers of the other half, slightly apart, for a 'step' effect, and position with cut side against the front of the slab cake.
2. Roll out 450 g (1 lb) of the *Sugar Paste* and use to loosely cover the cakes. To make the three towers, secure quarter of a mini roll to a whole one with a little dampened *Sugar Paste*. Wrap in a rectangle of thinly rolled *Sugar Paste*, dampening edges to secure. Cover a second whole mini roll, and three-quarters of a mini roll. Position towers on cake and mark on the bricks with a knife. Cut semi-circles from rice paper and shape into cones, then dampen the edges to secure and place on the towers as roofs.
3. Slice each marshmallow into three rounds. Halve and use for steps. Break up the meringues and scatter around the base with the mints. Blend the icing sugar with a little water to make a smooth paste and use to pipe 'foliage', adding silver balls and sugar decorations.
4. Secure the silver balls around the base of the castle and the top of the turrets. Shape the windows from grey *Sugar Paste*, using a little black colouring, and make a small pink door.

HEART-SHAPED SANDWICHES

Makes 12

Thin slices of brown, white or soft-grain bread
Butter, to spread
Ham spread or taramasalata
Radishes, sliced
Small tin pink salmon or cheese spread

1. Cut 18 heart shapes from the bread, and butter thinly.
2. Spread 6 of the slices with the ham spread or taramasalata and garnish with the radish.
3. Sandwich the remaining slices with finely mashed salmon or cheese spread.

BEJEWELLED CRISPS

Prawn cocktail-flavoured crisps or prawn crackers
Tub of small pink sugar flowers

1. Arrange the crisps or crackers in a dish then add the flowers as decoration.

MARSHMALLOW NECKLACES

Makes 8

2 packets pink and white marshmallows
4 packets Polo mints
8 red liquorice 'bootlaces'

1. Cut each of the marshmallows through to the centre only.
2. Divide the Polo mints and thread them evenly on to the 'bootlaces'.
3. Tuck the marshmallows around the laces, between the Polo mints.
4. Knot each end of the necklace to prevent the mints from falling off.

CHOCOLATE-COVERED STRAWBERRIES

Makes 20

50 g (2 oz) white chocolate
20 strawberries, with stalks

1. Melt the chocolate in a heatproof bowl set over a pan of barely simmering water.
2. Dip the strawberries diagonally in the chocolate and leave to set on a wire rack in the fridge until ready to serve.

PINK DRINKS

Strawberry milkshake or ice-cream soda
Raspberry or cranberry juice

1. Serve any of the above in tall glasses and well chilled.

SPECIAL OCCASIONS

When family and friends gather for Christmas, Easter, a wedding anniversary, a baby's christening or a lazy afternoon tea, why not prepare one of these splendid menus? It's always wonderfully satisfying to do something memorable to celebrate special occasions.

From the left: *Stir-fried Brussels Sprouts with Lemon and Bay Cream (page 142)*, *Roast Turkey with Mango and Pistachio Rice Stuffing (page 140)*, *Ginger and Sesame Carrots (page 142)*, *Port and Red Wine Gravy (page 142)*, *Cranberry and Orange Sauce (page 142)*, *Sausage and Chestnut Patties (page 140)*, *Bacon, Prune and Red Pepper Kebabs (page 141)* and *Herby Spiced Potatoes (page 141)*

CHRISTMAS TURKEY DINNER

ROAST TURKEY WITH MANGO AND

PISTACHIO RICE STUFFING

SAUSAGE AND CHESTNUT PATTIES

BACON, PRUNE AND RED PEPPER KEBABS

HERBY SPICED POTATOES

STIR-FRIED BRUSSELS SPROUTS WITH

LEMON AND BAY CREAM

GINGER AND SESAME CARROTS

PORT AND RED WINE GRAVY

GIBLET STOCK

CRANBERRY AND ORANGE SAUCE

ROAST TURKEY WITH MANGO AND PISTACHIO RICE STUFFING

For fan ovens, cook from cold in a 160C oven for 20 minutes per 450 g (1 lb), plus 20 minutes extra. There will be enough left-over turkey to make the *Chinatown Turkey Salad* in the Boxing Day menu with this size of turkey.

Serves 8

4.5–5.5 kg (10–12 lb) turkey, thawed if frozen
100 g (4 oz) melted butter or 4 tablespoons olive oil
8 rashers streaky bacon
Mixed fresh herbs, to garnish

For the stuffing
2 tablespoons olive oil
3 shallots, finely chopped
2 garlic cloves, finely chopped
2.5 cm (1 in) piece root ginger, finely chopped
2 teaspoons cumin seeds
175 g (6 oz) basmati rice
100 g (4 oz) shelled pistachio nuts, chopped
75 g (3 oz) dried mango, chopped
100 g (4 oz) chestnut mushrooms, chopped
450 ml (15 fl oz) vegetable stock
Salt and freshly ground black pepper

1. Pre-heat the oven to 180C/350F/Gas 4. Remove the giblets from the turkey and reserve to make

stock for the gravy (see page 142). Wash the turkey inside and out and dry well with kitchen paper.
2. To make the stuffing, heat the oil in a large pan, add the shallots, garlic and ginger and fry gently for about 5 minutes until softened but not browned. Add the cumin, rice and nuts and stir well until coated in oil.
3. Stir in the mango, mushrooms and stock, then bring to the boil. Reduce the heat, cover and simmer for 25 minutes until the rice is tender. Taste, adjust the seasoning and leave to cool.
4. Stuff the neck end of the turkey with the rice mixture, pushing it up between the flesh and skin towards the breast (not too tightly as it will expand during cooking). Sew up the neck skin or secure it with a skewer, then truss the turkey to give it a good shape. Weigh and calculate the cooking time, allowing 20 minutes per 450 g (1 lb), plus 20 minutes extra.
5. Place the turkey in a roasting tin and brush the breast and legs with the melted butter or oil. Season well all over. Cover loosely with foil and roast for the calculated cooking time.
6. Remove the foil for the last 30 minutes of the cooking time and cover the breast with the rashers of bacon. Add the *Sausage and Chestnut Patties* (see below) and the *Bacon, Prune and Red Pepper Kebabs* (see right) to the tin. If there isn't enough space, cook in a separate tin.
7. Test whether the turkey is cooked by inserting a skewer into the thickest part of the thigh – the juices should run clear not pink. Transfer to a large platter and allow to rest in a warm place for 15 minutes to make carving easier. Reserve pan juices to make the *Port and Red Wine Gravy* on page 142. Garnish with the herbs before serving.

SAUSAGE AND CHESTNUT PATTIES

Makes 12

450 g (1 lb) herbed sausages
175 g (6 oz) fresh white breadcrumbs
2 tablespoons sunflower oil
1 onion, finely chopped
2 celery sticks, finely chopped
240 g (8½ oz) can whole peeled chestnuts, chopped
1 egg, beaten
3 tablespoons chopped fresh parsley
12 bay leaves
6 rashers rindless streaky bacon, halved lengthwise
Salt and freshly ground black pepper

1. Pre-heat the oven to 180C/350F/Gas 4. Slit the sausages with a small, sharp knife and slip them out of their skins. Break up the meat in a bowl and combine with the breadcrumbs.

2. Heat the oil in a pan, add the onion and celery and fry gently for about 5 minutes until softened and lightly browned. Cool slightly, then add to the bowl with the chestnuts, egg, parsley and seasoning. Mix well until evenly combined.

3. Divide the mixture into 12 equal portions, shaping each one into a patty. Place a bay leaf on each patty and wrap in a strip of streaky bacon to secure. Arrange the patties around the turkey or in a roasting tin and cook for 30 minutes until they are crisp and lightly browned.

BACON, PRUNE AND RED PEPPER KEBABS

Makes 16

16 shallots, peeled
8 rashers rindless streaky bacon, halved widthways
16 stoned prunes
1 large red pepper, halved and seeded
16 cocktail sausages

For the glaze
2 tablespoons soy sauce
2 teaspoons wholegrain mustard
1 tablespoon clear honey

1. Pre-heat the oven to 180C/350F/Gas 4. Bring a pan of salted water to the boil, add the shallots and parboil for 15 minutes. Drain and leave to cool. Wrap each piece of bacon around a prune.

2. Cut the pepper into 2.5 cm (1 in) cubes. Thread on to each of 16 small wooden skewers a bacon-wrapped prune with a piece of pepper, a sausage and a shallot.

3. To make the glaze, blend the soy sauce, mustard and honey in a bowl. Brush over the kebabs and cook for 30 minutes.

HERBY SPICED POTATOES

 Serves 8

1.25 kg (2½ lb) potatoes
12 tablespoons olive oil
2 red chillies, seeded and finely chopped
½ teaspoon paprika
2 teaspoons dried rosemary
1 teaspoon dried oregano
4 garlic cloves
2 tablespoons chopped fresh parsley
Salt and freshly ground black pepper

1. Cut the potatoes into evenly-sized pieces. Dry well, then toss in oil until evenly coated. Season. Transfer half the potatoes to a separate bowl and toss with the chillies and paprika. Toss the remainder in rosemary and oregano.

2. Arrange the potatoes in a roasting tin in one layer, keeping the flavours separate. Tuck garlic cloves in between them and roast on a shelf above the turkey for 1–1¼ hours until crisp and golden brown. Garnish with parsley.

Christmas Turkey Dinner with all the trimmings

STIR-FRIED BRUSSELS SPROUTS WITH LEMON AND BAY CREAM

 Serves 8

3 tablespoons sunflower oil
2 garlic cloves, chopped
900 g (2 lb) Brussels sprouts, halved
4 tablespoons double cream
2 bay leaves
4 strips lemon rind
Salt and freshly ground black pepper

1. Heat the oil in a large pan, add the garlic and stir-fry briefly. Add the Brussels sprouts and stir fry for 2–3 minutes until they just start to soften. Pour in 3 tablespoons of water, season, then cover and cook gently for 8–10 minutes until just tender.
2. Warm the cream with the bay leaves and lemon rind for 5 minutes, then strain over the sprouts just before serving.

GINGER AND SESAME CARROTS

 Serves 8

900 g (2 lb) carrots, cut into thin sticks
25 g (1 oz) butter
1 teaspoon demerara sugar
2 teaspoons chopped root ginger
2 tablespoons toasted sesame seeds
Salt and freshly ground black pepper

1. Place the carrots, butter, sugar, ginger and seasoning in a pan. Add 3 tablespoons of cold water and bring to the boil. Cover and cook gently for 10–15 minutes until tender and the liquid has almost evaporated. Sprinkle over the sesame seeds.

PORT AND RED WINE GRAVY

Serves 8

4 tablespoons pan juices from the roast turkey
2 tablespoons plain flour
2 tablespoons Dijon mustard
4 tablespoons port
300 ml (10 fl oz) red wine
300 ml (10 fl oz) giblet stock (see page 140)
Salt and freshly ground black pepper

1. Heat the pan juices in the roasting tin or measure into a small pan. Add the flour, stir well and cook for 2 minutes. Add the mustard and port, then gradually add the wine and stock, stirring continuously until thickened. Simmer for 5 minutes, stirring until smooth and glossy. Season.

GIBLET STOCK

Makes 600 ml (1 pint)

Turkey giblets (liver removed)
1 onion, halved
1 celery stick, chopped
1 carrot, chopped
A few fresh parsley sprigs
4 cloves
1 bay leaf
6 black peppercorns
Salt

1. Rinse the giblets thoroughly, then place in a pan with the other ingredients and 600 ml (1 pint) water. Bring to the boil and skim off the scum with a slotted spoon. Reduce the heat and simmer for 45 minutes. Strain and cool.

CRANBERRY AND ORANGE SAUCE

 Serves 8

225 g (8 oz) cranberries, thawed if frozen
1 teaspoon grated orange rind
3 tablespoons fresh orange juice
75 g (3 oz) light muscovado sugar
2 tablespoons port (optional)

1. Place all the ingredients in a small pan with 3 tablespoons of water. Bring to the boil, reduce the heat and simmer uncovered for 7–10 minutes, stirring frequently until the cranberries soften and the sauce thickens. Serve warm or cold.

COUNTDOWN

Timings are for a 2.00 p.m. lunch.

Early December
• Order the turkey.
• Give some thought to general aspects of Christmas like when to ice your cake and bake mince pies, etc.

December 22–23
• Defrost the turkey. For a 4.5–5.5 kg (10–12 lb) turkey, allow 45–48 hours at a cool room temperature.
• Remove any giblets as soon as they are loose. Store in the fridge to make stock for the gravy.
• Make the *Cranberry and Orange Sauce*; chill until required.

Christmas Eve
• Store the turkey in the fridge, loosely covered with foil.
• Make *Giblet Stock* for gravy. Cool quickly, then chill until required.
• Make the *Mango and Pistachio Rice Stuffing* and *Sausage and Chestnut Patties*. Cover and chill.
• Prepare the carrots and Brussels sprouts. Store separately in a polythene bag at the bottom of the fridge.
• Prepare the *Bacon, Prune and Red Pepper Kebabs*. Wrap in foil in a covered container. Make the glaze and chill until required. Make sure that any cooked or perishable food is kept well away from the turkey to avoid the risk of cross-contamination.

Christmas Day
8.00 a.m.
Wash and dry the turkey. Stuff the neck end and secure with a large skewer. Truss into a neat shape or tie the legs together. Weigh and calculate the cooking time. The turkey should be cooked by 1.45 p.m. to allow for a 15-minute resting time.

8.30 a.m.
Pre-heat the oven to 180C/350F/Gas 4.

9.00 a.m.
Peel the potatoes and cover with cold water.

9.20 a.m.
A 5.5 kg (12 lb) turkey should now go into the oven.

10.00 a.m.
A 4.5 kg (10 lb) turkey should now go into the oven.

During the morning
• Lay the table, open the red wine, chill the white wine or champagne.
• Turn the *Cranberry and Orange Sauce* (unless serving warm) into serving dishes.

12.15 p.m.
Prepare and roast the *Herby Spiced Potatoes* on the shelf above the turkey.

1.15 p.m.
• Remove the foil from the turkey and cover the breast with bacon. Arrange the *Sausage and Chestnut Patties* and glazed *Bacon, Prune and Red Pepper Kebabs* in the roasting tin (or in a separate tin) and return to the oven.
• Remove cooking juices from the tin and make the *Port and Red Wine Gravy*. Keep warm.

1.25 p.m.
Make *Lemon and Bay Cream* to accompany the Brussels sprouts and keep warm. Cook the *Ginger and Sesame Carrots* and *Stir-fried Brussels Sprouts*.

1.45 p.m.
• Transfer the turkey to a serving platter, cover loosely with foil and leave to rest. Warm the plates and serving dishes.
• Heat through the *Cranberry and Orange Sauce*, if serving warm.

1.50 p.m.
• Remove the *Bacon, Prune and Red Pepper Kebabs*, *Sausage and Chestnut Patties* and *Herby Spiced Potatoes* from the oven. Sprinkle parsley over the potatoes.
• Arrange the *Bacon Kebabs*, *Sausage and Chestnut Patties* and potatoes around the turkey.

2.00 p.m.
Serve the turkey with all the trimmings, vegetables and gravy.

CHRISTMAS GOOSE DINNER

HONEY-GLAZED GOOSE
ROAST SWEDE, SWEET POTATOES AND CELERIAC
VEGETABLES WITH GARLIC, THYME AND BUTTER
ROAST APPLES WITH CRANBERRY SAUCE
RED WINE AND PORT SAUCE
GOOSE STOCK

HONEY-GLAZED GOOSE

Goose used to be a traditional Christmas bird until turkey superseded it in popularity. Try a taste of yesteryear, but with an oriental flavour. This dish will need long, slow marinating, so prepare the goose the night before.

Use a small, sharp knife to joint the bird. Place on a flat dish with legs pointing diagonally towards you, hold with a carving fork and cut through wing joints; carve legs the same way and divide in two. Use a long knife to carve the breast.

Serves 6

4.5 kg-5.5 kg (10-12 lb) goose

For the marinade
3 tablespoons clear honey
1 teaspoon chopped fresh thyme
1 teaspoon chopped fresh coriander
4 tablespoons soy sauce
3 garlic cloves, crushed
1 teaspoon finely grated root ginger
1 teaspoon Chinese five spice powder
1 teaspoon ground coriander
A pinch of ground cinnamon

1. Rinse the goose inside and out and dry with kitchen paper. Remove the wing tips and reserve with the neck and gizzard for a stock (see page 145). Truss and place in a non-metallic dish.
2. Mix the marinade ingredients and pour over the goose. Cover and leave overnight, turning and basting occasionally.
3. Pre-heat the oven to 220C/425F/Gas 7. Remove the goose from the marinade and pat dry. Weigh the bird, transfer to a rack in a roasting tin and cover with aluminium foil. Roast for 20 minutes,

then reduce the temperature of the oven to 200C/400F/Gas 6 and roast for 15 minutes per 450 g (1 lb). Transfer to a serving dish and leave to rest in a warm place.

ROAST SWEDE, SWEET POTATOES AND CELERIAC

Use orange-coloured sweet potatoes for this recipe. If you cannot find any, substitute ordinary waxy potatoes.

 Serves 6

450 g (1 lb) swede, cut into 2 cm (³/₄ in) chunks
450 g (1 lb) sweet potato cut into 2 cm (³/₄ in) chunks
450 g (1 lb) celeriac cut into 2 cm (³/₄ in) chunks
25 g (1 oz) butter
2 tablespoons olive oil
¹/₂ teaspoon grated nutmeg
Salt and freshly ground black pepper

1. Pre-heat the oven to 200C/400F/Gas 6. Parboil the vegetables in separate pans of boiling water until just tender. Add the seasoning.
2. Place the butter and oil in a large roasting dish and leave in the oven to heat for 5 minutes. Add the parboiled vegetables and grated nutmeg. Toss to coat in the hot butter and oil. Return to the oven and bake for 30–40 minutes or until tender and golden. Serve hot.

VEGETABLES WITH GARLIC, THYME AND BUTTER

 Serves 6

50 g (2 oz) butter
900 g (2 lb) courgettes, cut into 1 cm (¹/₂ in) thick slices
2 large red peppers, seeded and sliced
225 g (8 oz) baby sweetcorn
1 garlic clove, crushed
1 teaspoon light muscovado sugar
Salt and freshly ground black pepper
2 tablespoons chopped fresh thyme, to garnish

1. Heat the butter and stir-fry the courgettes, red peppers, sweetcorn and garlic over a high heat for 4–5 minutes or until just tender, then add the sugar and seasoning. Garnish with thyme.

From the left: *Roast Swede, Sweet Potatoes and Celeriac, Vegetables with Garlic, Thyme and Butter, Roast Apples with Cranberry Sauce* and *Honey-glazed Goose*

ROAST APPLES WITH CRANBERRY SAUCE

 Serves 6

3–6 Granny Smith apples, halved and cored
A little butter
675 g (1½ lb) cranberries
6 tablespoons orange juice
100 g (4 oz) sugar
8 tablespoons cranberry sauce

1. Pre-heat the oven to 200C/400F/Gas 6. Arrange the apple halves, cut sides down, in a greased baking dish, dot with a little butter and bake for 25–30 minutes or until soft.
2. Simmer the cranberries, orange juice and sugar for 5 minutes until soft. Strain off any excess juice and stir in the cranberry sauce. Spoon on to the apples and serve.

RED WINE AND PORT SAUCE

Serves 6

25 g (1 oz) butter
2 finely chopped shallots or 1 small red onion
150 ml (5 fl oz) red wine
150 ml (5 fl oz) port
300 ml (10 fl oz) Goose Stock (see following recipe)
1 tablespoon tomato purée
1 bay leaf

1. Melt the butter in a pan, add the shallots or onion and cook until soft. Stir in the red wine and port and bring to the boil. Add the *Goose Stock*, the tomato purée and the bay leaf and reduce by half. Season and serve hot.

GOOSE STOCK

Makes 600 ml (1 pint)

Goose giblets and left-over bones
1 small onion, halved
1 carrot, cut into chunks
1 celery stick, cut into chunks
A few bacon rinds, optional
1.2 litres (2 pints) water
6 black peppercorns

1. Place the giblets and any bones in a pan with the onion, carrot and celery. Add the bacon rinds (if using). Pour in the water and bring to the boil. Skim off any scum, then add the peppercorns. Cover and simmer for 2 hours. Strain and use for the *Red Wine and Port Sauce*, or gravy.

CHRISTMAS BAKING

RICH MINCE PIES

BRANDY BUTTER

CHRISTMAS PUDDING

CHRISTMAS CAKES:

CRYSTAL-TOPPED CAKE

GLITTERING STAR CAKE

NUT CLUSTER CHRISTMAS CAKE

GIFT-LADEN CHRISTMAS CAKE

Rich Mince Pies

RICH MINCE PIES

This recipe is suitable for vegetarians as long as the mincemeat used does not contain beef suet.

Makes 12

150 g (5 oz) butter, cut into pieces
225 g (8 oz) plain flour
50 g (2 oz) ground almonds
25 g (1 oz) caster sugar
A few drops almond essence
Grated rind of 1 orange
1 egg yolk
225 g (8 oz) mincemeat
1 egg white, lightly beaten
Caster sugar, for sprinkling
Brandy Butter (see right) or cream, to serve

1. Pre-heat the oven to 200C/400F/Gas 6. Rub the butter into the flour. Add the almonds, sugar, almond essence, orange rind, egg yolk and 2 tablespoons of water and mix to a firm dough.
2. Knead briefly on a floured surface, then wrap and chill for 30 minutes. Roll out thinly and stamp out 12 x 7.5 cm (3 in) rounds. Use the pastry to line 12 bun tins. Spoon in the mincemeat to come two-thirds of the way up the bun tins.
3. Stamp out holly leaves with the remaining pastry, making berries from the trimmings. Place over the mincemeat. Brush with egg white and dredge with caster sugar. Bake for 20 minutes until crisp and golden brown. Serve with cream or *Brandy Butter*.

BRANDY BUTTER

 Serves 8

100 g (4 oz) unsalted butter, softened
100 g (4 oz) caster sugar
50 g (2 oz) icing sugar, sifted
3 tablespoons brandy

1. Beat the butter until pale and soft. Gradually beat in the sugars, adding a little brandy with each addition. Beat in the remaining brandy until smooth. Transfer to a bowl, cover with foil. Chill for up to a week.

CHRISTMAS PUDDING

You can make Christmas puddings up to 1 year ahead but ideally make them around October or November to give them time to mature for Christmas. Each pudding serves 6-8.

 Makes 2 x 900 ml (1^1/$_2$ pint) puddings
each serving 8

100 g (4 oz) plain flour
2 teaspoons mixed spice
^{1}/$_2$ teaspoon ground ginger
^{1}/$_2$ teaspoon freshly grated nutmeg
175 g (6 oz) vegetable suet
100 g (4 oz) dark muscovado sugar
100 g (4 oz) fresh breadcrumbs
100 g (4 oz) blanched almonds, chopped
50 g (2 oz) hazelnuts, chopped
100 g (4 oz) glacé cherries, chopped
50 g (2 oz) candied peel, chopped
Grated rind of 1 lemon
Grated rind of 1 orange

Christmas Pudding

1 cooking apple, grated
225 g (8 oz) currants
275 g (10 oz) raisins
350 g (12 oz) sultanas
3 eggs, beaten
250 ml (8 fl oz) brown ale
2 tablespoons brandy or rum

1. Sift the flour and spices into a large bowl. Stir in the suet, sugar and breadcrumbs. Add the nuts, cherries, peel, rind, apple and dried fruit to the mixture. Stir, then add the eggs, ale and brandy or rum. Mix well.

2. Line the base of 2 x 900 ml (1½ pint) pudding basins with greaseproof paper. Pack in the mixture and smooth the top.

3. Cover each of the puddings with a round of double thickness greaseproof paper, pleated across the middle and tied down with string. Cover with a circle of foil, pleated in the middle, too.

4. Set each pudding in a large pan and pour in enough boiling water to come half way up them. Bring to the boil, reduce heat and cover with a tight-fitting lid. Steam for 4 hours, topping up with boiling water occasionally. Never let the water boil dry.

5. Remove from the pans and leave to cool. Take off the paper and tie down with fresh greaseproof paper. Store in a cool, dry place for up to 1 year.

6. To serve the pudding, steam as before for 3 hours. Turn out on to a plate, pour over warmed brandy and ignite. Serve when the flames have died down.

CRYSTAL-TOPPED CAKE

1 x 15 cm (6 in) round Basic Fruit Cake *(see page 210)*
1 x 20 (8 in) round cake board

For the decoration
*5 or 6 pieces of ribbon in different widths and designs,
each about 40 cm (16 in) long*
*100 g (4oz) mixed candied fruits such as pear, cherries,
apricots and angelica*
A few chocolate 'gold' coins

To cover the cake
Sieved apricot jam
Icing sugar, for dusting
350 g (12 oz) Almond Paste *(see page 211)*

1. Place the cake on the board and brush it all over
with apricot jam. Dust a work surface with a little
icing sugar, knead the *Almond Paste* lightly then roll
out a circle 7.5cm (3 in) larger than the cake.
2. Place the *Almond Paste* over the cake and ease
down over the sides. Smooth and trim.
3. Arrange the ribbons overlapping on top and
around the sides of the cake.
4. Slice the candied fruits, arrange on the cake with
the coins and decorate with a ribbon bow.

Glittering Star Cake

 GLITTERING STAR CAKE

The decorations on this cake are non-edible.

1 x 15 cm (6 in) Basic Fruit Cake *(see page 210)*
1 x 20 cm (8 in) cake board

To cover the cake
Sieved apricot jam
Icing sugar, for dusting
350 g (12 oz) Almond Paste *(see page 211)*
Gin, vodka or boiled water, to brush
350 g (12 oz) ready-to-roll Sugar Paste *(see page 212)*

For the decoration
150 g (6 oz) ready-to-roll Sugar Paste *(see page 212)*
Edible gold food colouring
White ribbon

1. To make the stars: roll out 100 g (4 oz) *Sugar
Paste* and cut out 8 different-sized stars using star
cutters. Leave the stars to dry overnight or longer,
if possible, on non-stick or waxed parchment.
2. Place the cake on the board and brush the cake
all over with apricot jam. Dust a work surface with
a little icing sugar, roll out *Almond Paste* to a circle
7.5 cm (3 in) larger than the cake. Place it over the
cake and ease down the sides. Trim off any excess
and leave overnight to dry.

Crystal-topped Cake

3. Brush the *Almond Paste* with the alcohol or cooled boiled water. Lightly dust the work surface with sugar and roll out the *Sugar Paste* to a circle large enough to cover the cake and board. Smooth the *Sugar Paste* down the cake and then over the board. Trim off any excess.

4. Tie the ribbon round the cake and fasten at the back. Decorate the stars, ribbon and cake board with the gold paint. Using the remaining *Sugar Paste*, mould into 8 balls of varying size and stick onto the cake with water or alcohol. Position the stars in front of the icing balls and stick into place. Pieces of screwed up kitchen paper can be placed behind the stars to keep them in positon while they are drying.

NUT CLUSTER CHRISTMAS CAKE

1 x 15 cm (6 in) round Basic Fruit Cake (see page 210)
1 x 20 cm (8 in) cake board

To cover the cake
350 g (12 oz) Almond Paste (see page 211)
Icing sugar, for dusting
Concentrated paste food colouring: red and green
Sieved apricot jam

For the decoration
18 pecan halves
6 whole Brazil nuts
7 whole almonds
1 hazelnut
Narrow ribbon for cake and board
Warmed apricot jam, to glaze

1. Colour half the *Almond Paste* green and the other half red. Measure round the cake and the height of the cake with a piece of string. Position on the board and brush the cake all over with apricot jam.

2. Roll out the green *Almond Paste* to a strip 1 cm (1/2 in) longer than the string and 1 cm (1/2 in) deeper than the cake. Wrap the *Almond Paste* round the cake so that it extends above the top. Smooth over the join.

3. Roll out the red *Almond Paste* 2 cm (1 in) longer than the string but the same height as the previous strip. Brush the green strip with apricot jam and press the red strip round it as before. Snip along the top edges at intervals with a small pair of scissors and bend in different directions.

4. Arrange the nuts on top of the cake and brush with jam, to glaze. Place the ribbon round the cake

and secure at the back. Stick remaining ribbon round the edge of the board, joinimg it at the back.

GIFT-LADEN CHRISTMAS CAKE

1 x 15 cm (6 in) Basic Fruit Cake *(see page 210)*
1 x 20 cm (8 in) cake board

To cover the cake
Sieved apricot jam
Icing sugar, for dusting
350 g (12 oz) Almond Paste *(see page 211)*
Gin, vodka or boiled water, to brush
350 g (12 oz) ready-to-roll Sugar Paste *(see page 212)*

For the decoration
150 g (6 oz) Almond Paste *(see page 211)*
Icing sugar, for dusting
Concentrated paste food colouring: red and green
Gold string
Gold edible balls
Silver edible balls
Ribbon

1. Follow steps 2 and 3 of *Glittering Star Cake* recipe opposite, to marzipan and ice the cake.

2. Colour half the *Almond Paste* green and the remainder red and knead until smooth. Mould the marzipan into small parcels and press a few gold and silver balls into them. Leave to dry before tying gold string round them and positioning onto the cake. Press more balls, lightly into the icing. Tie the ribbon round the cake and fasten with a bow at the front.

Nut Cluster Christmas Cake

BOXING DAY SPREAD

MUSTARD-GLAZED HAM WITH CRYSTALLISED FRUIT

CHINATOWN TURKEY SALAD

MIXED BEAN SALAD

HERBED POTATO SALAD

SATSUMA AND STILTON SALAD WITH ENDIVE

CARIBBEAN FRUIT SALAD WITH CHESTNUT CREAM

MUSTARD-GLAZED HAM WITH CRYSTALLISED FRUIT

Serves 8

225 g (8 oz) golden caster sugar
150 ml (5 fl oz) cider vinegar
120 ml (4 fl oz) water
3 tablespoons mustard seeds
3.5 kg (8 lb) bone-in half ham
350-450 g (12 oz-1 lb) whole crystallised fruit
Cloves
Bay leaves
Sprigs of thyme

1. Either boil or bake the joint. To boil, cover the joint with cold water, bring to the boil, drain off and cover with fresh water. Bring the water to the boil, reduce the heat, cover and simmer for 2 hours and 40 minutes or until cooked. Remove from the heat and leave in the liquid for 30 minutes. To bake, pre-heat the oven to 170C/325F/Gas 3. Wrap the joint in foil, place in a roasting tin and cook for 3-3$^1/_2$ hours or until the juices run clear.
2. Simmer together the sugar, vinegar and water for 10 minutes until syrupy. Remove from the heat before stirring in the mustard seeds and then allow to cool.
3. Cook the ham according to the supplier's instructions. Once cooked, slice off the rind but leave behind a thin layer of fat. Brush the ham with the syrup.
4. Thinly slice 225–350 g (8–12 oz) of the crystallised fruit and place it over the ham, securing the fruit with the cloves. Arrange the bay leaves and thyme between the fruit.
5. Finely chop the rest of the crystallised fruit and stir it into the remaining syrup. Serve this with the ham.

CHINATOWN TURKEY SALAD

Serves 8

225 g (8 oz) sugarsnap peas
50 g (2 oz) radishes
225 g (8 oz) can water chestnuts
175 g (6 oz) spring onions
350–450 g (12 oz–1 lb) turkey, cooked and sliced
4 tablespoons sunflower oil
3 tablespoons soy sauce
2 tablespoons clear honey
2 tablespoons fresh lime juice
1 tablespoon white wine vinegar
Toasted sesame seeds, to garnish

1. Steam the peas for 2 minutes and then drain.
2. Halve the radishes and drain the water chestnuts before mixing both with the peas in the serving dish.
3. Slice the spring onions lengthways and place these and the turkey slices over the other vegetables.
4. Blend together the oil, soy sauce, honey, lime juice and vinegar. Drizzle some of this over the salad but retain the rest to serve separately. Garnish with the sesame seeds.

MIXED BEAN SALAD

 ### Serves 8

1 shallot, finely chopped
2 garlic cloves, finely chopped
7 tablespoons olive oil
3 tablespoons cider vinegar
1 teaspoon chilli powder
$^1/_2$ teaspoon ground cumin
432 g (15 oz) can chick peas
213 g (7$^1/_2$ oz) can red kidney beans
283 g (10$^1/_2$ oz) can broad beans
220 g (8 oz) can butter beans
$^1/_2$ yellow pepper, seeded and sliced
1 small red chilli pepper, seeded and sliced
1 packet radicchio leaves
Salt and freshly ground black pepper

From the top left clockwise: *Mustard-glazed Ham with Crystallised Fruit, Herbed Potato Salad (page 153), Mixed Bean Salad, Satsuma and Stilton Salad with Endive (page 153)* and *Chinatown Turkey Salad*

1. Place the shallot and garlic in a screw-top jar and add the oil, vinegar, chilli powder, cumin and seasoning. Shake vigorously.
2. Drain the chick peas, kidney beans, broad beans and butter beans and place them in a bowl with the yellow pepper. Toss together with the dressing and the chilli.
3. Arrange the radicchio leaves on a serving plate and spoon the salad over them.

HERBED POTATO SALAD

Serves 8

900 g (2 lb) red potatoes, halved
7 tablespoons olive oil
1 red onion, cut into thin wedges
3 tablespoons tarragon vinegar
2 tablespoons fresh chives, snipped
2 tablespoons fresh tarragon, snipped
2 tablespoons fresh basil, chopped
2 tablespoons fresh parsley, chopped

1. Steam the potatoes for 15 minutes until just tender. Drain and place in a serving bowl.
2. Heat the oil in a small pan and add the onion, frying for 4 minutes until soft. Stir in the tarragon vinegar and cook for a further minute.
3. Remove the pan from the heat and allow to cool slightly before mixing with the potatoes.
4. Sprinkle the herbs over the potatoes and toss together gently.

SATSUMA AND STILTON SALAD WITH ENDIVE

Serves 8

1 curly endive, roughly torn
4 satsumas, peeled, sliced and seeded
225 g (8 oz) Stilton, cut into wedges
100 g (4 oz) fresh dates, stoned
100 g (4 oz) Brazil nuts, toasted and coarsely chopped
6 tablespoons walnut oil
3 tablespoons fresh lemon juice
2 tablespoons clear honey
Salt and freshly ground black pepper
Fresh flatleaf parsley, to garnish

1. Arrange the endive on a serving plate and layer the satsuma slices and Stilton wedges over it.

2. Sprinkle over the dates and nuts and garnish with the parsley.
3. Shake together the oil, lemon juice, honey and seasoning in a screw-top jar. Pour into a bowl and serve separately.

CARIBBEAN FRUIT SALAD WITH CHESTNUT CREAM

Serves 8

175 ml (6 fl oz) fresh orange juice
Juice of 1 lemon
25 g (1 oz) golden caster sugar
1 cinnamon stick
A pinch of nutmeg
1 mango, peeled, stoned and sliced
1 papaya, peeled, stoned and sliced
1 cantaloupe melon, halved and seeded before scooped into balls
1 small pineapple, peeled, cored and cut into wedges
175 g (6 oz) mixed green and red seedless grapes
Coconut slices, to decorate
Chinese gooseberries, to decorate

For the chestnut cream
300 ml (10 fl oz) whipping cream
250 g (9 oz) can sweetened chestnut purée
Ground cinnamon, to decorate

1. Heat the orange and lemon juice with the caster sugar and stir until dissolved.
2. Add the cinnamon stick and nutmeg and boil for 6 minutes. Remove from the heat and discard the cinnamon stick before allowing the syrup to cool.
3. Combine all the fruit, except the coconut slices and Chinese gooseberries, in a serving bowl and pour over the syrup. Cover the bowl and chill.
4. Once chilled, decorate the bowl with the coconut slices and Chinese gooseberries.
5. To make the chestnut cream, fold the chestnut purée into the cream and place in a serving bowl before sprinkling with the ground cinnamon.

Caribbean Fruit Salad with Chestnut Cream

NEW YEAR CELEBRATION

SCONE DOUGH

CREAMY MUSTARD SPLITS
WITH PICKLED HERRINGS

PARSLEY AND LEMON CREAM SPLITS

WITH POACHED SALMON

AVOCADO AND CRACKED PEPPERCORN SPLITS

WITH SMOKED SALMON

TOURTIÈRE

LEEK CHIFFONADE SALAD

RED SALAD

ATHOLL BROSE ICE-CREAM

SCONE DOUGH

This dough makes a lovely base for savoury splits
(see following recipes).
To freeze, place the cooked scones in an airtight
container and freeze for up to 1 month. Return to
room temperature for filling, and split by pulling
apart rather than cutting.

 Makes about 36 scones or 72 splits

350 g (12 oz) self-raising flour
1½ teaspoons baking powder
½ teaspoon salt
75 g (3 oz) cold butter
175 g (6 oz) natural yoghurt
5–6 tablespoons milk
Butter, for greasing

1. Pre-heat the oven to 230C/450F/Gas 8 and
grease 2 baking sheets. Sift the flour, baking
powder and salt into a bowl, then coarsely grate in
the butter and rub in lightly.
2. Blend the yoghurt with 3 tablespoons of milk
and stir into the dry ingredients with a fork,
adding more milk if necessary to form a soft, but
not wet dough.
3. Using floured hands, lightly pat out the dough
on a floured surface to 1 cm (½ in) thick. Stamp out
scones with a 4 cm (1½ in) cutter and transfer to
the baking sheets. You can pat out the trimmings
for a second cutting, but don't do it more than

twice or the scones will be heavy and chewy.
4. Bake the scones for 8–10 minutes until risen and
golden, then cool on a wire rack.

CREAMY MUSTARD SPLITS WITH PICKLED HERRINGS

Makes 24

1 tablespoon wholegrain mustard
150 g (5 oz) Greek yoghurt
12 scones, split (see Scone Dough, left)
4 pickled herring fillets, drained and cut into 2.5 cm
(1 in) pieces
24 thin radish slices
4 cucumber slices, each cut into 6 wedges

1. Mix the mustard and yoghurt and spread over the scone halves. Top each half with a piece of herring and garnish with radish slices and cucumber wedges.

PARSLEY AND LEMON CREAM SPLITS WITH POACHED SALMON

Makes 24

6 fresh parsley sprigs
225 g (8 oz) fresh salmon
Juice and grated rind of 1 lemon
Salt
200 ml (7 fl oz) crème fraîche
12 scones, split (see Scone Dough, *left)*

1. Pull the leaves from the parsley sprigs. Place the stalks in a small pan with the salmon, lemon juice, salt and enough water to cover. Poach the salmon gently until just cooked, then cool on a plate. Skin, bone and coarsely flake the salmon.
2. Chop the parsley leaves and mix with the lemon rind. Spread each scone half with the crème fraîche, sprinkle with the parsley mixture and top with flaked salmon.

From the left: *Leek Chiffonade Salad (page 157), Red Salad (page 158),* Creamy Mustard Splits with Pickled Herrings, Parsley and Lemon Cream Splits with Poached Salmon, *Avocado and Cracked Peppercorn Splits with Smoked Salmon (page 156)* and *Tourtière (page 156)*

AVOCADO AND CRACKED PEPPERCORN SPLITS WITH SMOKED SALMON

The topping should be made no more than a couple of hours before serving as the avocados will discolour. Otherwise, store in a covered container with plastic film pressed on to the surface.

Makes 24

1 teaspoon black peppercorns
2 avocados, very ripe (but not discoloured), peeled, stoned and halved
Juice of 1 lime
2–3 tablespoons olive oil
12 scones, split (see Scone Dough *page 154)*
50 g (2 oz) smoked salmon, cut into thin strips
Salt and freshly ground black pepper
Snipped fresh chives, to garnish

1. Crack the peppercorns coarsely with a pestle and mortar. Mash the avocado flesh with the lime juice and enough olive oil to make a creamy mixture. Stir in the peppercorns and salt.
2. Spread each scone half with the avocado mixture and curl a strip of smoked salmon on top. Garnish with snipped fresh chives and freshly ground black pepper.

TOURTIÈRE

Tourtière, a rich, golden pie of mixed minced meats and sweet spices, is part of the Canadian Christmas tradition. It can be served at room temperature or warmed through, making it a dream dish for buffet party cooks.

Much of the preparation is done in advance, as both the pastry and meat must be chilled when the tart is assembled. Flaky pastry is time-consuming to make as it needs to be rolled several times at intervals of at least 20 minutes. Fortunately, it can be made several days in advance and kept chilled or frozen. You could also buy ready-made, frozen flaky pastry to defrost and roll out. Traditionally the meat filling is a mixture of pork and poultry or veal, but you can use left-over cooked turkey – add it at a later stage though. Wild boar, available from large supermarkets, makes a special contribution to the flavour, so does the pancetta or bacon, though bacon is not a traditional ingredient. Canadians use the distinctively

flavoured herb savory in the filling, but as it's not easy to obtain, dried sage is a good substitute.
Cook stage 1 for 20 minutes and stage 2 for 15 minutes at 200C if using a fan oven.
You can freeze the *Tourtière* unbaked for up to 1 month. To cook, thaw for 2 hours and bake as from step 8.

Serves 12

For the flaky pastry
300 g (11 oz) plain flour
1 teaspoon salt
100 g (4 oz) lard
1 teaspoon lemon juice
100 g (4 oz) butter

For the filling
500 g (1$^1/_4$ lb raw minced wild boar or pork
500 g (1$^1/_4$ lb raw or cooked minced turkey or chicken
2 tablespoons vegetable oil
1 large onion, finely chopped
50 g (2 oz) butter
2 garlic cloves
1 teaspoon dried savory or sage
1 teaspoon ground cinnamon
1 teaspoon ground allspice
$^1/_2$ teaspoon ground cloves
350 g (12 oz) potatoes, diced
400 ml (14 fl oz) poultry stock
25 g (1 oz) plain flour
4 tablespoons medium sherry
120g–150 g (4$^1/_2$–5 oz) pancetta or thinly cut streaky bacon, rinded
2 tablespoons milk
1 egg yolk
Salt and freshly ground black pepper

To garnish
Bay leaves
Rosemary sprigs

1. Make the pastry: sift the flour and salt together, then rub in 50 g (2 oz) lard. Add about 120 ml (4 fl oz) iced water and the lemon juice and mix to a soft but not sticky dough, adding more iced water if necessary. Knead until smooth, place in a plastic bag and chill for 20 minutes. Using a firm-bladed knife, mix the remaining lard and butter on a plate. Chill.
2. Roll out the dough on a floured surface to an oblong 60 x 20 cm (24 x 8 in), brushing off any surplus flour. Cut one third of the mixed fat into

small flakes and dot over two thirds of the length of the pastry, keeping within 1 cm (¹/₂ in) of the edge. Fold up the buttered or larded bottom third and fold down the top third to sandwich the fat in two layers. Press the edges with a rolling pin to seal, return to the plastic bag and chill for 20 minutes.

3. Uncover the pastry on a well-floured surface, turn the folded edge to the right and repeat rolling and dotting as before with half of the remaining fat. Fold as before, seal the edges and chill in the plastic bag for 20 minutes.

4. Repeat step 3, using the remaining fat. Chill in the plastic bag for at least 30 minutes or preferably overnight.

5. To make the filling, combine the meats if both are raw. If the turkey is cooked, reserve it for a later stage. Heat the oil in a large pan and gently fry the onion and half of the butter until it softens and starts turning golden.

6. Add the garlic and savory or sage and fry for a few seconds, then add the raw minced meat and spices and stir until the mince separates and changes colour. Add the potatoes and stock and bring to the boil. If you are using cooked turkey, add it for the last 5 minutes of the cooking time.

7. Strain the stock into a bowl and leave the meat to cool. Melt the remaining butter in a pan, stir in the flour and cook for 1 minute over a low heat. Remove from the heat and gradually add about half of the stock, stirring between each addition. Return to the heat and add the remaining stock. Bring to the boil, stirring, then add the sherry. Raise the heat a little and leave to bubble for 10–15 minutes until slightly thickened. Check the seasoning, leave to cool, then mix into the meat and chill before assembling the tart.

8. Pre-heat the oven to 220C/425F/Gas 7. Thoroughly grease a 30 cm (12 in) square baking sheet or a 35 cm (14 in) pizza plate. Cut the pastry in half and roll out one piece to a 35 cm (14 in) circle; transfer to the baking sheet or pizza plate. Spread half of the pancetta or bacon over the pastry to within 5cm (2 in) of the edge, then spread the meat evenly on top. Roll out the remaining pastry to a circle to cover the meat, then press the edges to seal, roll in and pinch or press with a fork to make a border. Re-roll the trimmings, cut into decorative leaves and stick to the pie using a little milk. Bake for 20 minutes.

9. Mix the remaining milk with the egg yolk in a small bowl. Carefully remove the pie from the oven (it may be safest to lift out the whole oven shelf, as

the pie is very brittle at this stage). Generously brush the surface of the pie with the egg mixture and continue until all of it is used up – this will give the pie a rich, golden glaze. Return the pie to the oven for about 20 minutes until the pastry is firm and shiny, then leave to cool slightly. Serve warm or at room temperature on the baking sheet or plate, garlanded with several bay leaves and rosemary sprigs.

Tourtière

LEEK CHIFFONADE SALAD

                    Serves 12

1 kg (2¹/₄ lb) trimmed leeks, cut into thin strips, lengthways
120 ml (4 fl oz) olive oil
Juice of 2 lemons
4 tablespoons chopped fresh parsley
3 eggs, hard boiled
50 g (2 oz) black olives, pitted
Salt and freshly ground black pepper

1. Bring a large pan of lightly salted water to the boil and drop in the leek strips. Return to the boil and cook for 3 minutes. Turn and push down the strips with a wooden spoon to keep them submerged. Drain, then dry in a salad spinner or squeeze gently in a tea towel. Transfer to a bowl and dress with the oil, lemon juice, parsley and seasoning.

2. Place the leeks in a wide bowl or spread them out on a serving platter. Chop the eggs roughly and scatter over, then dot with the black olives.

RED SALAD

Serves 12

12 large radicchio leaves
1 kg (2¼ lb) cooked beetroot, thinly sliced
2 red onions, thinly sliced

For the dressing
50 g (2 oz) walnuts, finely chopped
3 tablespoons cranberry sauce
juice of 1 large orange
1 tablespoon fresh lemon juice
2 teaspoons raspberry vinegar
3 tablespoons walnut oil
5 tablespoons olive oil
1 teaspoon ground coriander
Salt and freshly ground black pepper

1. Spread the radicchio leaves on a wide platter and fill each leaf with beetroot slices. Arrange a ring or two of red onion on top.

2. To make the dressing, shake together the dressing ingredients in a screw-top jar. Pour over the salad to serve.

ATHOLL BROSE ICE-CREAM

This is an old-fashioned Scottish dessert.

Serves 12

600 ml (1 pint) milk
1 vanilla pod or 2–3 drops vanilla essence
5 egg yolks
100 g (4 oz) vanilla sugar or caster sugar
50 g (2 oz) medium oatmeal
50 g (2 oz) granulated sugar
300 ml (10 fl oz) double cream

For the sauce
3 tablespoons clear honey
3 tablespoons whisky
450 g (1 lb) frozen raspberries, thawed

1. Add the vanilla pod, if using, to the milk and bring to the boil in a large pan. Whisk the egg yolks with the vanilla or caster sugar in a heatproof bowl until pale and thick, then stir in the hot milk.

2. Place the bowl over a pan of simmering water and stir until the mixture thickens to coat the back of a wooden spoon – this will take about 30 minutes. Leave to cool.

3. Remove the vanilla pod or stir in the vanilla essence and freeze the mixture in its bowl for 1 hour. Meanwhile, mix the oatmeal and granulated sugar on a baking sheet and toast under a pre-heated grill, stirring frequently with a fork, until the sugar caramelises. Break into large crumbs with a fork. Leave to cool, then chill.

4. Whip the cream to soft peaks. Beat the partially frozen custard to loosen it slightly, stir in the oatmeal and fold in the cream. Return to the freezer for 1 hour.

5. Beat the ice-cream again, transfer to a 1.5 litre (2¹/₂ pint) ring mould, slide it into a freezer bag and freeze until firm.

6. On the day of the party, warm the honey and whisky in a pan and stir until blended, then leave to cool. Chill a serving plate big enough to take the ring mould.

7. Just before serving, remove the ice-cream from the freezer and run a thin knife around the inner and outer edges of the mould. Invert on to the chilled serving plate while pressing a tea towel, wrung out in hot water, on to the top of the mould for 30 seconds. Carefully lift the mould from the ice cream, heap raspberries into the centre and drizzle over the whisky sauce.

Atholl Brose Ice-cream

COUNTDOWN

Up to 1 month in advance
- Make the *Atholl Brose Ice-cream* and freeze.
- Prepare and assemble the *Tourtière* and freeze unbaked.
- Make and bake the *Scones*. Freeze in bags.

Up to 2 days in advance
- If you haven't already frozen the *Tourtière*, make the pastry, place in a sealed plastic bag. Chill.
- Prepare and cook the filling for the *Tourtière*. Chill.

The day before
- Prepare, cook and dress the leeks for the *Leek Chiffonade Salad*; chill in a covered dish.
- Make the dressing for the *Red Salad*. Chill.
- Make the *Creamy Mustard* and *Parsley and Lemon Cream* fillings. Chill until required.
- Allow the *Tourtière* to thaw in the fridge if it is frozen; otherwise assemble and chill.
- Chill the white wine.

1–2 hours before
- Thaw the scones and raspberries.
- Make the whisky sauce.
- Cook the fresh salmon.
- Make the *Avocado and Cracked Peppercorn* filling and chill.
- Bake the *Tourtière*.
- Prepare the *Red Salad* and arrange in a serving bowl.
- Hard boil the eggs and garnish the *Leek Chiffonade Salad*.
- Assemble the fish splits.
- Open the red wine and leave it to come to room temperature.

Just before serving
- Garnish the *Tourtière*.
- Dress the *Red Salad*.
- Unmould the ice-cream and decorate with the raspberries. Pour over the whisky sauce.

EASTER LAMB LUNCH

MIXED MUSHROOMS IN BREAD CASES

SPICED PRAWNS WITH MANGO SALAD

ROAST LAMB WITH A HERB AND PINE NUT CRUST

CARROT, RED PEPPER AND PARSNIP BUNDLES

PEAS WITH SPINACH AND SHALLOTS

WHITE AND DARK CHOCOLATE MOUSSE

TROPICAL CARAMEL CREAM

There is a choice of starters, one more substantial than the other, for this Easter menu with lamb.

MIXED MUSHROOMS IN BREAD CASES

Some supermarkets now sell packets of mixed mushrooms which are ideal for this starter.

 Serves 6-8

6-8 soft white bread rolls
75 g (3 oz) butter
1 shallot, chopped
350 g (12 oz) mixed mushrooms, such as chestnut,
oyster and shiitake
1 tablespoon Madeira
150 ml (5 fl oz) double cream
Salt and freshly ground black pepper
A selection of salad leaves, to serve
1 tablespoon snipped fresh chives, to garnish

1. Pre-heat the oven to 200C/400F/Gas 6. Cut the tops off the bread rolls and, using kitchen scissors or a small sharp knife, snip around 1 cm (1/2 in) inside the top of each roll. Scoop out the centres of each one to make a case.
2. Melt 50 g (2 oz) of the butter and brush all over the bread cases. Bake for 10–12 minutes or until crisp and golden.
3. Melt the remaining butter and fry the shallot until softened. Add the mushrooms and cook gently for 5 minutes. Stir in the Madeira and cream and season to taste. Cook for a few minutes until the cream reduces and thickens.
4. Fill the bread cases with the warm mushroom mixture and arrange on individual plates with the salad leaves. Sprinkle over the chives and serve hot.

Spiced Prawns and Mango Salad and *Mixed Mushrooms in Bread Cases*

Roast Lamb with a Herb and Pine Nut Crust, Carrot Bundles
(page 162) and *Peas with Spinach and Shallots (page 163)*

SPICED PRAWNS WITH MANGO SALAD

Bags of ready-prepared salad leaves are available in most large supermarkets, making this starter particularly quick to make.

Serves 6-8

50 g (2 oz) mixed salad leaves
5 cm (2 in) piece cucumber, sliced
1 large mango, peeled and thinly sliced

For the dressing
4 tablespoons Greek yoghurt
1 tablespoon lime juice
1 tablespoon groundnut oil
25 g (1 oz) butter
1 garlic clove, crushed
2 teaspoons mild curry paste
675 g (1½ lb) large cooked peeled prawns, thawed if frozen
Salt and freshly ground black pepper
Chopped fresh coriander, to garnish

1. Divide the salad leaves among 4 individual plates and scatter over the cucumber. Arrange the mango on top, then chill until ready to serve.
2. To make the salad dressing, mix together the yoghurt, lime juice, oil and seasoning in a small bowl, then chill.

3. Melt the butter in a large frying pan and fry the garlic for 30 seconds. Stir in the curry paste, toss in the prawns and fry until heated through.
4. Arrange the warm prawns over the mango salad mixture. Drizzle over the dressing and sprinkle with the coriander. Serve at once.

ROAST LAMB WITH A HERB AND PINE NUT CRUST

Because lamb tends to be rather fatty, it is ideal served with steamed or boiled new potatoes. If you are cooking the whole menu make sure you read the *Carrot, Red Pepper and Parsnip Bundles* recipe on page 162 as the vegetables need to be cooked with the lamb.

Serves 6–8

½ tablespoon olive oil
2 garlic cloves, chopped
50 g (2 oz) fresh white breadcrumbs
25 g (1 oz) pine nuts, finely chopped
25 g (1 oz) fresh parsley, chopped
15 g (½ oz) fresh rosemary, chopped
2 kg (4½ lb) leg of lamb
Salt and freshly ground black pepper

For the gravy
2 tablespoons pan juices
1 tablespoon plain flour
1 teaspoon wholegrain mustard
150 ml (5 fl oz) red wine
300 ml (10 fl oz) vegetable water or stock
1 tablespoon redcurrant jelly

1. Pre-heat oven to 180C/350F/Gas 4. Heat the oil, add the garlic and cook for 2 minutes until well softened. Stir in the breadcrumbs, pine nuts and herbs and cook for 1–2 minutes. Season well.
2. Place the lamb in a roasting tin and press the herb mixture evenly over the skin. Roast for 20 minutes per 450 g (1 lb) plus 20 minutes (approximately 2 hours for a 2 kg (4$^{1}/_{2}$ lb) joint).
3. Check the lamb after an hour and cover loosely with foil if it has become too brown.
4. When the lamb is cooked, keep it warm while you make the gravy. Pour the roasting pan juices into a pan and stir in the flour and mustard. Continue to stir over a low heat for 2 minutes until the gravy thickens.
5. Gradually add the wine and water or stock to the pan, stirring until smooth. Bring to the boil, then simmer for 10 minutes.

6. Stir in the redcurrant jelly, season to taste and simmer for 2 minutes. Serve with the lamb and vegetable accompaniments.

CARROT, RED PEPPER AND PARSNIP BUNDLES

 Serves 6–8

450 g (1 lb) each of parsnips cut into sticks, 7.5 cm (3 in) long
450 g (1 lb) carrots cut into sticks, 7.5 cm (3 in) long
1 red pepper, seeded and sliced into sticks
2 long leeks, split in half lengthways and separated into leaves

1. Blanch all the vegetables in boiling water for about 1 minute.
2. Tie bundles of the vegetables with strips of leek. Arrange around your leg of lamb and cook for 45 minutes, basting with pan juices.

Tropical Caramel Cream and *White and Dark Chocolate Mousse*

PEAS WITH SPINACH AND SHALLOTS

 Serves 6–8

450 g (1 lb) spinach
25 g (1 oz) butter
3 shallots, sliced
450 g (1 lb) frozen peas
2 tablespoons crème fraîche
A pinch of nutmeg
Salt and freshly ground black pepper

1. Rinse the spinach well, then drain and cook in a covered pan with no extra water for about 5 minutes until tender. Drain well and chop roughly.
2. Heat the butter in a pan and fry the shallots for 5 minutes until tender, add the peas and cook for 3–4 minutes. Stir in the spinach and heat through. Stir in the crème fraîche and seasoning and sprinkle with nutmeg.

WHITE AND DARK CHOCOLATE MOUSSE

 Serves 6-8

175 g (6 oz) Madeira cake
2 tablespoons brandy
1 tablespoon cold, strong, black coffee
175 g (6 oz) plain chocolate, broken into pieces
175 g (6 oz) white chocolate, broken into pieces
450 ml (15 fl oz) double cream

For the decoration
50 g (2 oz) plain chocolate, broken into pieces
50 g (2 oz) white chocolate, broken into pieces

1. Grease and line the base of a 20 cm (8 in) loose-bottomed cake tin. Line the sides with a strip of foil. Slice the Madeira cake and use to line the base and sides of the cake tin, cutting it to fit. Mix the brandy and coffee and drizzle over the base.
2. Melt the chocolate in 2 separate heatproof bowls over 2 pans of hot water. Whip the cream until it holds its shape, then divide between 2 bowls. Stir the plain chocolate into 1 bowl of cream and the white chocolate into the other.
3. Spoon alternate blobs of white and plain chocolate mousse into the cake tin and swirl into each other with a skewer. Smooth over the top, then chill for at least 2 hours before serving.
4. To decorate, melt the plain and white chocolate in 2 separate bowls over hot water. Cover a rolling pin with a piece of oiled foil and drizzle the chocolate on to it in alternate zig-zag lines. Leave it to set at room temperature.
5. Carefully remove the mousse from the tin and peel off the foil. Place on a serving plate and press the chocolate decorations around the sides. Chill until ready to serve.

TROPICAL CARAMEL CREAM

 Serves 6-8

2 bananas, cut into chunks
1 pineapple, cored and cut into chunks
1 Charentais melon, halved, seeded and cut into chunks
2 passion fruit, halved, with the flesh and pips scooped out
2 tablespoons dark rum
5 tablespoons orange juice
300 ml (10 fl oz) double cream
300 g (10 oz) Greek yoghurt
100 g (4 oz) caster sugar

1. Mix together the banana, pineapple, melon and passion fruit, flesh and pips in a glass bowl. Sprinkle over the rum and orange juice.
2. Whip the cream and fold into the yoghurt. Spread over the fruit mixture and chill.
3. Place the sugar into a small pan with 2 tablespoons of water. Heat gently, stirring until the sugar has dissolved. Boil rapidly, without stirring, until the syrup turns a light caramel colour.
4. Remove the pan from the heat and leave to stand for about 2 minutes or until the caramel darkens to a rich golden brown, then drizzle uneven shapes over a sheet of oiled foil.
5. Leave to cool and harden for at least 30 minutes. Peel off the foil and stick the caramel shapes into the cream mixture just before serving.

EASTER BAKING

HOT CROSS BUNS

EASTER BISCUITS

ALMOND CUSTARD TARTS

SPICED FRUIT RING

EASTER CAKE

When we think of Easter, we tend to conjure up images of all kinds of chocolate confections, but there is much traditional Easter fare that is well worth baking. Make our spicy hot cross buns, fruit ring with its luscious glaze and rich fruit cake and the chocolates will stay in their boxes while your guests come back for second helpings of your Easter baking!

HOT CROSS BUNS

                    Makes 12

450 g (1 lb) strong plain white flour
75 g (3 oz) butter, diced
1 sachet easy-blend dried yeast
1 teaspoon salt
1 teaspoon ground cinnamon
1¹⁄₂ teaspoons mixed spice
50 g (2 oz) golden caster sugar
50 g (2 oz) currants
25 g (1 oz) sultanas
25 g (1 oz) chopped mixed peel
1 egg, beaten
300 ml (10 fl oz) warm milk
50 g (2 oz) plain flour

For the glaze
4 tablespoons each milk and water, mixed
3 tablespoons golden caster sugar

1. Pre-heat the oven to 200C/400F/Gas 6. Sift the strong plain flour into a warm mixing bowl. Rub in the butter, then stir in the yeast, salt, spices, sugar, fruit and mixed peel, mixing well.
2. Gradually add the egg and enough milk to mix to a smooth dough. Turn on to a floured surface and knead for 5 minutes.
3. Divide the dough into 12 and roll the pieces into

rounds. Place well spaced on an oiled baking sheet. Leave, covered with a tea towel, in a warm place for about 1 hour to double in size.
4. Make a dough with the plain flour and a little water. Roll out thinly and cut into strips. Using a little water, fix pastry crosses to the risen buns
5. Bake for 15–20 minutes until golden brown, then transfer to a wire rack. Heat the milk and water with the sugar until the sugar dissolves, then brush over the warm buns. Leave to dry for a few minutes, then glaze again. Serve warm or toasted.

EASTER BISCUITS

                    Makes 12

50 g (2 oz) butter, diced
25 g (1 oz) white vegetable fat, diced
100 g (4 oz) plain flour
50 g (2 oz) golden caster sugar
100 g (4 oz) currants
15 g (¹⁄₂ oz) chopped mixed peel
Juice and grated rind of ¹⁄₂ lemon
¹⁄₄ teaspoon ground cinnamon
1 egg, beaten
1 tablespoon brandy, optional

1. Pre-heat the oven to 200C/400F/Gas 6. Cut the butter and fat into the flour using a round-bladed knife, then stir in the sugar, currants, peel, lemon juice and rind and cinnamon.
2. Add the egg and brandy (if using) and mix to a firm dough. Roll out thinly and stamp out 7.5 cm (3 in) rounds. Bake on a greased baking sheet for 15–20 minutes until pale golden brown. Leave for 5 minutes, then transfer to a wire rack to cool. Store in an airtight container.

ALMOND CUSTARD TARTS

                    Makes 6

40 g (1¹⁄₂ oz) butter
75 g (3 oz) plain flour
85 ml (3 fl oz) milk
1 egg, beaten
2 tablespoons golden caster sugar
¹⁄₄ teaspoon almond essence
Grated rind of ¹⁄₂ lemon
15 g (¹⁄₂ oz) flaked almonds
Icing sugar, for dusting

1. Pre-heat the oven to 200C/400F/Gas 6 and grease six 7.5 cm (3 in) brioche tins.
2. Rub the butter into the flour, then bind to a firm dough with about 2 tablespoons of water. Roll out the pastry thinly and cut out 6 rounds large enough to line the brioche tins (roll again as necessary). Prick all over, chill for 10 minutes, line with baking paper and fill with baking beans.
3. Bake the pastry cases for 10 minutes. Remove the paper and beans and bake for a further 10 minutes. Remove from the oven and reduce the temperature to 180C/350F/Gas 4.

4. Whisk the next 5 ingredients and pour into the cases. Scatter with almonds and bake for about 15–20 minutes until just set. Dust with icing sugar and serve warm or cold.

From the top left clockwise: *Almond Custard Tarts, Easter Biscuits, Hot Cross Buns, Easter Cake (page 166)* and *Spiced Fruit Ring (page 166)*

SPICED FRUIT RING

Makes one 25 cm (10 in) cake

225 g (8 oz) strong plain flour
2 teaspoons easy-blend dried yeast
1/2 teaspoon salt
25 g (1 oz) light muscovado sugar
1 teaspoon finely grated lemon rind
25 g (1 oz) butter, melted
1 egg, beaten
100 ml (4 fl oz) hand-hot milk
25 g (1 oz) golden caster sugar, for glazing
75 g (3 oz) icing sugar, sifted

For the filling
75 g (3 oz) glacé cherries, washed and chopped
25 g (1 oz) sultanas
50 g (2 oz) ready-to-eat dried apricots, chopped
25 g (1 oz) angelica, washed and chopped
75 g (3 oz) flaked almonds, chopped
25 g (1 oz) light muscovado sugar
1 teaspoon ground cinnamon
1/2 teaspoon mixed spice

1. Sift the flour into a bowl, stir in the yeast, salt, muscovado sugar and rind, then stir in the melted butter, egg and enough milk to form a soft dough. Knead for 5–10 minutes until smooth. Leave in a warm place to rise for 30 minutes, then knock back the dough and roll out into a 30 x 45 cm (12 x 18 in) rectangle.
2. To make the filling, mix together the fruit, angelica and almonds. Reserve 3 tablespoons and mix the rest with the sugar and spices. Sprinkle over the dough and roll up from one long side.
3. Place the roll on a greased baking sheet and curve into a circle. Dampen the ends and stick together. Snip halfway through at 2.5 cm (1 in) intervals and turn each section slightly.
4. Cover with oiled cling film and leave in a warm place for 1 hour or until doubled in size. Pre-heat the oven to 200C/400F/Gas 6. Remove the film and bake for 25 minutes or until golden.
5. Dissolve the caster sugar in 2 tablespoons of water and bring to the boil. Brush over the ring, leave to dry, then repeat.
6. Blend the icing sugar with a little water and drizzle over the top. Scatter with the reserved fruit and nuts and leave to set.

EASTER CAKE

Petal or flower paste and the flower cutters are available from cake decorating suppliers. You could also use ready-to-roll icing but it won't roll out as thinly or set hard.

Makes 1 x 20 cm (8 in) cake

225 g (8 oz) butter or margarine, softened
225 g (8 oz) light muscovado sugar
4 eggs, lightly beaten
275 g (10 oz) plain flour
1/2 teaspoon baking powder
1 1/2 teaspoons ground mixed spice
500 g (1 1/4 lb) dried mixed fruit
175 g (6 oz) Almond Paste (see page 211)

To decorate
2 tablespoons apricot jam, melted
370 g (12 oz) Almond Paste (see page 211)
100 g (4 oz) Flower Paste (see page 212)
Concentrated paste food colouring: burgundy, violet, black, yellow and green
Cornflour, for dusting
1 anenome-shaped flower cutter
2 teaspoons golden caster sugar
1 egg white, lightly beaten
1 primrose-shaped flower cutter

Spiced Fruit Ring

1 ivy leaf-shaped cutter
Florist's wire
Green dusting powder
Glacé icing, made from icing sugar with a little water

1. Pre-heat the oven to 160C/325F/Gas 3. Grease and line a 20 cm (8 in) hexagonal cake tin. Beat the fat and sugar until pale and fluffy, then beat in the eggs a little at a time. Fold in the flour, baking powder and mixed spice, then stir in the dried fruit.
2. Spoon half of the mixture into the tin. Roll out the *Almond Paste* to fit neatly inside and place on top of the mixture. Spoon in the remaining cake mixture and smooth.
3. Bake for 3–3¹/₂ hours or until a skewer comes out clean from the centre. Leave to cool in the tin, then turn out and wrap in greaseproof paper and foil until ready to decorate.
4. To decorate, place the cake on a cake board. Brush the jam over the top. Draw around the tin on greaseproof paper and, using a saucer as a guide, draw semi-circles against each straight edge to make scallops. Roll out the *Almond Paste* and cut out to the shape on the paper. Lift and smooth down over the cake. Use the trimmings to make long thin ropes and twist together. Press on to the cake to form an edging to the *Almond Paste*.
5. Divide the *Flower Paste* into quarters, colour 1 piece burgundy and 1 piece violet. Roll out each one on a surface dusted with cornflour. Using the flower cutters, cut out 6 anenomes from each colour. Thin the edge of each petal with a balling tool or the end of a paintbrush. Keep the other flowers covered with clingfilm to prevent drying out. Press together in pairs so that the petals alternate and place in bun trays lined with non-stick baking paper.
6. Colour small amounts of the anenome trimmings black and roll into 6 balls. Mix half of the sugar with black colouring, then roll the balls in egg white, then in black sugar. Place in the centre of the anenomes.
7. For the primroses, colour half of one of the remaining pieces of *Flower Paste* pale yellow and the other half an even paler yellow. Make 8 large darker and 25 small paler cones of paste. Flatten the thick ends and pinch the edges until really thin to make Mexican hat shapes. Roll out the thin edges with a round pencil. Place primrose cutters over the cones and stamp out flowers. Press the end of a thin knitting needle into the centre of each to make a star and paint the centres with yellow colouring. Place these in bun trays lined with non-

Easter Cake

stick baking paper.
8. To make the mimosa, roll yellow trimmings into 6 small balls. Mix the remaining sugar with yellow colouring, and then roll balls in egg white, then in yellow sugar.
9. Colour the remaining paste pale green and roll out on a surface dusted with cornflour. Using the ivy cutter, stamp out 26 leaves, pinch very lightly to shape and insert florist's wire into 18 of them. Place the leaves on non-stick baking paper.
10. Allow the leaves and flowers to dry overnight. Brush the ivy leaves with green dusting powder. Twist together the wired leaves into sprays of 3, snip the wires and arrange on the cake with the other leaves and flowers, as pictured, securing with the glacé icing.

SILVER WEDDING CELEBRATION

SILVER WEDDING CAKE

STUFFED SALMON FILLETS WITH GRAPES

LITTLE GEM SALADS

LEEK AND ONION SCONES WITH SMOKED MACKEREL

CHICK PEA AND PIMIENTO DIP IN BREAD BOWLS

CELEBRATION KING PRAWNS

PROSCIUTTO AND PARMESAN TARTLETS

HERBY BRIE TART

SAVOURY CHOUX PYRAMID

SUMMER FRUIT GALETTES

RASPBERRY AND AMARETTI TRIFLES

SILVER WEDDING CAKE

This cake can be frozen, uniced, for up to 3 months.

 Serves 24

500 g (1¹/₄ lb) butter, softened
500 g (1¹/₄ lb) caster sugar
10 eggs
500 g (1¹/₄ lb) self-raising flour, sifted
Finely grated rind of 4 lemons

For the decoration
50 cm (20 in) round cake board
350 g (12 oz) apricot jam
1.75 kg (4 lb) ready-to-roll Sugar Paste (see page 212)
Cornflour, for dusting
Icing sugar
2.5 metres (2¹/₂ yards) silver ribbon
Fresh edible flowers, such as roses, pansies, marigolds
1 egg white, beaten
50 g (2 oz) caster sugar

1. Pre-heat oven to 180C/350F/Gas 4. Make the numbers one at a time. To make the number 2: grease a 20 cm (8 in) ring tin and grease, line the base and assemble two 7.5 x 13–15 cm (3 x 5–6 in) rectangles or one 15 cm (6 in) square cake tin.
2. Beat together half the butter and half the sugar until pale and fluffy. Beat in 5 eggs, one at a time. Fold in half the flour, then stir in half the lemon rind.

Silver Wedding Cake shapes

3. Divide the cake mixture among the prepared tins and spread level. Bake for 30–35 minutes until well risen and springy to the touch. Leave to cool in the tins for 2 minutes, then turn out on to a wire rack. Remove the lining papers and leave the cakes to cool completely.
4. To make the number 5: grease and line the base of the tins again and make up the cake mixture as before using remaining cake ingredients. If using 15 cm (6 in) square tins, cut each cake in half to make 4 oblongs.
5. To make the numbers, cut the cakes (as shown in the picture, top) and assemble on the cake board. Heat the jam with 1 tablespoon of water, then press through a sieve. Brush all over the cakes.
6. Roll out 900 g (2 lb) of the *Sugar Paste* to a 38 cm (15 in) circle and carefully lift it over one of the cakes. Start by easing it into the recess areas, smoothing the paste downwards and stretching it

Silver Wedding Cake

out at the same time until it covers the sides. Roughly trim off excess. Dust your hands with cornflour and smooth the paste to eliminate any creases. Trim excess paste from around the base of the cakes.

7. Use the remaining *Sugar Paste* to ice the second cake in the same way. Blend a little icing sugar with a few drops of water until stiff. Use tiny dots of the icing to stick the silver ribbon around the base of the cakes.

8. To crystallise the flowers: brush with a little egg white, then dip in caster sugar. Shake off the excess sugar; place on greaseproof paper and leave to dry in a cool place for 1–2 hours. Stick the flowers on to the cakes with icing.

Stuffed Salmon Fillets with Grapes

To skin and fillet salmon, lay it on a board and cut off the head just below the gills. Ease the top fillet away from the backbone with a sharp knife, then remove bones. Cut the skin along the belly to free it. To loosen bottom fillet, cut through the backbone at tail end. Lift the backbone and pull it up gently, taking as many small bones as possible – any remaining bones can be removed with tweezers or pliers. To skin fillets, loosen the skin at the tail and grip firmly. Insert a knife between the flesh and skin then push flesh away with a sawing action.

Serves 24

2 salmon, weighing about 2 kg (4½ lb) each, skinned and filleted

600 g (1 lb 5 oz) full-fat soft cheese
175 g (6 oz) white seedless grapes, halved
175 g (6 oz) red or black seedless grapes, halved
3 tablespoons chopped fresh tarragon
150 ml (5 fl oz) apple juice
2 teaspoons pink peppercorns, crushed

To garnish
Tarragon sprigs
Salad leaves
Grapes

1. Pre-heat the oven to 180C/350F/Gas 4. Lay the salmon on a board and trim if necessary.

2. Beat the cheese until soft, add the grapes and tarragon then mix well. Spread the mixture evenly over 2 salmon fillets. Lay the remaining fillets on top to enclose the filling, reversing them so that the thick and thin edges touch. Cut each fillet into 12 slices with a sharp knife. Lay the slices flat in an ovenproof dish and shape into neat ovals. Chill.

3. Pour some apple juice around the salmon, brushing a little over the flesh but not the filling. Sprinkle with the crushed pink peppercorns.

4. Cover with foil and bake for 15–20 minutes. Remove the foil, brush the salmon with apple juice, then leave to cool in the liquid. To serve, transfer to a serving platter and garnish with tarragon sprigs, salad leaves and grapes.

From the left: *Stuffed Salmon Fillets with Grapes, Little Gem Salads (page 170), Leek and Onion Scones with Smoked Mackerel (page 170)* and *Chick Pea and Pimiento Dip in Bread Bowls (page 170)*

LITTLE GEM SALADS

Little Gem lettuces are small, crisp and well
flavoured, like tiny Cos. Use any other crisp lettuce
if they're unavailable.

 Makes 24–30

*1.5 kg (3 lb) mixed mushrooms, such as oyster, brown
cap, button and shiitake*
550 ml (18 fl oz) olive oil
6 garlic cloves, crushed
2 tablespoons wholegrain mustard
6 tablespoons raspberry vinegar or lemon juice
8 Little Gem lettuces
50 g (2 oz) sesame seeds, toasted
225 g (8 oz) cherry tomatoes
Salt and freshly ground black pepper
400 g (14 oz) Greek yoghurt, to serve

To garnish
Chopped fresh herbs
Paprika

1. Slice the mushrooms and place in a large bowl –
don't slice them too thinly or it will spoil the
texture of the salad. Shake together the oil, garlic,
mustard, vinegar or lemon juice and seasoning in a
screw-top jar. Pour over the mushrooms and stir to
coat. Cover and chill overnight.
2. Separate the lettuce leaves, wash and shake dry.
Arrange on a serving plate, placing 2 leaves
together to form cups. Lift the mushrooms from the
marinade and spoon into the lettuce cups. Sprinkle
with sesame seeds and scatter the tomatoes
around.
3. Spoon the yoghurt into a small side dish and
garnish with chopped fresh herbs and paprika.

LEEK AND ONION SCONES WITH SMOKED MACKEREL

For vegetarian friends, omit the mackerel and use
puréed, cooked mushrooms or red pesto to flavour
the fromage frais. These scones can be frozen for
up to 1 month.

Makes 60

1 tablespoon olive oil
1 onion, chopped

1 leek, sliced
A pinch of sugar
450 g (1 lb) self-raising flour
1 teaspoon salt
100 g (4 oz) butter, diced
300 ml (10 fl oz) milk
200 g (7 oz) natural fromage frais
225 g (8 oz) smoked mackerel fillet, skinned and mashed
Salt and freshly ground black pepper
Fresh dill sprigs, to garnish

1. Pre-heat the oven to 220C/425F/Gas 7. Heat the
oil and fry the onion, leek and sugar until softened.
Whizz in a food processor until finely chopped.
2. Sift together the flour and salt. Add the butter
and rub in until the mixture resembles fine
breadcrumbs. Stir in the onion mixture and enough
milk to form a soft dough. Turn out on to a floured
surface and knead lightly. Roll out to 1 cm (1/2 in)
thick then stamp out 2.5 cm (1 in) rounds.
3. Place the pastry rounds on to a floured baking
sheet and brush with milk. Bake for 12 minutes
until golden then cool on a wire rack.
4. Stir the fromage frais and seasoning into the
mackerel. Split the scones and spread one side with
the mackerel mixture. Garnish and replace the lids.

CHICK PEA AND PIMIENTO DIP IN BREAD BOWLS

Uncooked bread bowls can be frozen for up
to 1 month.

 Makes 2 bowls, each serving 12

2 large round white loaves
50 g (2 oz) butter, melted
2 x 400 g (14 oz) cans chick peas, drained
2 x 400 g (14 oz) cans pimientos, drained
4 tablespoons tomato purée
1–2 teaspoons hot chilli sauce
600 ml (1 pint) natural fromage frais
Crudités, to serve

1. Pre-heat the oven to 220C/425F/Gas 7. Cut off
the flat undersides of the loaves with a serrated
knife. Scoop out the insides to make 2 bowls.
2. Brush melted butter over the bowls, inside and
out. Bake for 10–15 minutes until crisp and golden,
covering with foil to prevent them from over-
browning. Leave to cool. Blend together half of the
chick peas, pimientos, tomato purée and chilli

sauce in a food processor.

3. Reserve 4 tablespoons of fromage frais for the garnish. Add half the remaining fromage frais to the blender and process to a rough purée. Make a second batch of dip with the remaining ingredients. Place the dip in small dishes and spoon reserved fromage frais on top. Place the dishes in the bread bowls and surround with the crudités.

CELEBRATION KING PRAWNS

Adjust the size of the ice bowl and quantity of prawns to suit the number of guests you are serving. To make the ice bowl, use 2 freezerproof bowls, one about 4 cm ($1^{1}/_{2}$ in) smaller in diameter than the other. Using previously boiled water will give clear ice while tap water will be opaque.
Allow 150 g (6 oz) 2–3 prawns per person.

2 freezerproof bowls
Sprigs of herbs
Lemon slices
King prawns
Lime slices
Sprig of flatleaf parsley

1. Pour cold water and ice cubes into the large bowl and float the smaller bowl inside. Fix the bowls with tape so the rims are level. Top up with iced water.

2. Slide the herbs and some of the lemon slices into the gap between the bowls, arranging them to make a pattern. Place the bowls on a baking sheet and freeze overnight.

3. To unmould, remove the bowls from the freezer and detach the tape. Pour warm water into the small bowl to loosen it, then lift it out. Dip the

Celebration King Prawns, Prosciutto and Parmesan Tartlets (page 172) and Savoury Choux Pyramid (page 173)

large bowl in hot water and tip out the ice bowl. Return the ice bowl to the freezer until required.
4. To serve, fill the bowl with king prawns, arranging them so that they hang over the side of the bowl. Garnish with the slices of lemon and lime and a sprig of flatleaf parsley.

PROSCIUTTO AND PARMESAN TARTLETS

These can also be made with 225 g (8 oz) cooked puréed chicken, sprinkled with 400 g (14 oz) tinned chopped asparagus spears. Fill with 225 g (8 oz) sautéed leeks, mushrooms or chopped fresh broccoli for vegetarians. They can be frozen for up to 1 month.

Makes 48

400 g (14 oz) filo pastry, thawed if frozen
100 g (4 oz) butter, melted
50 g (2 oz) Parmesan, freshly grated
1 tablespoon olive oil
4 garlic cloves, crushed
175 g (6 oz) prosciutto (Parma ham), finely chopped
3 eggs, beaten
275 ml (9 fl oz) milk
6 tablespoons double cream
Salt and freshly ground black pepper
Chopped herbs, to garnish

1. Pre-heat the oven to 180C/350F/Gas 4. Cut 1 sheet of filo into 7.5 cm (3 in) squares. Layer the filo squares in stacks of 3, brushing each layer with butter and arranging them at angles to create a star effect then use them to line a bun tin. Brush the cases with butter and sprinkle over some

Parmesan. Repeat with the remaining sheets to make 48 pastry cases.
2. Heat the oil and fry the garlic for 1–2 minutes. Remove from the heat and stir in the prosciutto. Leave to cool, then beat the eggs with the milk, cream, remaining Parmesan and seasoning. Spoon the mixture into the cases. Bake in batches for 10–12 minutes until the pastry is crisp and the filling has set. Cool and garnish with herbs.

HERBY BRIE TART

These tarts can be frozen for up to 1 month.

 Makes 2, each serving 12

450 g (1 lb) ripe Brie, rind removed
300 ml (10 fl oz) double cream
2 pinches saffron powder
675 g (1½ lb) plain flour
pinch of salt
350 g (12 oz) butter, diced
4 tablespoons chopped fresh thyme
50 g (2 oz) fresh parsley, chopped
4 tablespoons milk, plus extra to glaze
1 tablespoon wholegrain mustard
6 eggs, beaten
Salt and freshly ground black pepper

To garnish
Fresh herbs
Nasturtium flowers

1. Pre-heat oven to 140C/275F/Gas 1. Put the Brie, cream and saffron in an ovenproof dish and warm in the oven for 10 minutes. Remove and beat lightly.
2. Increase the oven temperature to 180C/350F/Gas 4. Sift the flour and salt, add the butter and rub in until the mixture resembles fine breadcrumbs. Stir in the herbs and about 175 ml (6 fl oz) cold water to make a firm dough. Chill for 30 minutes.
3. Halve the dough and roll out 1 piece to a 35 cm (14 in) circle, place a plate on top and cut out a 25 cm (10 in) round. Transfer the dough to a baking sheet. Knead the trimmings, halve and roll each piece to an 86 cm (34 in) sausage. Twist each strip separately, then twist 2 strips together to make a rope. Dampen the edge of the pastry circle with some water and place the twisted pastry strip on top: it should be thick and high enough to make a

Herby Brie Tart

good edge around the pie.

4. Seal the ends with water and brush with milk to glaze. Line pastry case with greaseproof paper and fill with baking beans. Bake blind for 20 minutes, then remove the paper and beans and bake for 5 minutes. Repeat with the remaining dough to make another pastry case.

5. Beat the Brie mixture with the milk, mustard, eggs and seasoning. Pour into the pastry cases and bake for 25 minutes until the filling is golden. Leave to cool, then garnish with herbs and flowers.

SAVOURY CHOUX PYRAMID

Remember to split the choux buns once cooked, to allow the steam to escape, then return them to the oven so they can dry out completely.
Unfilled choux buns can be frozen for up to 1 month.
You can use a vegetarian paté for this if you prefer, or grill 350 g (12 oz) smoked streaky bacon until crisp, then snip into small pieces. Beat together 600 g (1 lb 5 oz) full-fat soft cheese and 175 ml (6 fl oz) fromage frais. Stir in the bacon and use to fill the choux buns.

Makes 60–70

For the filling
225 g (8 oz) smooth Brussels paté
450 ml (15 fl oz) double cream
4 tablespoons snipped fresh chives
Salt and freshly ground black pepper
Fresh herb sprigs, to garnish

For the pastry
150 g (5 oz) plain flour
¼ teaspoon salt
100 g (4 oz) butter
4 eggs, beaten
Paprika, for sprinkling

1. Pre-heat oven to 190C/375F/Gas 5. To make the pastry, sift the flour and salt on to a sheet of greaseproof paper. Gently heat the butter and 300 ml (10 fl oz) water until the butter has melted, then bring to the boil. Remove from the heat and tip in the flour and salt immediately. Beat well with a wooden spoon.

2. Continue beating over a low heat until the mixture is smooth and forms a ball. Remove from the heat then leave to cool slightly before gradually adding the eggs.

3. Drop teaspoonfuls of the mixture on to dampened baking sheets. Alternatively, spoon into a piping bag fitted with a 1 cm (½ in) nozzle and pipe small bun shapes on to the baking sheets.

4. Sprinkle with paprika and bake for 15 minutes until well risen and golden brown. Make a small slit in the side of each bun, then return to the oven for a further 5 minutes to dry out. Leave to cool on a wire rack.

5. Whisk the paté and cream until thick and smooth. Fold in the chives and season. Spoon or pipe filling into choux buns. Pile the buns into a pyramid and garnish with fresh herb sprigs.

Summer Fruit Galettes

SUMMER FRUIT GALETTES

The unfilled cooked pastry cases can be frozen for up to 1 month.

        Makes 3, each serving 8–10

3 x 375 g (13 oz) packets flaky pastry, defrosted if frozen
Milk, to glaze
6 teaspoons arrowroot
900 ml (1½ pints) cranberry juice
6–8 tablespoons light muscovado sugar
600 ml (1 pint) crème fraîche
900 ml (1½ pints) double cream
6 passion fruit
About 1.5 kg (3 lb) soft summer fruit, such as blue-berries, blackberries and redcurrants

1. Pre-heat the oven to 220C/425F/Gas 7. Roll out a block of pastry to a 25 x 35 cm (10 x 14 in) rectangle. Trim edges, then cut a 2.5 cm (1 in) strip from each side. Place the pastry on a damp baking sheet and brush the edges with water.

2. Place a pastry strip along each edge, dovetail the corners and mark with a sharp knife. Prick the centre with a fork and brush the edges with milk, to glaze.

3. Line the pastry case with greaseproof paper and fill with baking beans. Bake for 15 minutes, remove the paper and beans and return to the oven for a further 5 minutes, then leave to cool. Repeat with the remaining pastry to make 3 galettes.

4. To make the glaze, blend the arrowroot with some cranberry juice. Heat the remaining juice with the sugar, then pour in the arrowroot, stirring constantly until clear and thickened. Cool slightly.

5. Whisk the crème fraîche and cream to form soft peaks. Halve the passion fruit, scoop out the pulp, with the pips, then fold it into the cream mixture.

6. Spoon the passion fruit cream into the pastry cases and arrange the fruit on top. Spoon over the glaze and leave to set.

RASPBERRY AND AMARETTI TRIFLES

The fruit sauces can be frozen for up to 1 month.

 Makes 24

1.5 kg (3 lb) cooking apples, peeled, cored and sliced
100–175 g (4–6 oz) granulated sugar
1.5 kg (3 lb) raspberries
Juice of 4 limes
120 ml (4 fl oz) crème de framboise
Icing sugar, to taste
48 boudoir biscuits, halved
350 g (12 oz) Amaretti biscuits, crushed
1.2 litres (2 pints) ready-made custard
900 ml (1½ pints) double cream
Fresh mint sprigs, to decorate

1. Put the apples, sugar and 150 ml (5 fl oz) water in a pan and bring to the boil. Cover and cook gently for 15 minutes or until soft. Beat with a wooden spoon until smooth, then add sugar to taste. Leave to cool.

2. Purée 1 kg (2 lb) raspberries with the lime juice

and crème de framboise. Sieve the fruit and add the icing sugar to taste. Spoon into 24 dishes; scatter over some of the whole raspberries and reserve the rest for the trifle tops.

3. Divide the boudoir biscuits among the dishes and sprinkle over some Amaretti biscuits. Spoon over the apple sauce, then the custard. Whip the cream to form soft peaks and spoon it on to the trifles. Sprinkle over the raspberries and finish with the Amaretti biscuits. Decorate with the mint.

COUNTDOWN

One month before
• Make and freeze the unfilled choux buns, bread bowls, apple and raspberry sauces for trifles, *Herby Brie Tart*, unfilled *Fruit Galette* cases, *Leek and Onion Scones* and *Prosciutto and Parmesan Tartlets*.
• Make the *Silver Wedding Cake* sponges, wrap in foil and freeze.

One week before
• Check there is enough clean cutlery, crockery, glasses, napkins and tablecloths. Arrange the room layout and buffet table.
• Make plenty of ice cubes.
• Make the ice bowl for the *Celebration King Prawns* and freeze. Make and bake the cake (if not already frozen) and store in an airtight container.

Two days before
• Make the mackerel filling for the *Leek and Onion Scones*; cover and chill.
• Ice the cake, but don't decorate it.
• Crystallise the fresh flowers and store in a cool, dry place.

The day before
• Remove everything from the freezer, except the ice bowl, and leave to defrost.
• Toast the sesame seeds and make the marinade for the *Little Gem Salads*. Leave the mushrooms to marinate overnight.
• Wash the lettuce, tie in bags and chill, prepare the crudités for the *Chick Pea and Pimiento Dip*, tie in bags and chill.
• Stuff the salmon and cut into slices, cover and chill.
• Make the filling for *Savoury Choux Pyramid* and chill.

On the day
• Cook and chill the *Stuffed Salmon Fillets with Grapes*.
• Assemble the *Raspberry and Amaretti Trifles*.
• Re-heat the choux buns and pastry cases for the *Summer Fruit Galettes* to crisp them; leave to cool, then fill.
• Make the *Chick Pea and Pimiento Dip* and arrange in the bread bowls with the crudités.
• Warm the *Herby Brie Tart* and *Prosciutto and Parmesan Tartlets* to crisp the pastry, leave to cool and garnish.
• Halve and fill the *Leek and Onion Scones with Smoked Mackerel*, chill wine and make up *Little Gem Salads* and dressing.
• Decorate the cake with crystallised flowers.
• At the last minute, take the ice bowl from the freezer and fill with the prawns.

Silver Wedding Cake (page 168),
Summer Fruit Galettes (page 173) and *Raspberry and Amaretti Trifles*

RUBY WEDDING ANNIVERSARY

RUBY WEDDING CAKE

SMOKED SALMON AND PRAWN ROULADES

LAYERED CHICKEN PIE WITH CREAMED
HORSERADISH SAUCE

MIXED LEAF SALAD WITH TANGY DRESSING

BABY NEW POTATOES WITH CHIVES AND OLIVES

HEAVENLY CHOCOLATE TART

FROSTED REDCURRANTS

RED FRUIT AND GINGER SALAD

Celebrate a ruby wedding with the rich colours of fresh summer fruits. Redcurrants and raspberries can be picked in advance, spread out on trays and frozen before being packed loosely into boxes. If you cannot pick your own from your garden or a local farm then check out the availability of frozen ones from larger supermarkets. The remaining fruits should be bought or picked fresh in order to look and taste really good.

 ## RUBY WEDDING CAKE

Enhance your celebration with this beautifully decorated cake. You will need to start several weeks in advance to make the simple *Flower Paste* bouquet but it will be well worth the time and you can keep it afterwards as a memento of the occasion. While the flowers are simple to make, they may take practise if you have never made flowers before. *Flower Paste* is available from cake decorating shops and rolls out very thinly. If you prefer, buy a silk or fresh flower arrangement. You can use a mould or cutters to make the lettering and numbers but if you have a steady hand, you can pipe on the message with royal icing. You will find all the equipment available from a good cake decorating shop. If you cannot buy cream-coloured *Sugar Paste*, you can colour white *Sugar Paste* with a little concentrated paste food colouring. There are recipes for making your own *Almond Paste* (see page 211), *Sugar Paste* (see page 212) and *Flower Paste* (see page 212), if desired.

The instructions are for a square cake, but you could make a 23 cm (9 in) round cake with a 25 cm (10 in) round gold cake board, if you prefer.

1 x 23 cm (9 in) square Basic Fruit Cake *(see page 210)*
1 x 25 cm (10 in) square, gold cake board

To cover the cake
4 tablespoons warmed, sieved apricot jam
Icing sugar, to dust
900 g (2 lb) Almond Paste *(see page 211)*
1.5 kg (3 lb) cream-coloured ready-to-roll Sugar Paste *(see page 212)*

1. Place the cake upside down on the board. Measure the top and sides of the cake with string. Brush the top and sides with apricot jam. Dust the work surface with a little icing sugar. Then roll out the *Almond Paste* to a square or round large enough to cover the top and sides. Lift it over the cake and smooth down with your palms, easing it around the corners. Trim the edges.
2. Dust a work surface with icing sugar and roll out the *Sugar Paste* to a square or round large enough to cover the top and sides of the cake. Drape over the cake then smooth over with the palms of your hands. Trim off any excess.

Decorating the cake
To make the lace edge
350 g (12 oz) cream-coloured ready-to-roll Sugar Paste *(see page 212)*
25 g (1 oz) Flower Paste *(see page 212)*
Concentrated paste food colouring: burgundy
1½ metres (4¾ feet) burgundy ribbon
Lace cutter
Icing nozzle

1. Knead together 25 g (1 oz) cream *Sugar Paste* with 25 g (1 oz) *Flower Paste*. Divide in half and colour one half with burgundy food colouring. Roll out very thinly into a long strip and cut 4 strips of *Paste* 2.5 cm (1 in) wide by 25 cm (10 in) long using the lace cutter (or you could cut long strips of *Paste* and cut a pattern along one edge with the end of a piping nozzle).
2. Place one burgundy strip on the cake board around or against each side of the cake and cut the corners diagonally to mitre. Using the remaining *Paste*, roll out and cut 4 strips of cream lace, each about 5 mm (¼ in) narrower than the previous ones. Make small holes in the lace with the point of an icing nozzle and place on top of the burgundy lace. Tie ribbon around the cake and make a bow at one corner.

Ruby Wedding Cake

To make the lettering and numbers

Burgundy coloured, ready-to-roll Sugar Paste
(see page 212)
Alphabet and number moulds or cutters
Egg white

Roll out a little burgundy *Sugar Paste* and press into
the alphabet mould. Turn out and place on the cake,
securing each by painting the back with a tiny dot
of egg white. Make the numbers in the same way.

To make the flowers

75 g (3 oz) Flower Paste *(see page 212)*
*Concentrated paste food colourings: burgundy
and green*
Burgundy food colouring powder
*1 bunch of 26-gauge paper-covered florist's wire cut
into 7.5 cm (3 in) lengths, with a tiny hook on one end*
5-petal blossom cutter
Small, medium and large ivy cutters
Small ball tool (if available)
Small artist's paintbrush

Oasis or bath sponge
Nail scissors
Florists' tape

To make the roses

1. Colour half of the *Flower Paste* with burgundy
paste food colouring. Wrap tightly in cling film.
2. Make a small cone of *Flower Paste* and place over
the hook. Roll out a little *Flower Paste* very very
thinly on a non-stick surface with a slight dusting
of cornflour. Cut out one set of petals with the 5-
petal blossom cutter, place in the palm of your
hand and using your little finger or a small ball
tool thin the edges of the petals slightly. Paint a
little egg white all over one petal and just at the
edge of each of the other petals. Place the wire
down through the centre of the petals, and place
the glued petal around to cover the cone. Then
place each petal around to form a bud. To make a
fuller rose place another set of petals around in the
same way, curling the edges of the petals out. Stick
into a sponge or Oasis to dry overnight. You need 10
roses. Paint calyxs on bases with the green colouring.

To make the finger flowers

1. Shape a small long cone of white *Flower Paste* between your fingers. Make a hole in the top with the end of a paintbrush or cocktail stick. Using tiny nail scissors, cut the hole into 4 sections to make four petals. Pinch and flatten each petal between your finger and thumb. Push a hooked wire down through the centre to secure and leave to dry overnight. Make a small long cone of *Flower Paste* and place on wire for a bud. Make at least 14 flowers and 12 buds.

2. When dry, lightly dust the backs of the petals with the burgundy food colouring powder.

To make the leaves

1. Roll out a little white *Flower Paste* very thinly and cut out at least 14 small and 16 medium ivy leaves. Hold the base of each leaf and push the hook of the wire up through it to secure. Use a little green food colouring to paint the variegations.

Colour the remaining *Flower Paste* green and roll out to make at least 14 medium and 18 large ivy leaves. Add the wires as before and twist the leaves slightly to give a natural look. Then leave the ivy to dry overnight. When dry brush lightly with burgundy food colouring powder in the centre and on the edges.

2. Use any remaining green *Flower Paste* to cut out rose leaves using either a veiner or a paintbrush to mark the veins. Wire and twist as for the ivy leaves.

To make up the flower bouquet

1. Make up 2 long trails of green ivy and 2 of white ivy first. Twist a little florists' tape around a small ivy leaf, starting as close to the leaf as possible and twisting tightly down the wire just a short way to secure. Add another couple of ivy leaves and continue twisting the tape around the wire to secure. Continue adding the larger leaves and

finish off by wrapping the tape to the end of the wire. The remaining leaves can be incorprated into the bouquet as it is assembled.

2. Beginning at one side of the bouquet, twist the tape around one white bud as for the leaf sprays adding ivy leaves and flowers and twisting the tape tightly to secure. Continue adding flowers and leaves using the largest flowers in the centre of the bouquet and the smaller ones at either side. As you build up the bouquet, you can bend the wires to create the oval shape and make the flowers move. You may find it easier to join together smaller sprays before assembling them in one large bouquet.

To finish
1 metre (about 3 feet) thin gold, ribbon

Cut the ribbon in half and loop a piece loosely through each end of the bouquet. Place the bouquet on top of the cake just before the guests arrive. The finished bouquet can be stored in a dry box (not airtight) for up to 1 year in a dark place.

SMOKED SALMON AND PRAWN ROULADES

Serves 12

450 g (1 lb) cooked peeled prawns
2 teaspoons powdered gelatine
250 g (9 oz) Mascarpone cheese
4 tablespoons mayonnaise
Finely grated rind of 1 lime
2 tablespoons finely chopped fresh tarragon or dill
400 g (14 oz) smoked salmon slices
Salt and freshly ground black pepper
Salad leaves, to serve
Brown bread and butter, to serve

To garnish
Lime slices
Dill sprigs

1. Thoroughly drain and dry the prawns, then chop roughly. Sprinkle the gelatine over 2 tablespoons of water in a small bowl and leave to soften.

2. Beat the Mascarpone in a bowl with the mayonnaise, lime rind, herbs and seasoning. Stand the softened gelatine in a pan containing a little simmering water and leave until dissolved. Cool slightly, then beat into the Mascarpone mixture. Stir in the prawns.

3. Separate the salmon slices and divide into 12 rectangles, each about 18 x 5 cm (7 x 2 in), dividing and reshaping the trimmings, if necessary. Spread the prawn mixture along each piece of salmon, then roll up, starting at the thinnest ends. Cover the rolls loosely with clear plastic film and chill for several hours or overnight.

4. Cut the rolls into thin slices, about 5 mm ($1/4$ in) thick, using a sharp knife and arrange on plates. Garnish with lime slices and dill sprigs and serve garnished with salad leaves and a plate of thin slices of buttered brown bread.

From the left: *Layered Chicken Pie with Creamed Horseradish Sauce (page 180), Baby New Potatoes with Chives and Olives (page 182), Mixed Leaf Salad with Tangy Dressing (page 180)* and *Smoked Salmon and Prawn Roulades*

LAYERED CHICKEN PIE WITH CREAMED HORSERADISH SAUCE

Serves 12

For the pie
900 g (2 lb) boneless chicken breasts, skinned
8 tablespoons olive oil
6 garlic cloves, crushed
2 tablespoons chopped fresh oregano or 2 teaspoons dried
2 tablespoons chopped fresh parsley
3 large onions, sliced
450 g (1 lb) courgettes, sliced
450 g (1 lb) aubergines, thinly sliced
675 g (1½ lb) puff pastry, thawed if frozen
3 beef tomatoes, skinned, quartered and seeded
Salt and freshly ground black pepper
1 beaten egg, to glaze
Bay leaves, to garnish

For the sauce
40 g (1½ oz) butter
2 teaspoons plain flour
450 ml (15 fl oz) double cream
6–8 tablespoons horseradish sauce
6 tablespoons white wine

1. Using a sharp knife halve each chicken breast horizontally. Heat 4 tablespoons of oil in a large frying pan, then add half the breasts and sprinkle with half the garlic and herbs. Season lightly. Fry the chicken on both sides to seal and remove with a slotted spoon. Fry the remaining chicken, garlic and herbs. Remove from the pan with a slotted spoon and reserve.
2. Add the onions to the pan and fry gently for 5 minutes, then add the courgettes and aubergines and fry for a further 5 minutes, adding more oil when needed. Leave to cool.
3. Pre-heat the oven to 220C/425F/Gas 7. Lightly grease a large baking sheet. Roll out a third of the pastry on a lightly floured surface to a 41 x 20 cm (16 x 8 in) rectangle and place on the baking sheet. Lay half the chicken to within 2.5 cm (1 in) of the pastry edges, cover with half the vegetable mixture, then arrange half the tomatoes over the vegetables. Repeat layering to use all the ingredients. Brush the pastry edges with beaten egg.
4. Thinly roll half the remaining pastry to a 41 x 28 cm (16 x ll in) rectangle. Cut diagonally into 2.5 cm (1 in) strips and lay over the filling, leaving a 5 mm (¼ in) gap between the strips. Press the ends to seal. Brush with beaten egg. Roll out the remaining pastry, cut strips and lay them over the pie in a lattice pattern. Press the edges of the pastry firmly together to seal then trim off the excess with a knife. Brush with egg and bake for 15 minutes. Reduce the oven temperature to 180C/350F/Gas 4 and bake for a further 40 minutes until risen and golden.
5. Meanwhile, make the sauce. Melt the butter in a small pan and blend in the flour. Cook for 1 minute, stirring. Remove from the heat and stir in the cream, horseradish and seasoning. Return the pan to the heat and cook, stirring, until thickened, then add the wine.
6. Carefully transfer the pie to a large plate or board, garnish with bay leaves and serve in thick slices accompanied by the sauce.

MIXED LEAF SALAD WITH TANGY DRESSING

Serves 12

1 iceberg lettuce
1 radicchio
½ small frisée
A small bunch of watercress
6 tablespoons olive oil
2 tablespoons red wine vinegar
Finely grated rind of 1 lemon
1 tablespoon clear honey
Salt and freshly ground black pepper

1. Tear the salad leaves into pieces and toss together in a serving bowl.
2. Beat together the oil, vinegar, lemon rind, honey and seasoning. Pour over the salad just before serving and toss lightly.

Red Fruit and Ginger Salad (page 182) and Heavenly Chocolate Tart with Frosted Redcurrants (page 182)

BABY NEW POTATOES WITH CHIVES AND OLIVES

Serves 12

1.75 kg (4 lb) baby new potatoes
50 g (2 oz) butter
A small bunch of fresh chives, chopped
50 g (2 oz) black olives

1. Cook the potatoes in boiling salted water until tender. Drain and toss with the butter, chives and olives, then transfer to a serving dish.

 ## HEAVENLY CHOCOLATE TART

Serve very small portions of this delicious dessert – it's extremely rich.

Serves 12

500 g (1¹/₄ lb) plain chocolate
1¹/₂ teaspoons powdered gelatine
150 g (5 oz) light muscovado sugar
2 tablespoons cornflour
3 egg yolks
450 ml (15 fl oz) milk
1 tablespoon ground espresso or after dinner coffee
900 ml (1¹/₂ pints) double cream
100 g (4 oz) white chocolate, broken into pieces
Frosted Redcurrants, *to decorate*

1. Break 275 g (10 oz) of the plain chocolate into a heatproof bowl and melt over a pan of simmering water. Cut a large square of foil and use it to line the base and sides of a 23 cm (9 in) spring-release or loose-bottomed tin.
2. Pour the melted chocolate into the tin and spread over the base and up the sides. Chill until set, then carefully peel the foil away from the sides, then the base of the case. If the case becomes warm while working, chill it for a few minutes.
3. Sprinkle the gelatine over 2 tablespoons of water in a small bowl and leave to soften. Whisk the sugar in a bowl with the cornflour, egg yolks and a little milk until smooth.
4. Put the remaining milk in a pan with the coffee and bring to the boil. Pour over the egg mixture, whisking well. Return to the pan and cook for about 1 minute over a very gentle heat, stirring, until thickened and bubbling. Do not allow to boil. Beat in the softened gelatine. Break the remaining

plain chocolate into chunks and beat into the mixture until melted and smooth.
5. Heat 150 ml (5 fl oz) of the cream in a pan, then stir in the white chocolate until melted and smooth. Chill until cooled.
6. Stir 450 ml (15 fl oz) of the remaining cream into the dark chocolate mixture. Whisk until thick and softly peaking then spoon half into the chocolate case. Lightly beat the white chocolate mixture and spoon over the dark. Cover with the remaining dark chocolate mixture. Swirl a skewer through the mixtures to lightly marble. Chill overnight.
7. Whip the remaining cream until just peaking and place spoonfuls over the filling before decorating with the *Frosted Redcurrants*.

FROSTED REDCURRANTS

Brush redcurrants with a little lightly beaten egg white, then toss in caster sugar and leave to dry on non-stick baking parchment.

RED FRUIT AND GINGER SALAD

Serves 8–10

50 g (2 oz) caster sugar
25 g (1 oz) stem ginger, drained and thinly sliced
6 tablespoons ginger wine
1 medium Charentais melon
100 g (4 oz) redcurrants
225 g (8 oz) fresh cherries
450 g (1 lb) strawberries
4 figs
225 g (8 oz) seedless red grapes
225 g (8 oz) raspberries

1. Place the sugar in a small pan with 175 ml (6 fl oz) of water and heat gently, stirring, until the sugar dissolves. Remove from the heat and stir in another 175 ml (6 fl oz) water, the ginger and ginger wine. Leave to cool.
2. Halve the melon, discard the seeds and use a melon baller to scoop out the flesh or cut the flesh into small cubes, and place in a serving bowl.
3. Pull the redcurrants from their sprigs using a fork and stone the cherries. Hull and halve any large strawberries and cut the figs into wedges. Add to the bowl with the grapes and raspberries and toss lightly to combine. Pour the syrup over the fruits and keep cool until ready to serve.

COUNTDOWN

Three months before
• Make *Basic Fruit Cake*, wrap it in foil and store in a cool, dry place.
• Send out invitations.

Two months before
• Start making the flowers and leaves for the bouquet. Allow to dry completely before storing between sheets of tissue paper in a box (not airtight). Store in a cool, dry, dark place.

One month before
• Unwrap the cake, pierce with a cocktail stick and pour over a little brandy. Repeat 2 or 3 times during the next 2 weeks.
• Make the *Layered Chicken Pie*. Cook and freeze it. Make the *Heavenly Chocolate Tart* and freeze.

Two weeks before
• Cover cake with *Almond Paste*. Leave to set in a dry airy place. Place a sheet of greaseproof over the top to keep off dust.
• Begin to assemble the bouquet, storing as before.

One week before
• Make the shopping list. Check out the availability of fresh fruits and salmon and order if necessary.
• Cover the cake with *Sugar Paste* and add the letters and numbers when the surface is dry. Store as before.

Two days before
• Buy the non-perishable ingredients and drinks.
• Check on tablecloth, cutlery, glasses.

One day before
• Buy the fruit and vegetables.
• Make the *Heavenly Chocolate Tart* or remove from freezer to defrost.
• Remove the prawns, chicken and pastry from the freezer (if frozen) and place in the refrigerator to thaw or defrost ready-made *Layered Chicken Pie* and *Chocolate Tart*.
• Make the *Smoked Salmon and Prawn Roulades*

up to the end of step 3, and chill whole.

On the day
• Frost the fruit and leave to dry then decorate the *Heavenly Chocolate Tart* with them.
• Make the *Red Fruit and Ginger Salad*.
• Prepare all ingredients for the *Layered Chicken Pie* (if not frozen earlier), chill well before layering pie. Cover with cling film and keep chilled until ready to cook.
• Wash the potatoes and prepare the dressings for the potatoes and salad.
• Lay the table. Place the flower bouquet on the cake.

Two hours before
• Wash and prepare the salad.
• Slice the *Smoked Salmon Roulades*, garnish the plate, cover with cling film and chill.
• Whip the cream and place over the *Heavenly Chocolate Tart*, chill.
• Set oven to 220C/425F/Gas 7.
• Prepare the bread and butter for the starter and cover with cling film.

One hour before
• Brush the *Layered Chicken Pie* with beaten egg and place in the oven.
• Make the *Horseradish Sauce* and keep warm.
• Reduce the oven temperature to 180C/350F/Gas 4.
• Cook the potatoes, garnish and keep warm.
• Check on the *Layered Chicken Pie*, remove and keep warm when cooked.

To serve
Toss the salad and place the frosted fruits on the *Heavenly Chocolate Tart* just before bringing to the table.

CHRISTENING TEA

CHRISTENING CAKE

LEEK AND GOAT'S CHEESE TARTLETS

SAVOURY SCONES WITH SMOKED SALMON FILLING

TURKEY AND SUN-DRIED TOMATO BRIOCHE LOAF

SANDWICHES

DOLCELATTE, CELERY AND APPLE FILLING

ROAST BEEF AND PRAWN FILLING

NON-ALCOHOLIC ICED TEA PUNCH

FRESH FRUIT DIP

PEANUT BRITTLE CHOUX BUNS

BLACK AND WHITE CHOCOLATE BROWNIES

PECAN FIG FINGERS

 ## CHRISTENING CAKE

20 cm (8 in) round Basic Fruit Cake (see page 210)
30 cm (12 in) round silver cake board
3 tablespoons apricot jam
675 g (1½ lb) Almond Paste (see page 211)
Icing sugar and cornflour, for dusting
1.2 kg (3 lb) ready-to-roll Sugar Paste (see page 212)
Concentrated paste food colourings: ivory, pale green, navy blue, pink and brown
Small blossom cutters

1. Cut the top of the cake so that it is level, then invert on to cake board. Use a little Almond Paste to fill any gaps between the base of the cake and board. Heat the jam in a small pan with 1 tablespoon water. Press through a sieve and brush over top and sides of the cake.
2. Measure from the board over the top and down the other side of the cake with a piece of string. Lightly dust a work surface with icing sugar and roll out the Almond Paste to a round large enough to drape over top and sides of the cake using the string as a guide. Lift the Almond Paste over the cake and smooth the cake with your palms, easing out any creases. Trim off excess.
3. Knead a small dot of ivory food colouring into 1.4 kg (2½ lb) of the Sugar Paste to tint it. Wrap the paste in cling film to keep it moist while tinting the remaining paste: 175 g (6 oz) pale green, 40 g

(1½ oz) navy blue and 15 g (½ oz) very pale pink. Wrap each coloured bit of icing in cling film.
4. Lightly knead 900 g (2 lb) of the ivory Sugar Paste on a surface dusted with a little icing sugar. Roll out to a circle large enough to cover the top and sides of the cake. Lift over the cake and ease the icing to fit, smoothing out any creases using your palms, dusted with cornflour. Trim off any excess around base. Thinly roll the trimmings and use to cover the surface of the cake board, trimming off any excess around edges. Leave the icing to set overnight.
5. Cut a strip of greaseproof paper the circumference and depth of the cake. Fold into seven equal pieces. Open out the strip and wrap round the cake. Mark each fold with a pin around the top edge of the cake.
6. Very thinly roll out a small piece of green Sugar Paste and trim to 5 mm (¼ in) wide and 12 cm (5 in) long. Dampen the cake between 2 pin marks. Twist the strip of Sugar Paste and secure to the side of the cake between the 2 pin marks so the remainder forms a loop. Repeat all round the cake ensuring all the loops are equal in length and the ends meet at the pins. Use more twists of green Sugar Paste to decorate the bottom edge of the cake and make tassels around the sides.
7. From the remaining ivory Sugar Paste shape a very simple oval cradle about 7.5 cm (3 in) long, 5 cm (2 in) wide and 2.5 cm (1 in) deep tapering slightly at the base. Mould a small pillow and place in position. Shape the baby's head, hand and body out of pink Sugar Paste and lay in the cradle. Thinly roll a rectangle of ivory Sugar Paste and lay over cradle as a blanket. For frills, thinly roll 5 mm (¼ in) strips of ivory icing and roll a cocktail stick along one edge to frill. Secure around the pillow and edge of the blanket. Place the cradle on a sheet of greaseproof paper to dry.
8. Shape the remaining accessories such as rattle, bib, teddy, booties, building blocks, balls and about 12 parcels in various sizes from the remaining ivory Sugar Paste. Leave to dry with the cradle for 24 hours.
9. To decorate the parcels, first paint stripes or spots on to them using diluted food colourings. Use a small piece of foam sponge, dipped in colouring to create the stippled effect. Finish with icing bows in contrasting colours. Paint more colour on to the building blocks and rattles.
10. To assemble the decorations, place a dome of leftover ivory Sugar Paste on the centre of the cake. Lightly dampen top of dome with water and gently

press the cradle into position at a slight angle. Arrange all the shaped parcels and accessories around the cradle, securing with a dampened paintbrush. Fill the gaps with more ribbons of green *Sugar Paste* and place one on the pillow.
11. Thinly roll out the blue *Sugar Paste* and cut out simple blossom shapes using the cutter. Use to decorate the side of cake and scatter a few over the top. Use a very fine brush and diluted brown colouring to paint features on to the baby's and teddy's faces.

LEEK AND GOAT'S CHEESE TARTLETS

These are made in individual tartlet tins.

 Serves 12

350 g (12 oz) plain flour
175 g (6 oz) margarine, cut up

For the filling
50 g (2 oz) butter
900 g (2lb leeks, cut into 5 mm (¹/₄ in) slices
225 g (8 oz) rindless goat's cheese

3 eggs
75 g (3 oz) raisins
3 tablespoons milk
50 g (2 oz) pine nuts
Salt and freshly ground black pepper

1. Place the flour and fat in a bowl and rub in with your fingers until the mixture resembles fine breadcrumbs. Mix to a soft dough with about 4 tablespoons cold water. Knead lightly and divide into 12 equal pieces. Roll out and use to line 12 x 10 cm (4 in) fluted tartlet tins. Chill for 30 minutes.
2. Pre-heat the oven to 200C/400F/Gas 6. Melt the butter in a large pan and gently cook the leeks for about 10 minutes until soft but with no excess liquid. Leave to cool.
3. Bake the pastry cases blind for 15 minutes until pale brown. Remove from the oven and reduce the temperature to 180C/350F/Gas 4.
4. Mash the cheese then add the eggs and mix together well. Add the leeks, raisins, milk and seasoning, to taste. Divide the filling between the pastry cases and sprinkle with the pine nuts. Bake for 20–25 minutes until set and serve warm.

Christening Cake

SAVOURY SCONES WITH SMOKED SALMON FILLING

For vegetarians, replace the smoked salmon with the flesh of a roasted red pepper.

Makes 12

For the scones
450 g (1 lb) plain flour
2 teaspoons baking powder
1 teaspoon salt
75 g (3 oz) butter, cut up
90 g (3½ oz) Parmesan, grated
2 tablespoons coarse grain mustard
300 ml (10 fl oz) milk

For the filling
225 g (8 oz) cream cheese
3 tablespoons milk
Juice and grated rind of 1 lemon
225 g (8 oz) smoked salmon, chopped
2 tablespoons freshly chopped chives

1. Pre-heat the oven to 220C/425F/Gas 7. Sift the flour, baking powder and salt into a bowl, add the butter and rub in until the mixture ressembles fine breadcrumbs. Stir in 75 g (3 oz) of the Parmesan. Mix the mustard and milk together, add to the flour and mix to form a soft dough.
2. Lightly knead the dough on a floured surface until smooth then roll out to 1 cm (½ in) thick. Cut out 5 cm (2 in) rounds and place them on to a greased baking sheet. Brush with a little milk and

sprinkle over the remaining cheese. Bake for 12–15 minutes until golden brown, then transfer on to a cooling rack. When cold, split in half horizontally.

3. To make the filling, mix the cream cheese, milk and lemon juice together until creamy then fold in the smoked salmon, chives and lemon rind. Spread the filling on the scones and sandwich together.

TURKEY AND SUN-DRIED TOMATO BRIOCHE LOAF

The turkey filling is cooked and chilled before being wrapped in the bread dough. Slow proving in the fridge overnight ensures a good rise and freshly baked bread on the day.

Serves 12

225 g (8 oz) minced raw turkey
25 g (1 oz) fatty smoked bacon, finely chopped
1 tablespoon chopped fresh tarragon
Salt and freshly ground black pepper
1 tablespoon olive oil

For the bread
225 g (8 oz) strong plain flour
6 g (1/4 oz) sachet easy-blend dried yeast
1/2 teaspoon salt
1 tablespoon sugar
50 ml (2 fl oz) olive oil or oil from sun-dried tomatoes
85 ml (3 fl oz) warm water
6 sun-dried tomatoes, chopped

1. Place the turkey, bacon and tarragon into a bowl and season well. Mix thoroughly and shape into a 20 cm (8 in) long sausage. Heat the oil in a frying pan and fry the turkey roll for 20–25 minutes turning frequently until golden and cooked through. Cool then chill.

2. Grease a loaf tin that measures 23 x 10 cm (9 x 4 in). Sift the flour into a bowl, add the yeast, salt, sugar, oil and water and mix to a smooth and elastic dough then knead in the sun-dried tomatoes until evenly mixed in.

3. Knead the dough on a floured surface then roll

From the top left clockwise: *Turkey and Sun-dried Tomato Brioche Loaf, Savoury Scones with Smoked Salmon Filling, Roast Beef and Prawn Sandwiches, Leek and Goat's Cheese Tartlets (page 185) and Dolcelatte, Celery and Apple Sandwiches*

out into a rectangle 25 x 18 cm (10 x 7 in). Place the chilled turkey sausage on the dough and wrap round to cover. Seal the ends and place join side down in the prepared tin. Brush the inside of a large plastic bag with oil and place the tin inside. Leave in the fridge overnight to prove and rise.

4. Pre-heat the oven to 220C/425F/Gas 7 and allow the bread to come to room temperature before baking. Brush the loaf with milk, slash the top with a sharp knife and bake 35–40 minutes until well risen and golden. The bread should sound hollow when tapped. Serve warm or cold.

SANDWICHES

Each filling makes sufficient for 6 sandwiches.

DOLCELATTE, CELERY AND APPLE FILLING

1 red eating apple, cored
1 tablespoon lemon juice
225 g (8 oz) Dolcelatte
1 tablespoon soured cream
2 sticks celery, finely chopped
Salt and freshly ground black pepper
12 slices brown bread

1. Finely chop the apple and sprinkle with some of the lemon juice. Mash the cheese and soured cream together until creamy then stir in the celery, apple and any remaining lemon juice. Season to taste.

2. Spread the mixture over 6 slices of bread, place another slice on top and press down lightly. Trim off the crusts and cut each sandwich into 4 triangles.

ROAST BEEF AND PRAWN FILLING

12 slices medium cut white bread
butter for spreading, softened
6 lettuce leaves, washed and dried
225 g (8 oz) thinly sliced roast beef
100 g (4 oz) cooked, peeled tiger prawns, chopped
4 tablespoons mayonnaise
1 tablespoon creamed horseradish

1. Spread each slice of bread with the softened butter. Place a lettuce leaf on 6 slices and divide the beef between them.

2. Mix the prawns into the mayonnaise with the horseradish and spread over the beef. Press a buttered piece of bread on top, trim off the crusts and cut each sandwich into 4 triangles.

NON-ALCOHOLIC ICED TEA PUNCH

   Makes 3.25 litres (5½ pints)

3 oranges
3 lemons
4 limes
8 Earl Grey teabags
275 g (10 oz) caster sugar
2 cinnamon sticks
1.2 litres (2 pints) boiling water
30 ice cubes
1.75 litres (3 pints) soda water

To serve
Citrus fruit slices
Mint

1. Using a potato peeler remove the zest from all the fruit and place it into a heatproof jug with the teabags, sugar and cinnamon sticks. Pour over the boiling water and stir until the sugar has dissolved then leave to infuse until cold.
2. Squeeze the juices from the fruit and add to tea.
3. Strain the punch into a large serving bowl. Just before serving, add the ice cubes, soda water, fruit slices and mint.

FRESH FRUIT DIP

   Serves 12

For the dip
225 g (8 oz) fresh raspberries
75 g (3 oz) caster sugar
2 tablespoons freshly chopped mint
2 tablespoons lemon juice
450 g (1 lb) Mascarpone cheese
Mint, to garnish

Fruit for dipping
½ medium pineapple
225 g (8 oz) large strawberries
4 sharon fruit
½ cantaloupe melon
4 kiwi fruit

1. Either purée the raspberries with the sugar and mint in a liquidiser and then sieve, or press the raspberries and mint through a sieve then stir the sugar into the purée. Stir in the lemon juice.
2. Place the Mascarpone in a bowl and beat in the raspberry purée, then transfer to a serving dish and garnish with mint.
3. Prepare the fruit and cut into chunks, wedges or thick slices and serve with the dip.

PEANUT BRITTLE CHOUX BUNS

   Makes 24 small buns

For the buns
100 g (4 oz) plain flour
75 g (3 oz) butter, cut up
3 eggs, size 3, beaten

For the filling
175 g (6 oz) peanut brittle, crushed
300 ml (10 fl oz) double cream
1 tablespoon icing sugar

1. Pre-heat the oven to 200F/400F/Gas 6. Sift the flour on to a sheet of paper. Place the butter and 200 ml (7fl oz) water in a pan over a medium heat and bring to the boil. Remove from the heat and immediately add all the flour and beat vigorously until a smooth dough is formed. Cool the dough slightly then add the eggs, a little at a time and beat vigorously after each addition.
2. Lightly grease 3 baking sheets and run some cold water over them. Shake off the excess. Place 24 teaspoonsfuls of mixture on to the prepared sheets allowing plenty of room for spreading. Bake for 30–35 minutes until golden brown and crisp. Split each bun in half and allow to cool.
3. Grind the peanut brittle in a food grinder. Whip the cream until it is thick then fold in the peanut brittle powder. Fill the buns with the cream and dust with icing sugar before serving.

From the top clockwise: *Black and White Chocolate Brownies (page 190), Pecan Fig Fingers (page 190), Peanut Brittle Choux Buns* and *Fresh Fruit Dip*

BLACK AND WHITE CHOCOLATE BROWNIES

Makes 24 small squares

50 g (2 oz) plain chocolate, broken
175 g (6 oz) unsalted butter, cut up
50 g (2 oz) white chocolate
4 eggs
275 g (10 oz) soft brown sugar
175 g (6 oz) plain flour, sifted
120 ml (4 fl oz) soured cream

1. Pre-heat oven to 160C/325F/Gas 3. Line a 28 x 18 cm (11 x 7 in) shallow baking tin with baking parchment. Melt the plain chocolate with 75 g (3 oz) butter over a gentle heat then allow the mixture to cool slightly. Melt the white chocolate with the remaining butter and leave to cool.
2. Beat the eggs with the sugar until light and fluffy and divide between 2 bowls. Stir the plain chocolate into one bowl and the white chocolate into the other. Carefully fold half the flour and then half the soured cream into each bowl.
3. Place alternate spoonfuls of mixture into the prepared tin and then lightly stir to give a marbled effect. Bake for 30–35 minutes until firm to the touch. Leave to cool before carefully turning out and cutting into squares.

PECAN FIG FINGERS

Makes 24 fingers

225 g (8 oz) dried figs, chopped
100 g (4 oz) clear honey
50 g (2 oz) mixed peel
Juice and grated rind of 1 orange
225 g (8 oz) pecan nuts, coarsely chopped
250 g (9 oz) plain flour
175 g (6 oz) unsalted butter, cut up
75 g (3 oz) caster sugar

1. Pre-heat oven to 180C/350F/Gas 4. Line a 28 x 18 cm (11 x 7 in) shallow baking tin with non-stick baking parchment. Place the figs, honey, peel, orange rind and juice into a small pan and heat gently until thick, stirring frequently. Add the pecan nuts and allow to cool.
2. Sift the flour into a bowl, add the butter and rub in until the mixture resembles fine breadcrumbs. Add the sugar and press three-quarters of the mixture into the prepared tin. Spread the fig mixture evenly over and sprinkle over the remaining crumb mixture. Bake for 40 minutes until pale brown. Leave to cool completely before cutting into fingers.

Black and White Chocolate Brownies and *Pecan Fig Fingers*

COUNTDOWN

Two months before
• Make the *Basic Fruit Cake* and drizzle brandy over it several times during the next 6 weeks. Wrap in greaseproof paper and foil and store in a cool dry place.
• Send out invitations and check details of christening service.

Two weeks before
• Cover the cake with *Almond Paste*.
• Make the decorations for the cake and leave to dry.
• Make the *Leek and Goat's Cheese Tartlets*, and store in the freezer.
• Make scones for *Savoury Scones with Smoked Salmon* and store in a plastic bag in freezer.
• Make the buns for *Peanut Brittle Choux Buns* and store in a plastic bag in the freezer.
• Make the *Black and White Brownies* and store, uncut, in the freezer.
• Make the *Pecan Fig Fingers* and store, uncut, in the freezer.

One week before
• Cover cake with *Sugar Paste*. When dry add decorations. Store in a cool dry place lightly covered with greaseproof to protect from dust.
• Buy any remaining unperishable foods and drinks. Order extra milk.
• Organise the tablecloth, napkins, cutlery, glasses, plates, serving plates, seating etc.
•Ensure you have sufficient tea towels, kettles, jugs and helpers on the day.
• Order the flowers.

Two days before
• Clear out the fridge.
• Buy the perishable foods.
• Grind the peanut brittle and store in an airtight container.

One day before
• Make up and cook the turkey filling for *Turkey and Sun-dried Tomato Brioche Loaf* and when cold, chill in the fridge.
• Make both types of sandwiches and place, uncut, back into the plastic bread bags and store in the fridge.
• Make up the filling for *Savoury Scones* and store in the fridge.
• Prepare step 1 of *Non-alcoholic Iced Tea Punch* and leave the fruit to infuse.
• Prepare step 1 of *Fresh Fruit Dip* and store in the fridge.
• Lay the table and collect the serving plates. Wash the green salad leaves or garnish and store in a plastic bag.

Before going to bed
• Make up the yeast dough for the *Turkey and Sun-dried Tomato Brioche Loaf*. Shape the round turkey roll and place in the tin lightly covered with greased plastic and leave to rise. Place in the fridge to prove overnight.
• Remove the scones, choux buns, *Chocolate Brownies*, *Pecan Fig Fingers* and *Leek and Goat's Cheese Tartlets* from freezer.

On the day
• Finish the tea punch except for adding the ice cubes, and mint. Prepare the fruit for adding later.
• Fill the scones, and arrange on a serving plate. Cover with plastic and keep chilled.
• Cut up the *Chocolate Brownies* and *Pecan Fig Fingers* and arrange on serving plates. Cover.
• Cut sandwiches, arrange on plates and cover with greaseproof paper and a damp tea towel.
• Finish *Peanut Brittle Choux Buns*. Chill.
• Finish *Fresh Fruit Dip*. Keep chilled. Prepare the fresh fruit for serving.

One hour before serving
• Remove the *Turkey and Sun-dried Tomato Brioche Loaf* from the fridge and allow to come to room temperature. Pre-heat the oven to 220C/425F/Gas 7.
• Bake *Turkey and Sun-dried Tomato Brioche Loaf* for 35–40 minutes or until golden brown and well heated through in the middle. Remove from the oven, cool slightly and slice.
• Place the *Leek and Goat's Cheese Tartlets* in the oven immediately after removing the *Brioche Loaf* and turn off heat. Leave for 5–8 minutes until heated through.
• Arrange all the food on the table.
• Add the soda water, ice cubes, mint and sliced fruit to the *Non-alcoholic Iced Tea Punch* and serve.

SUNDAY TEA

GOLDEN SCENTED FRUIT CAKE

TEATIME BAGUETTE

STILTON AND CELERY SCONES

BLUEBERRY AND HAZELNUT SLICES

BANANA AND PINE NUT LOAF

CHOCOLATE CAKE WITH RICH CHOCOLATE ICING

GOLDEN SCENTED FRUIT CAKE

 Makes 12 slices

This cake is wonderfully scented. Try to buy semidried fruits which have even more flavour than dried ones. This recipe is a light alternative to the traditional fruit cakes with an exotic combination of flavours.

350 g (12 oz) mixed semi-dried fruits, such as mango, papaya, pear and pineapple, chopped

40 g (1½ oz) flaked coconut, toasted
250 ml (8fl oz) strong fruit tea
175 g (6 oz) butter, softened
175 g (6 oz) golden caster sugar
3 eggs, beaten
225 g (8 oz) self-raising flour
2 tablespoons milk

For the topping
175 g (6 oz) icing sugar
Pinch of saffron strands

1. Set aside 50 g (2 oz) of the dried fruit and 2 tablespoons of the coconut flakes to decorate. Soak the remaining dried fruit in the tea for 1–2 hours or overnight if more convenient.
2. Pre-heat the oven to 180C/350F/Gas 4. Lightly grease and line the base of a deep 20 cm (8 in) round cake tin. Cream the butter and sugar with an electric whisk until light and fluffy. Gradually beat in the eggs, then fold in the flour followed by the milk.
3. Drain the soaked fruit and fold into the creamed mixture with the flaked coconut. Spoon the mixture into the prepared tin and bake for 1 hour. Cover with foil and bake for a further 20 minutes or until

well risen and a skewer inserted into the centre comes out clean. Cool in the tin for about 10 minutes, then turn out on to a wire rack and cool completely.

4. Make the topping: sift the icing sugar into a bowl. Mix the saffron with 5 teaspoons boiling water and break down the saffron with a teaspoon, allowing the vibrant yellow colour to disperse into the water. Gradually beat the saffron water into the icing sugar to give a smooth thick icing. Spoon over the cake, then scatter over the reserved fruit pieces and coconut flakes.

TEATIME BAGUETTE

Makes 18 slices

100 g (4 oz) sweetcure streaky bacon
1 baguette, about 46 cm (18 in) or 2 baguetines
12 tablespoons mayonnaise
6 eggs, hard boiled, shelled
Pinch of cayenne pepper
50 g (2 oz) cos lettuce, finely shredded
1-2 tablespoons snipped fresh chives
Salt and freshly ground black pepper

1. Grill the bacon under a hot grill until crispy, then chop. Slit the loaf lengthways down one side, taking care not to cut all the way through. Pull out some, but not all, of the soft bread to leave a hollow for the filling. Open up the loaf and spread the inside with 4 tablespoons of the mayonnaise.
2. Put the yolks and whites of the hard boiled eggs in separate bowls. Mash the yolks with 4 tablespoons of mayonnaise and the cayenne pepper. Spread on the top inside half of the loaf. Mash the egg white with the remaining 4 tablespoons of mayonnaise and seasoning. Spread on the bottom inside half of the loaf.
3. Lay the lettuce along the centre, then sprinkle over the bacon and chives. Press the two halves of the loaf together firmly. Cut into 2.5 cm (1 in) slices and serve.

STILTON AND CELERY SCONES

 Makes 8

225 g (8 oz) self-raising flour
50 g (2 oz) butter
75 g (3 oz) Stilton, crumbled
2 sticks celery, very finely chopped
2 teaspoons chopped fresh thyme

8 tablespoons milk
Salt and freshly ground black pepper

1. Pre-heat the oven to 220C/425F/Gas 7. Measure the flour into a bowl. Add the butter, cut into small pieces and rub in with the fingertips until the mixture resembles fine breadcrumbs.
2. Stir in the Stilton, celery, thyme and seasoning. Add the milk and mix lightly to form a soft dough. Do not overwork the mixture or it will be tough. Knead very briefly on a lightly floured surface, then roll out to a 20 cm (8 in) round. Cut into 8 wedges.
3. Transfer the scones to a baking sheet and bake for 12–15 minutes until the scones are risen and golden. Cool on a wire rack and serve warm, split and buttered.

From the left clockwise: *Banana and Pine Nut Loaf (page 194), Teatime Baguette, Golden Scented Fruit Cake, Chocolate Cake (page 195), Stilton and Celery Scones* and *Blueberry and Hazelnut Slices (page 194)*

BLUEBERRY AND HAZELNUT SLICES

Makes 18 slices

For the shortbread
225 g (8 oz) plain flour
150 g (5 oz) butter, diced
50 g (2 oz) caster sugar
1 egg yolk

For the filling
100 g (4 oz) unsalted butter, softened
100 g (4 oz) caster sugar
2 eggs, beaten

100 g (4 oz) ground hazelnuts
15 g ($^1/_2$ oz) plain flour
8 tablespoons blueberry jam
50 g (2 oz) hazelnuts, halved

1. Lightly grease a 23 x 30 cm (9 x 12 in) Swiss roll tin. Make the shortbread: put the flour in a bowl and rub in the butter with your fingertips until the mixture resembles fine breadcrumbs. Stir in the sugar, then make a well in the centre and mix in the egg yolk to bind. Gather up the shortbread mixture in your hand and press into a ball, wiping the bowl clean.
2. Press the dough into the tin with your fingers to evenly cover the base. Smooth the surface with the back of a metal spoon. Cover with plastic film and chill for 30 minutes while you make the filling.
3. Pre-heat the oven to 180C/350F/Gas 4. Make the filling: beat the butter and sugar with an electric whisk until light and fluffy. Beat in the eggs, ground hazelnuts and flour.
4. Spread the jam evenly over the chilled shortbread base to within 5 mm ($^1/_4$ in) of the edges. Carefully spoon the hazelnut mixture over the jam, using the back of a spoon and being careful not to disturb the jam. The mixture will spread in the oven so don't worry if there are little gaps. Sprinkle over the hazelnut halves. Bake for 20 minutes or until golden and firm to the touch. Cut into 18 x 5 x 7.5 cm (2 x 3 in) slices and cool on a wire rack.

BANANA AND PINE NUT LOAF

Makes 8 slices

100 g (4 oz) butter, softened
100 g (4 oz) light muscovado sugar
2 eggs, beaten
2 small ripe bananas, mashed
75 g (3 oz) pine nuts
175 g (6 oz) self-raising flour, sifted
3 tablespoons milk

1. Pre-heat the oven to 180C/350F/Gas 4. Lightly grease and line the base of a 900 g (2 lb) loaf tin. Cream the butter and sugar with an electric whisk until light and fluffy. Beat in the eggs, then fold in the bananas and half the pine nuts. Gently stir in the flour and milk. Spoon the mixture into the

Banana and Pine Nut Loaf

Chocolate Cake with Rich Chocolate Icing

prepared tin and level the surface.
2. Sprinkle over the remaining pine nuts and bake for 1–1¼ hours or until well risen and a skewer inserted in the centre comes out clean. Cool in the tin for 10 minutes, then turn out onto a wire rack and leave to cool completely. Slice and serve buttered if you like.

CHOCOLATE CAKE WITH RICH CHOCOLATE ICING

Makes 12 slices

100 g (4 oz) plain chocolate, broken into pieces
225 g (8 oz) self-raising flour
40 g (1½ oz) cocoa powder
1½ tablespoons baking powder
100 g (4 oz) butter, softened
175 g (6 oz) light muscovado sugar
2 eggs, beaten
100 ml (3½ fl oz) milk
8 tablespoons apricot jam

For the rich chocolate icing
225 g (8 oz) plain chocolate
100 g (4 oz) butter
150ml (¼ pint double cream)

1. Pre-heat the oven to 180C/350F/Gas 4. Grease and line the bases of 2 round 20 cm (8 in) tins. Place the chocolate in a bowl with 100 ml (3½ fl oz) boiling water and stir to melt. Sift the flour, cocoa powder and baking powder.
2. Beat together the butter and sugar in a bowl until pale and fluffy, then beat in the eggs a little at a time, beating well after each addition. Fold in the sifted ingredients alternately with the melted chocolate and milk. Spoon into the tins and bake for about 30 minutes or until well risen and just firm to the touch.
3. Leave the cakes in the tins for 30 minutes, then turn out on to a wire rack and cool completely. When cool, spread the jam over one of the cakes and sandwich the other cake on top.
4. Make the icing: break the chocolate into a heatproof bowl over a pan of simmering water and stir until it melts. Remove the bowl from the heat and stir in the butter until melted, then stir in the cream. The mixture should be fairly thick. Spread the icing over the top and sides of the cake with a palette knife.

WEDDINGS

There's no better gift to a bride than her wedding buffet, but it can be jolly hard work. Here are three delicious menus designed to be made at home with the minimum of fuss and easily multiplied to serve as many guests as you can cope with.

From the left: *Lemon and White Chocolate Wedding Cake (page 198), Asparagus Risotto Timbales (page 199), Apricot Bulgar Salad (page 202), New Potato Salad (page 203), Walnut Patties with Mango Relish (page 202), Pimiento Stuffed Turkey (page 200)* and *Saffron Potted Trout (page 200)*

MELLOW YELLOW WEDDING

LEMON AND WHITE CHOCOLATE WEDDING CAKE

ASPARAGUS RISOTTO TIMBALES

SAFFRON POTTED TROUT

PIMIENTO STUFFED TURKEY

WALNUT PATTIES WITH MANGO RELISH

APRICOT BULGAR SALAD

NEW POTATO SALAD

ROSY MOUSSE GATEAU

MARINATED SOFT FRUIT

A cold buffet is the perfect way to entertain a large number of guests if a wedding reception is being held at home. The following menus will serve 25 people, but the quantities can be doubled if you are planning a bigger event.

LEMON AND WHITE CHOCOLATE WEDDING CAKE

This cake can be frozen in advance (see method). Make the ganache in three batches for best results.

Serves 50

500 g (1¹/₄ lb) butter, softened
500 g (1¹/₄ lb) golden caster sugar
10 eggs
500 g (1¹/₄ lb) self-raising flour
275 g (10 oz) plain flour
Grated rind of 3 lemons
175 g (6 oz) white chocolate polka dots
6 tablespoons brandy

For the ganache
425 g (15 oz) white chocolate
75 g (3 oz) unsalted butter
3 tablespoons brandy
900 ml (1¹/₂ pints) double cream

For the decorations
450 g (1 lb) white chocolate
2 metres (2 yards) cream ribbon (5 mm (¹/₄ in) wide)
White and yellow roses

1. Pre-heat the oven to 160C/325F/Gas 3. Grease and line 3 cake tins, the smallest tin measuring 15 cm (6 in), with one of 20 cm (8 in) and one of 25 cm (10 in).
2. Beat the butter in a large bowl until fluffy, then beat in the sugar, eggs, flour and lemon rind until pale and creamy. Stir in the chocolate polka dots and divide the mixture among the tins, levelling the surface of each one.
3. Bake the smaller cakes in the centre of the oven, allowing 50 minutes for the 15 cm (6 in) cake and 1–1¹/₄ hours for the 20 cm (8 in) cake, or until just firm to the touch. Bake the largest cake for about 1¹/₂ hours. Leave the cakes in the tins for 5 minutes, then turn out on to wire racks to cool completely. Place the cakes on freezerproof plates and drizzle over the brandy.
4. To make the ganache, melt 150 g (5 oz) of the chocolate with 25 g (1 oz) of the butter and 1 tablespoon of the brandy in a heatproof bowl set over a pan of simmering water. Leave to cool slightly. Whip 300 ml (10 fl oz) of the cream and beat into the chocolate mixture. Spread over top and sides of the centre tier.
5. Make 2 more batches of ganache and spread over the other 2 cakes, using any excess from the top tier as extra for the bottom tier. Open-freeze the cakes until solid, then cover with clear film and freeze for up to 1 month.
6. To decorate, 2 days in advance, remove the cakes from the freezer and unwrap, but don't allow them to defrost. Cut three strips of greaseproof paper long enough to wrap around each cake and wide enough to stand 2.5 cm (1 in) above the top. Cut scallops along the edge of each strip and place flat on a work surface.
7. Melt the white chocolate in a bowl set over a pan of gently simmering water. Spread evenly over the greaseproof paper and leave until just beginning to set.
8. Stack the cakes on top of each other while still frozen. Wrap the greaseproof paper, chocolate side facing inwards, around the smallest cake, pressing gently. Leave for 5–10 minutes until the chocolate has hardened, then peel away the paper. Repeat on the other cakes, store in the fridge until completely thawed and ready to serve.
9. Two or three hours in advance, decorate the cake with the ribbon and roses. Keep chilled until ready to serve.

ASPARAGUS RISOTTO TIMBALES

There are two starters in this menu. You could use both the quantities given or double up either recipe and just serve one of them. If you don't have a dariole mould, use a 1.2 litre (2 pint) ring mould. To freeze, invert the timbales on to a freezerproof tray and freeze uncovered until firm, then cover with foil and freeze for up to 1 month. To thaw, leave in a cool place for 24 hours.

 Serves 14–16

400 g (14 oz) risotto rice
50 g (2 oz) wild rice
225 g (8 oz) thin asparagus spears
1 bunch spring onions, finely chopped
85 ml (3 fl oz) olive oil
2 tablespoons pesto
2 tablespoons white wine vinegar
50 g (2 oz) fresh Parmesan, finely grated
Salt and freshly ground black pepper

To garnish
Cherry tomatoes, quartered
Basil leaves
Flatleaf parsley sprigs

1. Cook the risotto rice and wild rice separately, according to the instructions. Rinse under cold water and drain thoroughly.
2. Trim the ends of the asparagus then remove and reserve the tips. Cook the asparagus stalks in boiling water for 2–3 minutes, then add the tips and cook for a further 1 minute. Rinse under cold water, drain and chop.
3. Mix together the rice, asparagus, spring onions, oil, pesto, vinegar, Parmesan and seasoning. Pack a little of the mixture into a lightly greased dariole mould and invert on to a plate. Repeat with the rest of the mixture. Serve garnished with cherry tomatoes, basil leaves and flatleaf parsley.

Lemon and White Chocolate Wedding Cake

Asparagus Risotto Timbales (page 199) and Saffron Potted Trout

SAFFRON POTTED TROUT

Ramekins are used as moulds for this dish, but you could use a 1.75 litre (3 pint) loaf tin lined with greaseproof paper – just turn out and cut into slices.
You can freeze the pots at the end of step 3. Cover the ramekins with clear film, then foil. Freeze for up to 1 month. To thaw, remove from ramekins and place in the fridge for 24 hours.

Serves 14–16

1.5 kg (3 lb) trout fillets
350 g (12 oz) butter
8 rashers streaky bacon, rinded and chopped
6 rosemary sprigs
2 teaspoons saffron strands, crushed
Salt and freshly ground black pepper
Rosemary sprigs, to garnish

1. Pre-heat the oven to 190C/375F/Gas 5. Place the fish, skin side down, in a large roasting tin, season lightly and add 3 tablespoons of water. Cover tightly with foil and bake for 12–15 minutes. Roughly flake fish, discarding skin and any bones.
2. Melt 15 g (1/2 oz) of the butter and fry the bacon, rosemary and saffron until crisp. Discard the rosemary, remove the bacon using a slotted spoon and add to the fish, reserving the pan juices.
3. Pack the trout mixture tightly in ramekins. Melt the remaining butter with the pan juices and pour over the ramekins. Cool until set.
4. Remove the trout from the ramekins and garnish with rosemary sprigs.

PIMIENTO STUFFED TURKEY

Ask your butcher to bone the turkey – you will probably need to give a couple of days' notice.
To freeze, wrap the turkey in a double thickness of foil at the end of step 5, and freeze for up to 1 month. To thaw, place in the fridge 3 days before serving. Complete the recipe from step 6. Make the glaze a day before you plan to serve the turkey

Serves 25

5.5 kg (12 lb) turkey, boned
(with drumsticks remaining)

For the marinade
150 ml (5 fl oz) dry white wine
4 tablespoons olive oil
Pared rind of 2 oranges
1 large onion, sliced
4 garlic cloves, sliced
3 bay leaves
1 tablespoon coriander seeds, lightly crushed
1 tablespoon black peppercorns

For the stuffing
450 g (1 lb) sausagemeat
100 g (4 oz) cashew nuts
15 g (1/2 oz) fresh mint, chopped
50 g (2 oz) fresh white breadcrumbs
2 eggs, lightly beaten
2 x 200 g (7 oz) cans pimientos, drained
350 g (12 oz) no-soak dried figs or apricots
Salt and freshly ground black pepper

For the glaze
Juice of 2 oranges
1 1/2 teaspoons cornflour
4 tablespoons dark muscovado sugar

To garnish
Fresh figs, halved
Fresh herb sprigs

1. Place the turkey, skin side down, in a non-metallic dish. Combine the marinade ingredients and pour over the turkey, turning to coat. Cover and chill for 24 hours, basting occasionally.
2. To make the stuffing, combine the sausagemeat, nuts, mint, breadcrumbs and seasoning, then bind together with the eggs.
3. Pre-heat the oven to 180C/350F/Gas 4. Remove the turkey from the marinade and place, skin side down, on a board. Spread half of the stuffing down the centre, cover with pimientos, then the figs or apricots and top with the remaining stuffing.
4. Bring up the sides of the turkey to enclose the stuffing and sew together with fine string. Tuck in the ends and sew to enclose completely.
5. Carefully invert the turkey on to a rack set over a roasting tin. Season well and roast in the oven for 2^1/$_2$ hours or until tender and the juices run clear when pierced with a skewer. Cover with foil if it starts to brown too quickly. Remove from the oven and leave in a cool place until completely cold. Cut off the string.
6. Make the glaze a day before serving. Blend the orange juice and cornflour in a small pan. Add the sugar and heat gently, stirring continuously, until it dissolves and the glaze has thickened. Leave to cool slightly, then brush over the turkey. Chill until ready to serve.
7. Serve the turkey garnished with halved figs and the herb sprigs.

Pimiento Stuffed Turkey

Walnut Patties with Mango Relish

WALNUT PATTIES WITH MANGO RELISH

These patties are a vegetarian alternative to the turkey main course. To freeze, pack the *Walnut Patties* into a rigid container at the end of step 2, and freeze for up to 1 month. To thaw, transfer to a cool place and leave for up to 24 hours before serving.

 Serves 14–16

2 teaspoons cumin seeds, crushed
450 g (1 lb) shelled walnuts, finely chopped
2 onions, finely chopped
2 garlic cloves, crushed
5 cm (2 in) piece root ginger, peeled and grated
50 g (2 oz) fresh white breadcrumbs
3 tablespoons chopped fresh coriander
3 carrots, finely grated
2 eggs, beaten
Salt and freshly ground black pepper

For the relish
2 mangoes, halved, skinned, stoned and thinly sliced
1 onion, cut into thin slivers
Juice and grated rind of 2 limes
4 teaspoons light muscovado sugar

To garnish
Lime halves
Fresh coriander sprigs

1. Pre-heat the oven to 180C/350F/Gas 4. Using your hands, mix together the cumin, walnuts, onions, garlic, ginger, breadcrumbs, coriander, carrots, eggs and seasoning.
2. Roughly shape the mixture into balls (about 4 cm (1½ in) diameter), then press between the palms of your hands to flatten slightly. Place on a baking sheet and bake for 12–15 minutes until golden brown. Set aside to cool.
3. To make the relish, mix together the mangoes, onion, lime rind and juice and sugar. Cover and chill for up to 3 days.
4. Garnish the patties with the lime halves and coriander sprigs. Serve with the mango relish.

APRICOT BULGAR SALAD

Bulgar wheat, pre-steamed cracked wheat grains, makes a light, summery salad.
To freeze, pack the salad (omitting the apricots) in a rigid container and freeze for up to 1 month. To thaw, transfer to the fridge a day before serving. Add the apricots as soon as the salad has thawed.

 Serves 25

450 g (1 lb) bulgar wheat (cracked wheat)
Juice and grated rind of 2 lemons
2 onions, finely chopped
6 celery sticks, finely sliced
65 g (2½ oz) fresh parsley, chopped
2 teaspoons ground allspice
1 teaspoon golden caster sugar
1½ teaspoons salt
1 tablespoon paprika
150 ml (5 fl oz) olive oil
6 fresh apricots, halved, stoned and sliced, or 12 no-soak dried apricots, sliced

1. Place the bulgar wheat in a large bowl, cover with cold water, add the lemon juice and leave to stand for 1 hour, then drain thoroughly.
2. Place the bulgar wheat in a large serving bowl and add the remaining ingredients, stirring well.

NEW POTATO SALAD

Serves 25

2.25 kg (5 lb) new potatoes, cooked
450 g (1 lb) baby broad beans, cooked
300 ml (10 fl oz) olive oil
4 tablespoons white wine vinegar
2 tablespoons golden caster sugar
6 tablespoons wholegrain mustard
10 tablespoons fresh chives, snipped
Salt and freshly ground black pepper

1. Mix together the potatoes and broad beans and place them in the serving bowl.
2. In a separate bowl, mix together the other ingredients before pouring over the salad. Toss thoroughly before serving.

ROSY MOUSSE GATEAU

Allow guests the luxury of both desserts by making two gateaux and serving them with the *Marinated Soft Fruit* on page 204. If you prefer a different flavour, use kirsch, Amaretto or Cointreau instead of the rosewater
To freeze, remove the gateau from the tin after step 7, wrap in clear film and freeze for up to 1 month. To thaw, leave in a cool place for 24 hours, then follow steps 8 and 9.

Serves 16

Rosy Mousse Gateau and *Marinated Soft Fruit (page 204)*

For the sponge
5 eggs, separated
150 g (5 oz) golden caster sugar
6 tablespoons ground almonds
25 g (1 oz) plain flour
1 tablespoon lemon juice

For the mousse
4 tablespoons rosewater
4 teaspoons powdered gelatine
500 g (18 oz) carton fresh custard
600 ml (1 pint) double cream

For the decorations
100 g (4 oz) golden caster sugar
Icing sugar, for dusting

1. Pre-heat the oven to 180C/350F/Gas 4. Grease and base-line a 25–28 cm (10–11 in) loose-bottomed cake tin.
2. To make the sponge, whisk together the egg yolks and sugar in a bowl until pale and thickened. Gently fold in the almonds, flour and lemon juice.
3. Whisk the egg whites in a separate bowl until just peaking. Gently fold a spoonful into the egg yolk mixture, then fold in the remainder. Turn into the prepared tin and bake for 20 minutes until well risen and just firm. Leave to cool in the tin for 5 minutes, then turn out on to a wire rack and cool completely.
4. Wash the tin and re-line the base and sides with non-stick baking paper. Carefully halve the sponge horizontally and place one half back in the tin.
5. To make the mousse, place the rosewater in a bowl with 2 tablespoons of water. Sprinkle over the gelatine and set aside. Set the bowl of gelatine over a pan of simmering water until dissolved.
6. Whip the cream until it just holds its shape. Fold the cream, and the custard together. Gradually pour the gelatine into the mixture stirring well all the time. Carefully pour the mixture into the prepared tin. Level the surface and cover with the other half of the sponge. Chill for several hours until the mousse has set.
7. To make the decorations, heat the sugar with 4 tablespoons of water until dissolved, then boil rapidly until it is golden brown. Using a teaspoon, drizzle the syrup across an oiled sheet of aluminium foil to make irregular squiggles. Leave to set in a cool, dry place for 30 minutes.
8. Using a sharp knife, mark the gateau into thin slices. Dust liberally with icing sugar and press the squiggles into the top.

MARINATED SOFT FRUIT

Use soft fruits which are in season such as strawberries, raspberries, blueberries and red-currants. Serve the fruits with whipped cream.

 Serves 20

2.25 kg (5 lb) mixed soft fruit
175 ml (6 fl oz) Cointreau or other orange-flavoured liqueur

1. Mix the fruits before tossing gently with the liqueur.
2. Chill for 24 hours and then toss again.

COUNTDOWN

One month in advance:
• Make and freeze the *Walnut Patties*, *Asparagus Risotto Timbales*, *Rosy Mousse Gateau* and iced (but not decorated) cakes for the *Lemon and White Chocolate Wedding Cake*.

One week in advance:
• Make and freeze the *Apricot Bulgar Salad* and *Saffron Potted Trout*.
•Make the dressing for the *New Potato Salad*. Chill.

Three days in advance
• Transfer turkey from freezer to fridge. Make the *Mango Relish*, cover and chill.
• Make caramel squiggles for gateau, cover with oiled cling film and store in a cool, dry place.

Two days in advance
• Remove the iced cakes from freezer and complete the chocolate decoration while still frozen.

One day in advance
• Glaze the *Pimiento Stuffed Turkey*. Prepare the *Marinated Soft Fruit* and *New Potato Salad*.
• Remove the *Asparagus Risotto Timbales*, *Saffron Potted Trout*, *Walnut Patties*, *Apricot Bulgar Salad* and *Rosy Mousse Gateau* from freezer.
• Chill *Saffron Potted Trout* and *Rosy Mousse Gateau*. Keep the rest in a cool place.

On the day
• Whip cream to accompany *Marinated Soft Fruit*. Add the apricots to the *Apricot Bulgar Salad*.
•Decorate the *Lemon and White Chocolate Wedding Cake* with the ribbon and roses and the *Rosy Mousse Gateau* with caramel shapes.

Rosy Mousse Gateau (page 203)

PINK LACE WEDDING

PINK AND WHITE WEDDING CAKE

SALMON IN ASPIC

INDONESIAN SALAD

SHREDDED SAVOY SALAD

MUSCAT MERINGUE

RASPBERRY MOUSSE

This is a light and easy meal to prepare for an informal gathering of about 20 guests. Serve the salmon with the two salads here, a third one chosen from one of the other weddings, such as *Apricot Bulgar Salad* (see page 202), *Orange Rice Salad* (see page 218) or *Green Summer Salad* (see page 217). If you require a second main course make the *Mediterranean Roasted Vegetable Ring* (see page 217).

PINK AND WHITE WEDDING CAKE

1 x 15 cm (6 in) round Basic Fruit Cake *(see page 210)*
1 x 20 cm (8 in) round Basic Fruit Cake *(see page 210)*
1 x 25 cm (10 in) round Basic Fruit Cake *(see page 210)*
1 x 15 cm (6 in), 1 x 20 cm (8 in) and 1 x 25 cm (10 in) round cake boards
2 kg (4¹/₂ lb) Almond Paste *(see page 211)*
2.25 kg (5 lb) Sugar Paste *(see page 212)*

ROYAL ICING

2¹/₂ teaspoons powdered egg albumen or 2 large egg whites
450 g (1 lb) icing sugar, sifted
1–2 teaspoons glycerine, optional

1. Put the egg albumen with 4 tablespoons of water (or the egg whites) in a clean bowl and whisk well with a fork.
2. Gradually beat in the icing sugar and glycerine, if using, until the mixture becomes very white and smooth – like softly whipped cream.

Pink and White Wedding Cake

Decorating the cakes

See page 210 to make the *Basic Fruit Cakes* and pages 211 and 212 to cover cakes with *Almond Paste* and *Sugar Paste*. Once the cakes have been covered with *Almond Paste* and *Sugar Paste*, you can begin to decorate them. Use a lace which has very raised embroidery – when pressed into soft icing it leaves a pattern which can be iced over. You can use lace from your wedding dress to copy this design. Or place a small piece of glass (removed from a small picture frame) over the lace and pipe the outline in *Royal Icing*. Leave to dry for 2–3 days. Press the icing on the glass into the cake and it will leave the pattern for you to copy.

450 g (1 lb) Royal Icing (see page 205)
Pink dusting powder
1 quantity Flower Paste (see page 212)

Equipment
30 cm (12 in) embroidered lace pieces
No. 2 plain piping nozzle
Greaseproof and waxed paper
Cake icing smoother
No. 4 mini 'm' shape crimper
Fine artist's paintbrush
Double-sided sticky tape
2 medium sized rose petal cutters or 2.5 cm (1 in) and
1 cm (½ in) round cutters
Small sponge and balling tool
Small rolling pin
Polystyrene apple tray or something similar
Cream fabric stamens
2 x 10 cm (4 in) squares fine white net
4 metres (4 yards) wide pink ribbon
Pink cotton thread to match the ribbon
1½ metres (1½ yards) thin pink ribbon
8 round solid cake pillars
8 lengths of plastic cake dowelling

1. As soon as the cake is covered with the *Sugar Paste*, apply the lace pattern.
2. Using a pin, prick the sides of one cake with the width of each lace piece. Press the lace or glass pattern firmly against the side of the cake. If using lace, it's best to use a flat, firm cake smoother to press on the lace, to avoid fingerprints! Cover the remaining cakes with the *Sugar Paste* and press the patterns on one at a time, as before.
Note: check that the lace flowers are arranged in either the same or regular alternating directions.

3. Place a little *Royal Icing* in a greaseproof paper piping bag fitted with a no. 2 nozzle. Pipe the outline of each flower, working on the outside petals first. Pipe a thick outline. Dip the artist's paintbrush in a little water, dry slightly, then brush the icing from the outline towards the inside of the petal. Try to leave the edge thicker to give depth. Pipe the next petal and continue brushing the icing towards the flower's centre.
4. Complete the flower by piping the dots in the centre of each flower. The leaves are brushed in the same way, and then over-piped to look like the leaf veins.
5. Pipe small dots of icing around the cake board. Secure the wide ribbon to the edge of the board with double-sided tape.

Making the flowers
You need the *Flower Paste* and 2 flower cutters. Make 12–13 flowers. Roll out a little piece of *Flower Paste* and cut 5 large petals. Keep covered to prevent drying. Place one petal in your palm and roll the edge with a balling tool until it gets thinner. Place the petal on the sponge and press down to 'cup' it. Allow it to dry in an apple tray. Continue

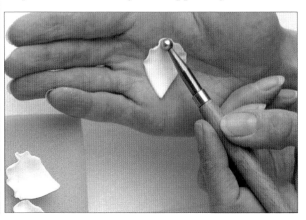

to make 60 large petals and 110 small petals and dry overnight in a cool place.

Assembling the flowers
Cut 12–13 squares of waxed paper. Slit the 4 corners and place in polystyrene apple trays. Pipe a circle of *Royal Icing* in the base. Arrange 5 petals on the edge. Pipe another circle of *Royal Icing* on top and arrange 4 small petals inside. Repeat. Pipe a blob of *Royal Icing* in the centre. Snip the stamens into short lengths and place 4–5 in the centre of each flower. Leave to dry for 2–3 days. Brush the edge of each petal (from the back) with dusting powder, peel off the paper and secure on the cake with the *Royal Icing*.

From the left: *Indonesian Salad (page 208), Salmon in Aspic, Shredded Savoy Salad (page 208)*

Net and ribbon loops
Join all 4 corners of the net squares. Pinch the base and wind cotton around it. Open out the top points. Wind a thin ribbon 3 times around 2 fingers, snip the end to neaten. Wind cotton around one end of the loops.

Completing the cake
Position the pillars and push dowelling into the cake to support them. Saw off excess dowelling. Arrange decorations and secure with *Royal Icing*.

To cut a wedding cake
Cut each round cake in half, then cut into 5 cm (2 in) sections straight across the cut edge of the halved cake. Cut each of these sections into 1 cm (¹/₂ in) slices.

SALMON IN ASPIC

Choose a salmon which will fit in either a fish kettle or a large roasting tin. The fish can be cooked a day in advance and kept in the fridge.

Serves 20

1 x 3¹/₂ kg (8 lb) whole fresh salmon
1 sachet aspic jelly crystals
4 tablespoons redcurrant jelly
¹/₄ – ¹/₂ teaspoon pink food colouring

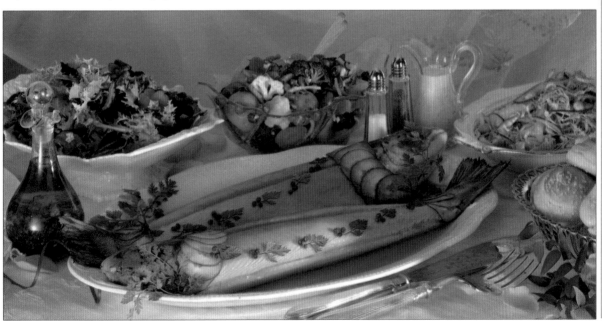

For the court bouillon
300 ml (½ pint) red wine vinegar
2 onions, sliced
A handful of parsley stalks
A few fresh thyme sprigs
3 bay leaves
12 peppercorns

To garnish
Cucumber
Fresh chervil
2 tablespoons pink peppercorns in brine, drained and rinsed

1. Put the court bouillon ingredients in a large pan, add 900 ml (1½ pints) of water and simmer for 20 minutes. Cool and strain through a sieve.
2. Place the salmon in a large, heavy roasting tin or fish kettle and pour over the cooled court bouillon. Cover the tin and poach the salmon very gently for 20–30 minutes. To test if the fish is cooked, pull away the dorsel fin; the flesh should be firm and no longer transparent. Leave to cool in the liquid, basting occasionally.
3. When completely cold, gently lift the fish out of the roasting tin. Cut through the skin along the sides of the fish and very carefully peel it off. Scrape off dark brown flesh.
4. Strain the cooking liquid through muslin or a tea towel, pour into a large pan and boil over a high heat until the liquid has reduced to 600 ml (1 pint). Add the aspic, redcurrant jelly and food colouring, stir to dissolve. Leave to cool. Chill until nearly set.
5. Pour a little of the aspic to a depth of 3 mm (⅛ in) on to a large serving platter and chill until it has completely set. Arrange the salmon decoratively on the platter and brush all over with a little aspic.
6. Place ultra thin slices of cucumber along the length of the salmon. Add the chervil and pink peppercorns and brush again with aspic. Chill before serving.

INDONESIAN SALAD

 Serves 20

900 g (2 lb) tiny new potatoes
750 g (1½ lb) baby carrots, scrubbed and thinly sliced
750 g (1½ lb) French beans, topped, tailed and halved
450 g (1 lb) cauliflower florets
450 g (1 lb) broccoli florets
450 g (1 lb) beansprouts

For the dressing and garnish
300 ml (½ pint) groundnut oil
225 g (8 oz) shelled unsalted peanuts
4 garlic cloves, crushed
2 fresh chillies, seeded and very finely sliced, optional
120 ml (4 fl oz) rice wine vinegar or white wine vinegar
50 g (2 oz) creamed coconut, finely grated
Salt and freshly ground black pepper

1. Simmer the potatoes in a large pan of boiling, salted water until tender. Drain and set aside.
2. Blanch the carrots, French beans, cauliflower and broccoli for 3–4 minutes until just tender. Drain, rinse in cold water and place in salad bowls with the potatoes and beansprouts, mixing well. Cover and chill.
3. Fry the peanuts in 4 tablespoons of oil until golden. Add garlic and chillies, if using, and fry for a few seconds more. Cool and set aside.
4. Mix together the remaining dressing ingredients. Before serving, pour dressing over the vegetables. Sprinkle the peanut mixture over the top and toss everything together.

SHREDDED SAVOY SALAD

 Serves 20

900 g (2 lb) Savoy cabbage, finely shredded
900 g (2 lb) Chinese leaves, finely shredded
900 g (2 lb) carrots, very finely grated
2 celery heads (including the leaves), finely sliced diagonally
2 red onions or 6 shallots, finely sliced
Grated rind of 2 oranges
100 g (4 oz) hazelnuts

For the dressing
300 g (11 oz) natural yoghurt
300 g (11 oz) mayonnaise
Juice of 2 oranges
4 tablespoons wholegrain mustard
Salt and freshly ground black pepper

1. Mix together all the ingredients for the salad and place in 2 or 3 large serving bowls. Cover and chill until ready to serve.
2. Mix together all the ingredients for the dressing and chill until ready to serve. Pour the dressing over the salad just before serving and toss together.

MUSCAT MERINGUE

Serves 10

4 egg whites
A pinch of salt
225 g (8 oz) caster sugar
3 teaspoons cornflour
1 teaspoon lime juice
1½ teaspoons vanilla essence
150 ml (5 fl oz) Muscat wine, such as Beaumes de
Venise or Frontignan
350 g (12 oz) Muscat grapes, halved and pipped
2 Galia or Ogen melons, peeled and cut into small slices
150 ml (5 fl oz) double cream
Grated rind of 1 lime

1. Pre-heat the oven to 120C/250F/Gas ½. Draw a 20 cm (8 in) circle on a sheet of non-stick paper and place on a baking sheet.
2. Whisk the egg whites with the salt until they are stiff and dry, then whisk in the caster sugar thoroughly, 1 tablespoon at a time. Once all the sugar is added, the meringue should be very stiff.
3. Fold 2 teaspoons of the cornflour, lime juice and vanilla essence into the meringue. Put 4 tiny blobs at each corner of the baking sheet to secure the paper, then spoon and swirl the remaining meringue on to the paper and spread out to fill the circle, leaving a dip in the centre.
4. Bake for 1 hour and leave to cool in the oven with the door ajar.
5. Blend the remaining cornflour with a little of the wine, then stir in the remaining wine and cook in a small pan, stirring until boiling and thickened. Add the grapes and melon and any of the juices, stir gently to coat the fruit in the sauce and then leave to cool.
6. Whip the cream until it holds soft peaks. Spoon fruit and sauce on to meringue and top with the cream. Scatter over the grated lime rind. Serve as soon as possible on a pretty plate.

RASPBERRY MOUSSE

You may prefer to make this a day in advance, in one large fruit bowl. Top with cream about an hour before serving.

Serves 10

30 ratafia biscuits
75 ml (3 oz) medium sweet white wine
450 g (1 lb) raspberries (225 g/8 oz puréed and sieved)
4 tablespoons crème de cassis
900 ml (1½ pints) double cream, whipped
6 tablespoons caster sugar
1 sachet gelatine

1. Combine the ratafias and wine and divide among 10 glasses. Mix the puréed raspberries and crème de cassis. Fold in 300 ml (5 fl oz) of the cream with 3 tablespoons of the sugar.
2. Sprinkle the gelatine over 3 tablespoons of water and leave to soften. Stand the bowl in a pan of hot water until the gelatine has dissolved, then stir into the raspberry mixture.
3. Fold the remaining raspberries into the mousse mixture and spoon into the glasses.
4. Mix the remaining cream and sugar, then spoon into the glasses and chill for 1 hour.

Raspberry Mousses and *Muscat Meringue*

MIDSUMMER WEDDING

MIDSUMMER WEDDING CAKE

SPINACH AND SUN-DRIED TOMATO PINWHEELS

SALMON FILO PIE

DILL SAUCE

GLAZED GAMMON

MEDITERRANEAN ROASTED VEGETABLE RING

GREEN SUMMER SALAD

MINTED MELON AND GRAPE SALAD

ORANGE RICE SALAD

RASPBERRY AND ORANGE MERINGUE ROULADE

CITRUS TART

CHOCOLATE PRALINE BOMBE

This is a small but elegant wedding, with enough food to serve about 16 guests, although the wedding cake will serve many more. Ready-made white almond paste and sugar paste are readily available.

TO MAKE BASIC FRUIT CAKE

1. Brush the tins with melted fat and line with a double thickness of greaseproof paper. Grease the paper.
2. Set the oven to 180C/350F/Gas 4. Place the butter and sugar in a large mixing bowl and beat together until light and creamy. Beat the eggs together in a bowl and add a little at a time to the butter mixture, beating well between each addition.
3. Add the dried fruit, the almonds, peel, cherries and lemon rind. Sift the flour and spice and add to the bowl with the treacle and sufficient lemon juice to make a soft dropping consistency.
4. Put the mixture into the prepared tin and level with the back of a spoon. Wrap several pieces of brown paper round the tin to protect the sides from overbrowning and place the tin just below the

To make cake sizes:	15 cm/6 in round 12 cm/5 in square	20 cm/8 in round 18 cm/7 in square	25 cm/10 in round 23 cm/9 in square
dark muscovado sugar	150 g (5½ oz)	250 g (9 oz)	400 g (14 oz)
butter	150 g (5½ oz)	250 g (9 oz)	400 g (14 oz)
eggs (medium, beaten)	3	4	7
currants	150 g (5½ oz)	250 g (9 oz)	400 g (14 oz)
sultanas	225 g (8 oz)	400 g (14 oz)	600 g (1 lb 5 oz)
raisins	75 g (2¾ oz)	125 g (4½ oz)	200 g (7 oz)
chopped almonds	50 g (1¾ oz)	75 g (2¾ oz)	100 g (3½ oz)
mixed peel	50 g (1¾ oz)	50 g (1¾ oz)	100 g (3½ oz)
glace cherries, chopped	75 g (2¾ oz)	150 g (5½ oz)	200 g (7 oz)
grated rind and juice of lemon	½	1½	1½
plain flour	175 g (6 oz)	300 g (10½ oz)	450g (1 lb)
mixed spice	¼ teaspoon	½ teaspoon	1 teaspoon
Total cooking time:	up to 3¾ hours	up to 4 hours	up to 4½ hours
To cover the cake:			
Almond Paste	550 g (1¼ lb)	1 kg (2¼ lb)	1.3 kg (3 lb)
Sugar Paste	700 g (1 lb 9 oz)	2.5 kg (2 lb 12 oz)	1.6 kg (3½ lb)

centre of the oven. If placing 2 tins on the same shelf, avoid touching the sides of the oven.

5. Reduce the oven to 160C/325F/Gas 3 and cook for 1 hour, then reduce oven one mark and cook another hour. Reduce the oven to 140C/275F/Gas 1 and test with a skewer after a further hour. Cover the surface of the cake with greaseproof if over-browning. When cooked the cake should be firm, deep golden brown and leave a skewer clean when poked into the centre. The larger cake may take up to an hour longer to cook (see timings in chart on the left).

6. Leave the cakes to cook in the tins overnight, then turn out and wrap in double thickness of greaseproof paper. Store up to 3 months. The cakes can occasionally be pricked and brandy drizzled over, but be sure to re-wrap well.

ALMOND PASTE

White almond paste is readily available in supermarkets if you prefer not to use raw egg. This quantity of *Almond Paste* is enough to cover a 20 cm (8 in) cake. You will need 350g (12 oz), or $^1/_2$ this quantity, for a 15 cm (6 in) cake and 900 g (2 lb), or $1^1/_2$ quantities, for a 25 cm (10 in) cake.

225 g (8 oz) ground almonds
225 g (8 oz) caster sugar
225 g (8oz) icing sugar
1 large egg or 2-3 yolks
A few drops of almond essence

1. Mix the dry ingredients together. Beat the egg or yolks with the almond essence and add to the dry mixture. Mix to a firm, rollable paste.

TO COVER THE CAKES WITH ALMOND PASTE

4-10 tablespoons boiled sieved apricot jam
Icing sugar, for dusting
Cake boards

1. Measure the top and down both sides of each cake with string. Turn cake upside down and place on board. Brush top and sides of cakes with jam and use little pieces of *Almond Paste* to fill in any gaps between the board and cake and to help make the cake level.

2. Dust clean work surface with icing sugar and

Midsummer Wedding Cake (page 212)

roll out each piece of weighed *Almond Paste* to a circle the diameter of the appropriate piece of string. Lay the *Almond Paste* over the cake and smooth it down the sides. Turn the cake over and push on to the work surface to level top. Turn up the correct way, trim edges and place on the cake board. Leave in a cool airy place to dry for at least 2 days.

SUGAR PASTE

Ready-to-roll sugar paste is available in shops. See chart on page 210 for quantities needed to cover all three tiers of the *Midsummer Wedding Cake*.

Makes 450 g (1 lb)

1 egg white, size 2
1 rounded tablespoon liquid glucose
450 g (1 lb) icing sugar, sifted
Concentrated paste food colouring: cream

1. Place the egg white and liquid glucose in a grease-free bowl. Mix in the icing sugar gradually with a wooden spoon. If the mixture feels too dry and crumbly, add a drop more egg white. If the mixture feels slack (it should be quite firm), add more icing sugar. Make each batch of *Sugar Paste* just before it is needed, as it tends to lose elasticity with time.
2. Knead until the mixture forms a ball. Drip on a little food colouring using a cocktail stick. Sprinkle the work surface with icing sugar and knead until pliable and evenly coloured.

TO COVER THE CAKES WITH SUGAR PASTE

2-4 tablespoons brandy
Icing sugar and cornflour, for dusting

1. Ensure the work surface and rolling pin are free from grease. Measure the cakes as for almond pasting. Brush the *Almond Paste* all over with a little brandy. Dust a work surface with icing sugar and lightly knead the weighed piece of *Sugar Paste* until smooth. Roll out into a circle to fit the measured string. Lay the *Sugar Paste* over the cake, smoothing down the sides as before.
2. Dust clean, dry hands with cornflour and smooth over the top with the ball of your hand or icing leveller. Trim round the bases of the cakes and reserve trimmings for attaching the flowers. Leave cakes in a dry, airy place to set.

FLOWER PASTE

This *Paste* is firm enough to roll out very thinly; it dries quickly and keeps its shape. It is ideal for modelling delicate roses. Keep it well-wrapped in cling film while not using it. Use small pieces at a time and dust the surface with a fine dusting of cornflour to prevent it sticking.

Makes 225 g (8 oz)

1 teaspoon powdered gelatine
1 rounded teaspoon white fat
225 g (8 oz) icing sugar

1. Heat the gelatine, fat and 5 teaspoons of water in a small pan until the gelatine has dissolved and the liquid is clear. Do not boil.
2. Gradually stir in the icing sugar until the mixture forms a firm ball. Turn out and knead in enough icing sugar until *Paste* is firm but pliable.

MIDSUMMER WEDDING CAKE

This lovely three-tiered wedding cake is easy to decorate as it requires no tricky piping or cake decorating skills. To make it even simpler you could use fresh or silk flowers.

15, 20, 25 cm (6, 8, 10 in) round Basic Fruit Cakes *(see page 210)*
33 cm (13 in) round thick cake board
20 and 23 cm (8 and 9 in) thin cake boards

1.75 kg (4$\frac{1}{4}$ lb) Almond Paste *(see page 211)*
2.5 kg (5$\frac{1}{2}$ lb) Sugar Paste *(see left)*
10 tablespoons boiled sieved apricot jam
Brandy, for brushing
Cornflour, for dusting
Icing sugar, for dusting

1. Place the 25 cm (10 in) cake on the thick 33 cm (13 in) board, the 20 cm (8 in) cake on the 23 cm (9 in) thin board and the 15 cm (6 in) cake on the 20 cm (8 in) cake board. Cover with *Almond Paste* and *Sugar Paste* as instructed on page 211 and left.

To decorate
100g (4 oz) Flower Paste (see left)
Concentrated paste food colourings: blue, yellow, green
Medium carnation cutter or 2.5 cm (1 in) fluted round pastry cutter
Medium ivy cutter
Fern cutter, optional
8-petal daisy cutter
Black fabric stamens (optional)
26-gauge paper-covered florist's wire

1 egg white, lightly beaten
Foil
Cocktail sticks
Oasis or foam sponge
Paintbrush
3 x 13 cm (5 in) solid white pillars
3 lengths plastic cake dowelling
250 g (8 oz) Royal Icing (see page 205)
75 g (3 oz) Sugar Paste (see page 212)
No. 8 or medium star piping nozzle

TO MAKE THE DAISIES

1. Colour a piece of *Flower Paste* the size of a
walnut with yellow food colouring and use it to
make 55 small mini pea-sized balls. Roll each one
over the small holes of a grater, flatten slightly,
then leave to dry.
2. Roll out a small pea-sized piece of white *Flower
Paste* thinly and cut out a daisy with the cutter. Cut
each petal in half lengthways and widen each petal
by rolling lightly with a cocktail stick. Stick a
yellow ball in the centre with a dot of egg white
and leave daisy to dry in a cup made out of foil.
You need to make 54 more daisies for the garlands.
3. Wired daisies: Cut 18 x 7.5 cm (3 in) lengths of
wire and bend each end over into a small hook.
Make 18 yellow centres as before. Thread a piece of
hooked wire through the centre of each and leave
to dry. Make 18 daisies and roll petals as before.
Push a wired yellow centre through the middle of
each daisy and secure with a dot of egg white.
Paint a green calyx on the base of the daisies, if
desired. Leave to dry. Insert the wires into Oasis or
a sponge and bend flowerheads down to dry.

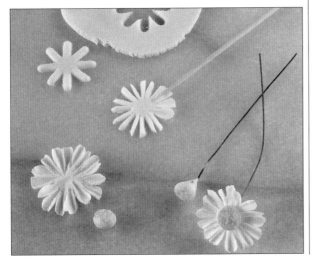

TO MAKE THE CORNFLOWERS

1. Colour half the *Flower Paste* with the blue food
colouring, knead well and roll out a pea-sized
piece thinly and using the carnation cutter, cut out
one cornflower. Using the index finger, roll the end
of a cocktail stick backwards and forwards round
the edge of the flower until it begins to frill.
2. Paint a dot of egg white in the centre and fold in
half, then add another dot of egg white and fold in
half again. Turn the flower over, paint a dot of egg
white in the centre and fold in half again. Pinch the
base. This makes one cornflower and you will need
to make 54 more for the garlands. Crumple up a
piece of foil, open out and leave the cornflowers to
dry overnight on the foil.
3. The flowers and leaves on the top decorations
are wired. Cut 18 x 7.5 cm (3 in) lengths of wire.
Bend the tops over to form small hooks. Make the
cornflower as before but thread a piece of hooked
wire down through the centre of the flower before
the last fold. After folding the cornflower insert 3
stamens into the centre of each before leaving the
cornflower to dry. Insert the wires in Oasis or a
sponge and bend the flowerheads down to dry.
Make 18 wired cornflowers.

TO MAKE THE IVY LEAVES

1. Cut 18 x 7.5 cm (3 in) lengths of wire. Roll out
small pieces of white *Flower Paste* and cut out an
ivy leaf. Hold the base of the leaf and push one end
of the wire up through the base and squeeze to
secure. Make another 17 leaves. When dry, use the
green food colouring to paint on the veins and
variegations.

To Make the Fern Leaves

1. Colour the remaining *Flower Paste* green. Cut 6 x 7.5 cm (3 in) wires. Roll out a small oval piece of *Paste,* push a wire three quarters through from the fattest end. Roll out *Paste* either side of the wire. Place the cutter over the *Paste* and cut out a fern leaf. Place the leaf on a piece of foam. Curl the leaves lightly by rolling with the handle of a paintbrush or a small ball tool and leave to dry on scrunched foil.

To Assemble the Tiers

1. Cut out a 20 cm (8 in) circle of greaseproof paper, fold it in half and then into 3 equal parts. Open out and use the creases to mark 3 points 7.5 cm (3 in) from centre of circle. This will give the positions for the dowelling supports.
2. Place the paper on the middle tier and transfer the marks. With the pointed end, push the dowelling through the cake to the board. Mark the height of the icing. Remove it. Cut the dowelling with a small saw, wipe and replace in the hole. Repeat with the remaining 2 dowels measuring each one in case cake is uneven.
3. Centre the middle tier on top of the largest cake. Make up the *Royal Icing*, place in a piping bag fitted with the star nozzle and pipe shells around the base of each cake. (This will help secure the middle tier in place and hide its cake board.) Press the daisies and cornflowers alternately into the *Royal Icing* around the cakes before it sets. At this point you may find it easier to assemble the decorations on the cakes (see right) before placing the pillars between the middle and top tier just before serving.

To Assemble the Cake Decorations

For the top cake's decoration
Use 12 wired daisies, 12 wired cornflowers, 12 ivy leaves and 12 fern leaves

1. Mould about 50 g (2 oz) *Sugar Paste* into a cone and secure on to the top of the smallest cake with a little egg white or *Royal Icing*.
2. Arrange the flowers and leaves around it, pushing the wires into the *Sugar Paste* and bending as required.

For the middle cake's decoration
Use the 6 wired cornflowers, 6 wired daisies and 6 ivy leaves

1. Using a smaller piece of *Sugar Paste* arrange the flowers and leaves as before on the middle tier.

Spinach and Sun-dried Tomato Pinwheels

Serves 16

For the base
450 g (1 lb) frozen chopped spinach
25 g (1 oz) butter
A pinch of nutmeg
8 eggs, separated
Salt and freshly ground black pepper

For the filling
350 g (12 oz) curd or full-fat soft cheese
175 ml (6 fl oz) mayonnaise
1 teaspoon tomato purée
100 g (4 oz) sun-dried tomatoes, drained and chopped
1 bunch of spring onions, thinly sliced
1 teaspoon dried tarragon

For the garnish (if desired)
Fresh edible flowers
Cherry tomatoes or boiled, halved quails' eggs

1. Pre-heat the oven to 180C/350F/Gas 4. Line 2 Swiss roll tins 40 x 27 cm (15$^1/_2$ x 10$^1/_2$in) with non-stick baking parchment (or use shallow baking tins).
2. Place the frozen spinach in a pan over a gentle heat to defrost, stirring occasionally. Drain, if necessary, then return to the pan and boil off the

excess liquid. Add the butter and the pinch of
nutmeg and stir until the butter has melted. Season
and remove from the heat.

3. Stir the egg yolks into the spinach, mix well.
Whisk the egg whites until stiff then gradually fold
into the spinach using a metal spoon. Divide the
mixture between the tins and spread evenly. Bake
for 12–15 minutes until set. Leave to cool.

4. To prepare the filling, mix together the cheese
and mayonnaise to form a firm paste and add a
little tomato purée to colour it pink. Add the
tomatoes to the cheese with the onions, tarragon
and seasoning to taste.

5. Place a piece of non-stick baking parchment on
top of each base and then a baking sheet and flip
over so that it turns out without breaking. Remove
the parchment. Divide the filling in half and
carefully spread over the 2 bases. Turn each one
widthways and cut in half from top to bottom. Roll
up each one, wrap tightly in cling film, then foil or
a clean cloth and place on a baking sheet in the
fridge until required.

6. To serve, unwrap the rolls and cut each into
about 8 slices. Arrange slices on serving plates and
add the garnishes.

SALMON FILO PIE

Each pie serves 8

Juice of 1 lemon
1.5 kg (3½ lb) salmon fillets
225 g (8 oz) fresh asparagus or 1 x 400 g (14 oz) tin
asparagus, drained
1 bunch watercress, washed and trimmed
450 g (1 lb) full-fat soft cheese
1 tablespoon chopped fresh dill
50 g (2 oz) butter, melted
2 tablespoons vegetable oil
2 x 275 g (10 oz) packet frozen filo pastry, thawed
Salt and freshly ground black pepper

1. Place the salmon fillets in a large pan with
150 ml/¼ pint of water and the juice of the lemon.
Cover and poach for 20 minutes. Drain. Remove
skin and bones and break the fish up slightly.

2. Trim the fresh asparagus and simmer in lightly
salted water until just tender. Drain and rinse well
in cold water. Leave to cool.

3. Plunge the watercress into boiling water for 1
minute, drain, dip into cold water and drain well.

4. Place the asparagus, watercress, soft cheese, dill

Spinach and Sun-dried Tomato Pinwheels

and seasoning into a blender or food processor
and blend well.

5. Mix the melted butter and oil together in a small
basin. Grease 2 x 23 cm (9 in) loose-bottomed flan
tins. Brush a sheet of filo pastry with melted fat
and lay it flat in the base of one tin leaving the
sides overlapping the edge. Repeat with 2 or 3
more sheets laid at different angles to completely
cover the base and sides. Repeat for the other tin.

6. Divide salmon between the 2 tins. Spread the
asparagus mixture over the fish covering it all.
Bring in the overlapping pastry edges to cover the
filling completely. Place another sheet of buttered
filo on top to neaten and seal.

7. Brush any remaining pastry with fat, cut into 6
cm (2½ in) wide strips and scrunch up into
rosettes. Brush the pies with fat and arrange the
rosettes on top. Chill until ready to cook.

8. To cook, pre-heat the oven to 180C/350F/Gas 4.
Brush the pies with fat and bake for 30–35 minutes
until golden brown. Serve hot or cold with *Dill
Sauce*.

DILL SAUCE

Serves 16

2 tablespoons chopped fresh dill
2 tablespoons French dressing
600 ml (1 pint) soured cream or crème fraîche

1. Mix the dill and French dressing together, stir in
the soured cream or crème fraîche and leave for
several hours to allow the flavours to develop.

GLAZED GAMMON

Gammon on the bone cooks better and looks good on the table, but a boned joint is easier to carve. If using smoked gammon, cover in cold water and leave to soak overnight before rinsing in fresh water and starting the recipe.

Serves 16

3 kg (7 lb) smoked or unsmoked gammon knuckle end on the bone or 2.25 g (5 lb) boned
1–2 teaspoons made mustard
50 g (2 oz) breadcrumbs
50 g (2 oz) demerara sugar
Cloves
150 ml (5 fl oz) apple or pineapple juice

1. Either boil or bake the joint. To boil, cover the joint with cold water, bring to the boil, drain off and cover with fresh water. Bring the water to the boil, reduce the heat, cover and simmer for 2 hours and 40 minutes until cooked. Remove from the heat and leave in the liquid 30 minutes. To bake, pre-heat the oven to 160/325F/Gas 3. Wrap the joint in foil, place in a roasting tin and cook for 3 hours or until the juices run clear.

2. Turn up or pre-heat the oven to 190C/375F/Gas 5. Remove the skin from the hot joint, score the fat and spread with the mustard. Mix together the breadcrumbs and sugar and press firmly over the fat. Stick cloves over the joint.

3. Place the joint in a roasting tin and cover the exposed meat end with foil. Pour the fruit juice and 150 ml (5 fl oz) cooking liquid round the joint. Bake 30–40 minutes until golden brown. Baste the breadcrumbs several times during cooking being careful not to dislodge them. Baste the meat well. Remove from oven and leave to cool before slicing.

From the top left clockwise: *Green Summer Salad, Glazed Gammon, Orange Rice Salad (page 218), Minted Melon and Grape Salad (page 218), Salmon Filo Pie (page 215) and Mediterranean Roasted Vegetable Ring*

MEDITERRANEAN ROASTED VEGETABLE RING

The vegetables can be roasted in advance when the oven is in use and chilled until required. Fills a 1.5 litre (2½ pint) ring mould, or 2 x 900 ml (1½ pint) ring moulds.

Serves 16

For the ring mould
2 small aubergines
500 g (1¼ lb) butternut squash
350 g (12 oz) courgettes
1 small red pepper
1 small green pepper
1 small fennel bulb
1 medium onion
2 cloves garlic
6 teaspoons olive oil
1 teaspoon cumin seeds, optional
A few sprigs fresh basil, shredded
4 tomatoes
A few black olives, halved
300 ml (10 fl oz) dry white wine or water
1½ sachets powdered gelatine
300 ml (10 fl oz) passata or tomato juice

For the filling
175 g (6 oz) bulgar wheat
4 tablespoons French dressing
50 g (2 oz) stoned black olives, halved
150 g (5 oz) feta cheese, cubed
7.5 cm (3 in) piece cucumber, finely diced
Salt and freshly ground black pepper

1. To prepare the vegetables, dice the aubergine, sprinkle with salt and leave 30 minutes. Skin the squash then halve it and remove the seeds and dice the flesh. Slice the courgettes. Halve the peppers, remove the seeds and dice the flesh. Roughly chop the fennel, onion and garlic.
2. Pre-heat the oven to 220C/425F/Gas 7. Rinse and pat dry the aubergine and place in a roasting tin with all the other prepared vegetables. Add the oil and mix well, to coat. Sprinkle with the cumin seeds and basil. Bake for 35–45 minutes or until the vegetables are tender and slightly browned, turning occasionally. Remove from the oven and leave to cool.
3. Skin and thinly slice the tomatoes. Brush a 1.5 litre (2½ pint) ring mould with oil (alternatively use 2 x 900 ml (1½ pint) ring moulds. Arrange the slices of tomato and halved olives on the base and fill with the roasted vegetables.
4. Place the wine or water in a small pan, sprinkle the gelatine over and leave for 5 minutes. Place the pan over a low heat until the gelatine has dissolved. Stir in the passata or tomato juice and mix well. Pour the liquid over the vegetables to fill the mould making sure there are no air pockets. Chill until set.
5. To make the filling, cover the bulgar wheat with cold water and leave to soak for 30 minutes. Drain and squeeze dry. Place in a bowl and mix in the French dressing with plenty of seasoning and leave for a further 30 minutes. Mix in the olives, feta cheese and cucumber.
6. To serve, prepare a pan of hot water. Loosen the vegetable mould round the edge and dip in hot water for a few seconds, then invert on to a wet serving plate. Pile the filling into the middle.

GREEN SUMMER SALAD

Serves 16

225 g (8 oz) French beans
225 g (8 oz) mangetout
1 iceberg lettuce
1 small curly endive lettuce
1 bunch watercress, washed
1 small red onion, halved and thinly sliced
2 avocados
50 g (2 oz) pine nuts, toasted

For the dressing
150 ml (5 fl oz) olive oil
50 ml (2 fl oz) balsamic vinegar
2 garlic cloves, crushed
1 teaspoon caster sugar
Salt and freshly ground black pepper

1. Trim the beans and mangetout, cut them in half and cook in boiling water for 2–3 minutes. Drain then plunge into cold water. Drain again and leave to cool. Shred the lettuce and break up the endive. Trim the watercress, wash again briefly in cold water and shake dry.
2. Place the beans, mangetout, endive, lettuce, watercress and onion into a large salad bowl.
3. To make the dressing, shake together the oil, vinegar, garlic, sugar and seasoning in a screw-top jar.

4. To serve, skin and slice the avocados just before serving, add to the salad bowl with the pine nuts and toss together. Shake the dressing vigorously and pour over the salad, tossing well, to coat.

MINTED MELON AND GRAPE SALAD

Vary the flavour and texture of this salad by using 3 different types of melon.

Serves 16

3 ripe melons
350 g (12 oz) seedless grapes
10 firm, ripe tomatoes
1½ cucumbers
For the dressing
150 ml (5 fl oz) olive oil
50 ml (2 fl oz) white wine vinegar
1 tablespoon chopped fresh mint
Salt and freshly ground black pepper
A few sprigs of mint, to garnish

1. Halve the melons, discard the seeds and scoop out the flesh with a melon baller or simply cut into evenly-sized chunks. Place in a bowl and add the grapes.
2. Thinly slice the tomatoes and cucumbers. Arrange the cucumber slices around the edge of a large flat platter or plate, then arrange a ring of tomato slices inside.
3. Shake together the oil, vinegar, seasoning and

Minted Melon and Grape Salad

chopped mint in a screw-top jar. Pour over the melon and toss lightly, to coat. Pile the melon mixture into the centre of the platter. Garnish with mint sprigs.

ORANGE RICE SALAD

Serves 16

600 ml (1 pint) fresh orange juice
1.2 litres (2 pints) chicken or vegetable stock
½ teaspoon salt
225 g (8 oz) brown rice, rinsed
450 g (1 lb) long-grain white rice
3 oranges
5 sticks celery, thinly sliced
2 bunches spring onions, sliced
225 g (8 oz) raisins
100 g (4 oz) pecan nuts

For the dressing
250 ml (8 fl oz) olive or vegetable oil
5 tablespoons white wine vinegar
1 teaspoon sugar
1 tablespoon chopped parsley
Salt and freshly ground black pepper

1. Place the orange juice and stock in a large pan with the salt. Add the brown rice and bring to the boil, cover and simmer for 15 minutes. Add the white rice and cook for a further 12–15 minutes until both rices are tender and the liquid has been absorbed. Drain and rinse them quickly under cold running water. Drain again, then spread the rices out on a tray to cool.
2. Remove the zest from one orange with a potato peeler and place in a bowl with the oil for the dressing. (The zest of another orange can be cut into fine strips, simmered in water for 3 minutes then drained and reserved for decoration, if desired.) Remove the white pith from all the oranges, divide them into segments and roughly chop the flesh. Mix into the rice with the celery, spring onions, raisins and nuts.
3. Remove the orange zest from the oil, squeeze out and discard. Shake together the vinegar, seasoning, sugar and parsley with the oil in a screw-top jar. Pour the dressing over the rice salad and mix well. Garnish with orange strips, if desired.

RASPBERRY AND ORANGE MERINGUE ROULADE

Four of the egg yolks can be kept in a small covered container in the fridge and used in the *Citrus Tart* recipe.

 Serves 8

For the roulade
6 egg whites
275 g (10 oz) caster sugar
2 teaspoons cornflour
¹/₂ teaspoon vinegar

For the filling
1 orange
600 ml (1 pint) double cream
2 tablespoons Grand Marnier liqueur or juice from 1 orange
2 passion fruit
Icing sugar, for dusting
400 g (14 oz) raspberries

1. To make the meringue base, pre-heat oven to 180C/350F/Gas 4. Line a 40 x 27 cm (15¹/₂ x 10¹/₂ in) Swiss roll tin with non-stick baking parchment.
2. Whisk the egg whites until stiff and dry, add 2 tablespoons sugar and whisk for a further 2–3 minutes. Gradually whisk in the remaining sugar, then fold in the cornflour and vinegar. Pile the mixture on to the prepared tin and spread over and into the corners. Bake for 35 minutes until crisp and golden then remove from the oven and leave to cool in the tin.
3. Grate the orange and place the rind in a bowl with 450 ml (15 fl oz) of the cream. Whip the cream until stiff then fold in the Grand Marnier or orange juice. Cut the passion fruit in half, scoop out the flesh and seeds and fold them into the cream.
4. Place a large piece of greaseproof paper on the work surface and sprinkle over some icing sugar and turn the meringue base on to it. Spread over the whipped cream and sprinkle with some of the raspberries, reserving a few for decoration.
5. Roll up the meringue from one of the short sides and transfer on to a serving plate.

CITRUS TART

Make and freeze this dessert before adding the sliced lemon and icing sugar.

 Serves 12

For the pastry
175 g (6 oz) plain flour
75 g (3 oz) firm butter
3 tablespoons caster sugar
3 egg yolks

For the filling
3 lemons
1 orange
2 eggs
1 egg yolk
350 ml (12 fl oz) double cream
175 g (6 oz) caster sugar

For the decoration
1 lemon
Icing sugar, for sifting

1. To make the pastry, sift the flour on to a board or clean work surface, make a well in the centre and place the butter, sugar and egg yolks into it. Work with the fingertips of one hand until these are blended then gradually work in the flour. Continue mixing until the pastry forms into a smooth ball, wrap in cling film and chill for 30 minutes. (Alternatively, make in a blender by mixing the flour and butter first then blending in the egg yolks and sugar. Pour the mixture on to a large piece of cling film, form into a ball and chill until firm.)
2. Pre-heat the oven to 190C/375F/Gas 5. Grease a 28 cm (11 in) flan dish or loose-bottomed flan tin. Roll out the pastry and use to line the tin. Prick the base well with a fork and bake blind for 15–20 minutes or until just brown. Cool and reduce the oven temperature to 160C/325F/Gas 3.
3. To make the filling, finely grate the rind from 1 lemon, place in a large bowl with the juice from all the lemons and the orange. Add the eggs and yolk, cream and sugar. Whisk the mixture together until the sugar has dissolved and the top is fluffy. Pour the filling into the pastry case and bake in the centre of the oven for 30–35 minutes or until the filling is set. If the filling begins to

boil, lower the oven temperature but do not move the tart until it is set. Leave to cool.

4. To serve, remove the tart from the loose-bottomed tin (if used). Prepare a hot grill. Halve the lemon lengthways and cut into thin slices. Arrange round the top of the tart, and sift the icing sugar over to cover. Protect the pastry with foil and place the tart under the hot grill for 1–2 minutes or until the sugar begins to brown.

CHOCOLATE PRALINE BOMBE

This dessert keeps well in the fridge for 2–3 days or freeze in its bowl, covered with cling film and foil. Turn out while still partially frozen and decorate with cream and chocolate shapes. (The chocolate shapes for decoration are optional and you could use thin chocolate mints instead.)

                        Serves 12–16

For the praline
225 g (8 oz) caster sugar
225 g (8 oz) whole almonds, unblanched
Oil, for greasing

For the bombe
500 g (1¼ lb) plain chocolate
75 ml (3 fl oz) strong black coffee, freshly made
150 g (5 oz) butter, chopped
2 tablespoons rum
750 ml (1¼ pints) double cream

For the decoration
150 ml (5 fl oz) double cream
25 g (1 oz) plain chocolate (optional)

1. To make the praline, brush a large baking sheet with oil. Place the sugar and nuts into a heavy-based pan over a low heat without stirring, until the sugar has melted and is just turning in colour. Now stir frequently until a good caramel colour has been reached and the almonds appear to be toasted. Turn the mixture immediately on to the oiled tin and leave until quite cold and set. Break into pieces then pound to a fine powder between sheets of baking parchment or place the caramel pieces in a food processor and process until fine.

From the top: *Chocolate Praline Bombe, Citrus Tart* (page 219) and *Raspberry and Orange Meringue Roulade* (page 219)

2. Break up the chocolate and place in a pan with the coffee over a low heat until melted. Remove from the heat and gradually stir in the butter until melted. Stir in the rum and leave in the fridge for several hours until firm.

3. Brush a 2.25 ml (4 pint) basin or bombe mould with oil. Stir the praline into the chocolate mixture. Whip the cream until it just holds its shape then fold into the chocolate. Pour the mixture into the mould and leave in the fridge for several hours or overnight until firm.

4. To serve, loosen round the edge of the *Bombe* with a round-bladed knife or spatula. Turn it on to a serving dish and place hot cloths round the bowl to help loosen it. Do not dip it into hot water as this will melt the chocolate. Whip the cream until it is thick and pipe it round the bottom edge of the *Bombe*. Decorate with chocolate shapes.

5. To make chocolate shapes, prepare a sheet of non-stick baking parchment. Melt the chocolate in a small basin over a pan of hot water, then spread quickly over the prepared parchment. When set, mark into squares or shapes and keep in a cool place until ready to use, then peel off the parchment when ready to serve.

COUNTDOWN

Two months to go
• Check on the tablecloth, cutlery, glasses, and china. Hire, if necessary. Check on serving platters and dishes for food and hire or borrow items as necessary including a few spares.
• Check out tables and seating arrangements and organise help for serving and clearing up afterwards.
• Bake *Midsummer Wedding Cake*.

One month to go
• Make a shopping list and plan the shopping, buying store-cupboard ingredients gradually over the next three weeks.
• Make and freeze *Citrus Tart* and *Chocolate Praline Bombe*.
• Complete *Midsummer Wedding Cake*.

One week to go
• Collect together all the tableware and arrange pick-up of hired equipment, if using.
• Fill condiments. Organise kitchen and make space in fridge and freezer. Ensure an adequate supply of teatowels, kitchen paper, cling film, foil and washing-up liquid etc.

Three days to go
• Soak gammon joint overnight, if necessary.
• Make and cook pastry base for *Citrus Tart* if not already frozen. Wrap in foil, to store.
• Buy fruit and vegetables and finish shopping.

Two days to go
• Cook the gammon joint and finish in the oven. When cold, store in the fridge wrapped in foil.
• Roast the vegetables for *Mediterranean Roasted Vegetable Ring* and chill.
• Make praline and prepare up to end of step 4 for *Chocolate Praline Bombe* if not already frozen. Make chocolate shapes for decoration, if desired. Store in a cool place.
• Make the dressings for *Green Summer Salad* and *Minted Melon and Grape Salad*.

One day to go
• Make *Spinach and Sun-dried Tomato Pinwheels*

and leave uncut and well wrapped in fridge.
• Make up *Salmon Filo Pie* and leave uncooked, covered in the fridge. Make *Dill Sauce*.
• Finish the *Mediterranean Ring* and leave to set. Make up bulgar wheat filling for the *Mediterranean Ring* and chill.
• Cook the beans for *Green Summer Salad*.
• Cook the brown and white rice for *Orange Rice Salad* and prepare the remaining ingredients but do not combine.
• Make the roulade base for *Raspberry and Orange Meringue Roulade*. Store overnight wrapped in foil, prepare all the fruit and leave ready to finish filling tomorrow.
• Finish *Citrus Tart* (or defrost it).
• Remove *Chocolate Praline Bombe* from freezer.
• Slice gammon, if desired, wrap slices in greaseproof and foil and leave in fridge.

On the day
• Pre-heat the oven to 180C/350F/Gas 4. Bake *Salmon Filo Pie*.
• Finish *Orange Rice Salad*.
• Prepare *Green Summer Salad* to end of step 4.
• Prepare all the ingredients for *Minted Melon and Grape Salad* but do not arrange on serving dish.
• Finish *Raspberry Meringue Roulade*.
• Place *Citrus Tart* on serving plate.
• Arrange sliced meat or joint on a serving platter.
• Slice *Spinach Pinwheels* and arrange on plate.
• Remove *Salmon Filo Pie* from tin, if necessary, and place on serving plate. Pour *Dill Sauce* into a sauce boat.

Two hours to go
• Prepare avocados, toss in the dressing. Place all the other ingredients in a serving bowl.
• Turn out *Mediterranean Ring* and pile filling into centre.
• Arrange *Minted Melon and Grape Salad* on to serving platter and add melon and dressing.
• Turn out *Chocolate Praline Bombe*, decorate with cream and keep cool.

To serve:
• Pour the dressing and avocados on to the *Green Summer Salad* and lightly toss, to coat them.
• Decorate *Raspberry Meringue Roulade* with raspberries and orange strips.